THE ROMANCE OF THE WORD

The Romance of the Word

One Man's Love Affair with Theology

three books by

ROBERT FARRAR CAPON

An Offering of Uncles
The Third Peacock
Hunting the Divine Fox

WILLIAM B. EERDMANS PUBLISHING COMPANY
GRAND RAPIDS, MICHIGAN

Original editions copyright as follows:

An Offering of Uncles: The Priesthood of Adam and the Shape of the World
  © 1967 by Sheed and Ward, Inc.

The Third Peacock: The Problem of God and Evil
  © 1971, 1986 by Robert Farrar Capon

Hunting the Divine Fox: An Introduction to the Language of Theology
  © 1974, 1985 by Robert Farrar Capon

This edition © 1995 Wm. B. Eerdmans Publishing Co.
255 Jefferson Ave. S.E., Grand Rapids, Michigan 49503
All rights reserved

00 99 98 97 96 95   7 6 5 4 3 2 1

Printed in the United States of America

ISBN 0-8028-4084-1

Contents

[v]

CONTENTS

The Third Peacock 167

Hunting the Divine Fox 239

Preface

The three books in this volume — *An Offering of Uncles* (1967), *The Third Peacock* (1969), and *Hunting the Divine Fox* (1974) — are among the earliest of some twenty theological works I've written over the past thirty years.

No, that's not quite accurate. Not all of them are formal theology; to be honest, none of them is a formal anything. I'm not a very proper person — or parson either, for that matter. My personal style alternates between preoccupied and relaxed: I go from bouts of work to cigars, wine, and jokes on a regular basis. Neither is my preaching style quite seemly: it is conversational in the extreme and consists almost entirely of teaching, not exhortation. Some people enjoy it, but few ever think of calling what I offer them "sermons."

As for my writing style . . . well, that too is informal, to say the least. It is made up largely of chats with the reader, interlarded with stories, images, and liberal doses of my own predilections. I am indeed a theologian, having taught the subject in a seminary for twenty-two years and in the pulpit for forty-five. But I am not an academic. I am a cook, a woodworker, a runner of the roads, and a reasonably competent linguist, administrator, canonist, and musician — but not the kind of reader a theologian is usually supposed to be. Someone once observed to the nineteenth-century American theologian William Porcher DuBose that he did not seem to have read very widely in the theological literature of his time. His reply has been mine ever since the day I first came across it: "I have made great use of a very few books."

To locate myself briefly for you, I am a lifelong Episcopalian who began as an old-fashioned high churchman and a Thomist to boot. With some minor attenuations of the rigors of those positions, I remain such to this day — though it's been a bit harder for the uninitiated to get a fix on them as the years have passed. The authors of whom I have made great use are C. S. Lewis, G. K. Chesterton, T. S. Eliot, W. H. Auden, and, just to prove I'm not hung up on Englishmen with two initials, Matthew, Mark, Luke, John, and Paul. More and more, it is the Bible that is my principal reading.

In any case, my books have come mostly out of my life, uneventful though it has been by the usual standards. I decided to study for the priesthood when I was seventeen (I used to say that was the last life-decision I ever made), and I finished college, graduate school, and seminary before I was twenty-four (I had to wait several months to reach the minimum age for ordination to the priesthood). Those were the bad, good old days when "experience in the world" was not thought to be a necessary preparation for life in the ministry. All of my experience in the world came after I was a priest — though a good deal of it was not exactly priestly and some of it less than reputable.

But all of it was grist for my writer's mill, and most of it has been retailed in one book or another. To the best of my knowledge, there isn't much I've held back. I am neither very open nor forthcoming as a person; but put a pencil in my hand and I am honest enough to alarm those who don't know me and dismay those who do. Accordingly, with a promise to you that I will eventually get around to the three books comprised by this volume, I think it would be useful to do two other things at some length. One is to give you a brief rundown of what I have done as a writer — of my *oeuvre,* as they say in the lit. crit. business (no one, to my knowledge, has done this, so I may as well blow my own horn). The other is to say what it is I think I've been doing all these years — to analyze the *oeuvre* and tout what I take to be its virtues (I'm positive no one has ever done this).

Of my books, eight and a half are hardly textbook theology at all — or textbook anything else, for that matter. Two of them are unconventional marriage manuals, two and a half are more or less faulty novels, and four are unorthodox cookbooks. All of them, however, are theological — at least according to my view of the theological enterprise. The remaining eleven are more recognizable as theological works, but only to people with open minds. I gave a paper once for a group of academic theologians. Since it was written in my usual combination of badinage and *shtick,* almost no one present "got" it. The one gentleman who did — and who kindly rose to its defense — felt obliged to preface his remarks with an apology: "Even though Capon writes in a kind of 'code' . . ." So much for my general reception in academe. If I am read at all in seminaries, I suspect it is more on the students' motion than the faculty's.

My only consolation is that I've seen that happen before. Back in the forties when I was a seminarian, we students had just taken up with a new writer, one C. S. Lewis. We were told in no uncertain terms not to waste our time on such a "mere popularizer" but to concentrate instead on certain Russians and Germans — authors whose prose style had all the fluidity of crankcase oil on a January morning. My hope is that in some small way I shall one day share in C. S. Lewis's revenge: we still read him; the Russians and Germans are mostly gathering dust.

But enough of that. In the interests of completeness, I shall give you a chronological list of all my books and then a few remarks on each of them — in whatever order strikes my fancy.

Bed and Board	1965
An Offering of Uncles	1967
The Supper of the Lamb	1969
The Third Peacock	1971
Hunting the Divine Fox	1974
Exit 36	1975
Food for Thought	1978
Party Spirit	1979

I started *Bed and Board* with the intention of writing a cookbook; but since life is what happens when you're making other plans, I lost my grip on the subject of cookery with the first sentence I wrote. Having begun with a hymn to the absurdity of the marital venture, I went on to write a kind of anti-marriage-manual marriage manual — a celebration of my own peculiar marriage. It was about my wife Margaret, my six children (Michael, Anne, Stephen, Patricia, Mary, and Virginia) — and of course about myself at shameless length. The book (even though it was unapologetically theological) was received well enough to become a best-seller and to encourage me to continue writing for publication. Some of its ethical strictures (at that time, for example, I was against contraception), I have since tempered; and since it was written before public consciousness of sexism had been raised (certainly before mine had), its language and a few of its attitudes were masculine to a fault. Nevertheless, the theology of the book — and above all its good-humored gratitude for having been allowed to embark on the leaky love boat of marital life — still, I think, stands up well.

Mark the word "leaky." Thirty years after *Bed and Board,* I am divorced from Margaret and at varying distances from my long-since-grown children. As it has turned out, there were a lot of departments in which I was not a success, not to mention several in which I was, and still am, a failure. Even such successes as I had were absurdly different from anything I had in mind. I dedicated a great deal of time and effort to my children's religious formation, only to find them now mostly uninterested and non-practicing. On the other hand, I cooked almost entirely to please myself and produced a whole family of good cooks and happy omnivores: we have at least the stove and the table in common. For the rest, our life together has proceeded not by triumphant goodness or heroic efforts but almost entirely by dumb luck and forgiveness. Which, it seems to me, is more or less the way even God operates — and which, by my own internal logic, brings me to another book: *A Second Day*.

After twenty-seven years of marriage to Margaret, I asked for a divorce and married my wife Valerie, acquiring two more children, Laura and Erik, in the bargain. At the time, the bishop took a dim view of my plans. Since I was beholden solely to him for my two jobs (dean of the diocesan seminary and priest-in-charge of a mission church), and since he gave me a resign-or-be-fired ultimatum, I resigned politely, took the severance pay, and went freelance as a writer. I was not deposed or suspended from the priesthood, so I still continued to function as an occasional Sunday-supply priest; but for a number of years, Valerie's and my income consisted almost entirely of what I could earn by my food-writing wits.

Back in 1969, I had written my first cookbook, a left-handed theological extravaganza entitled *The Supper of the Lamb*. Since that too was a best-seller, I was able (after a few months of floundering around at the time of my divorce) to land a twenty-five-thousand-dollar contract for *Food for Thought*, which turned out to be an equally offbeat venture. It did not sell well, however, nor did anything after it for a long while: my decision to go freelance threatened constantly to become a license to starve. Not only that, but from then till now, publishers' advances to me for books have in fact gone straight downhill — and not in adjusted 1969 dollars, either: advances for my eight most recent books have ranged from six thousand dollars down to zero. What saved us back then was writing numerous articles on food for *The New York Times, Newsday, Redbook, Working Mother, Connoisseur, Eating Well*, and other publications. But all the while, I continued to write books and to have the good luck to find publishers willing to gamble on an author who was, with each passing year, more "mid-list" than best-seller. *Party Spirit* and *Capon on Cooking* (even worse-selling cookbooks than *Food for Thought*) followed it into quiet oblivion.

But back to *A Second Day*. Since Valerie's and my rented home was in an out-of-the-way place called Shelter Island (located between the two forks at the eastern end of Long Island and accessible only by ferry), it became a kind of safe house for divorcing and remarrying clergy. Of these, there were quite a few at the time — my bishop having decided to counteract what he saw as his leniency toward me by severity toward anyone who, as he thought, was following my baleful example. Therefore, having written an unorthodox marriage manual in *Bed and Board,* I undertook to produce an equally non-conformist divorce-and-remarriage manual in *A Second Day*. It too sold like coldcakes. But even though it has long since been out of print, I still think it a good piece of work and still hear from people who find it sane and helpful. Perhaps its best insight is its refusal to give houseroom to the words "ex-wife" and "ex-husband." No marriages ever really end — not even the marriages of those who think they do. We simply go on adding more relationships to our already cluttered lives. We do not chuck one wife or husband for another, any more than we get rid of children in favor of stepchildren. I now have two wives and eight children — and such affinities with each of them as I can manage to muddle through. If we cannot (for all their faults and ours) have ex-parents, there is no sense in trying to "ex" anyone else out of our lives.

I know. This is rambling. But since life is a ramble, let it pass. Prior to the divorce, I had written the three explicitly theological works contained in this volume. Leaving those for the end of this preface, I think I should address what I still see as the major turning point in both my life and my theologizing.

In 1975, still firmly in place as mover and shaker in both the diocese and the General Convention of the Episcopal Church — and still close enough to best-sellerdom to be riding high — I took a crack at writing a novel, *Exit 36*. It was about the suicide of a priest as dealt with by a fellow priest who had known him slightly. Not surprisingly, the narrator was a seminary professor and parish priest; even less surprisingly, he was a cigar-smoking bon-vivant with a considerable sensitivity to women. I even gave him my name while writing the book. But just before publication, my wife, family, friends, and publisher ganged up and insisted he be at least thinly veiled as "Bill Jansson." Candor in print, they felt, was not wise. At the time, I had my doubts; but in the present overheated ecclesiastical climate, with its sexual harassment monsoons, I am finally convinced. The days of my public honesty are over — at least until the church wakes up and repents of its current unwillingness to tolerate sinners in its midst. True enough, the whole brouhaha has a skin of reason on it insofar as it tries to deal with victims of abuse. But for the rest, it is childish. I use the word precisely. The hardest thing to teach a two-year-old is that a long stick has two ends: the one she's holding with a short grip to move her doll furniture around on the coffee table, and the other that's knocking her mother's Limoges off the mantelpiece. Fuss long enough with running sinners out of ministerial employment, and you'll knock all the crockery of grace off the church's shelf.

Anyway, back to the turning point. Simply put, something I took as a personal tragedy occurred in my life in late 1974. I give you no details, except to say that what happened was largely my fault and that the experience was devastating. But I didn't even begin to understand it until, in 1975, I attended a clergy conference conducted by Jim Forbes (who is now the Senior Pastor of Riverside Church in New York City). Over three days he hammered home the message that the only reason the church cannot rise from its moribund condition is that it will not die — that for as long as it tries to hang on to the life it thinks it has, it will never enjoy the gift of resurrection from the dead that God gives it in Jesus. "Jesus came to raise the dead," he said — not to teach the teachable, reform the reformable, or improve the improvable. As I later came to put it myself, the only ticket anyone needs to God's party of grace and forgiveness is, by great good luck, the one ticket everybody has: death.

Only after that — and only bit by bit — did I begin to understand the tragedy. I was not just devastated, or hurt, or ill-used, or broken; I was *dead*. Unless you have been through such an experience, you may find this overblown; but my life, as I had known it, was over, gone, kaput. If I ever lived again — and it was inconceivable to me that I could — it would not be by my hand.

You want to ask me, of course, "But what about all the positive parts of your life that were still in place: wife, children, work, success? Was it fair of you simply to write all that off as gone?" You miss the point. All those goodnesses remained exactly as they were. I did not write them off; I *died* — just as suddenly and certainly as if I had been run over by an eighteen-wheeler. Fairness or unfairness, guilt or innocence, blame or exculpation had nothing to do with the case. My life-designing capabilities were not impaired or in need of remedial treatment; I just didn't have my life anymore.

But far from being a sad state of affairs, that turned out to be the best news I had ever heard. My death was not the tragedy I first thought; it was my absolution, my freedom. Nobody can blame a corpse — especially not the corpse itself. Once dead, we are out from under all the blame-harrows and guilt-spreaders forever. We are free; and free above all from the messes we have made of our own lives. And if there is a God who can take the dead and, without a single condition of credit-worthiness or a single, pointless promise of reform, raise them up whole and forgiven, free for nothing — well, that would not only be wild and wonderful; it would be the single piece of Good News in a world drowning in an ocean of blame. It was *not* all up to me. It was never up to me *at all*. It was up to someone I could only trust and thank. It was salvation by grace through faith, not works.

The writing out of this radical doctrine of grace began when I started *Between Noon and Three*, directly after the clergy conference. The book took a year to write and five years to find a publisher — and even at that, it was never published in its original form. The first part of the book, called *Parable*, was published (mostly intact) as *Between Noon and Three*, and it included some sections of the second part of the original, which was entitled *Coffee Hour*. The third part, called *The Youngest Day*, was published a year later, but only after I had completely rewritten it as a piece of nature-writing designed to serve as a vehicle for dealing with what a radical acceptance of the doctrine of grace does to our views of Eschatology: of Death, Judgment, Heaven — and above all, of the Hell we know and love only too well.

Between Noon and Three took so long to see print partly because it was too salty, and thus (as both publishers and friends saw it) too revealing on my part. But the principal reason was that it was too uncompromisingly Pauline: it proclaimed, perhaps even more than Paul did, that there is nothing we can or need to do to earn the gift of acceptance by God except trust that we already have it in Jesus, free of charge. It refused to announce unqualified grace in one breath only to load it up with conditions in the next. *Faith plus nothing* was the message of the book: no ifs, no ands, no buts. Again and again, almost *ad nauseam,* it recurred to Romans 8:1: "There is therefore now no condemnation to those who are in Christ Jesus." I was accused of being a universalist, and of not believing in the scriptural doctrines of hell and eternal punishment.

To answer the first of those charges: I am and I am not a universalist. I am one if you are talking about what God in Christ has done to save the world. The Lamb of God has not taken away the sins of *some* — of only the good, or the cooperative, or the select few who can manage to get their act together and die as perfect peaches. He has taken away the sins of the *world* — of every last being in it — and he has dropped them down the black hole of Jesus' death. On the cross, he has shut up forever on the subject of guilt: "There is therefore now no condemnation. . . ." All human beings, at all times and places, are home free whether they know it or not, feel it or not, believe it or not.

But I am not a universalist if you are talking about what people may do about accepting that happy-go-lucky gift of God's grace. I take with utter seriousness everything that Jesus had to say about hell, including the eternal torment that such a foolish non-acceptance of his already-given acceptance must entail. All theologians who hold Scripture to be the Word of God must inevitably include in their work a tractate on hell. But I will not — because Jesus did not — *locate hell outside the realm of grace.* Grace is forever sovereign, even in Jesus' parables of judgment. No one is ever kicked out at the end of those parables who wasn't included in at the beginning.

Alas, though, the church has always had a tough time latching on to that truth. More often than not, it has expounded the offer of free grace as a bait-and-switch proposition, like the offer of a ninety-nine-dollar airfare to Orlando — which turns out to mean that there are only three seats on the plane at that bargain price, the rest being at the same old you've-got-to-have-the-wherewithal price of two hundred seventy-five. The church gives (and, worst of all, the world understands it to be giving) the clear impression that grace works only on the early birds and eager beavers who cooperate with it. But that's dead wrong. Grace works without requiring *anything* on our part. It's not expensive. It's not even cheap. It's *free.*

Our enjoyment of grace, of course, is another matter. If we want to hang on to our precious guilt (or, worse yet, to hang on to everybody else's), we are free to act as if grace was never given at all — and to suffer the consequences of such stupidity. But even then, God never takes it back. He's slipped us his last ace of trumps under the table of Jesus' death, and we've won. *He's lost the God game for our sakes!* If we insist on crying in our beer over such a happy issue out of all our afflictions, so much the worse for us: we've still won, but we won't pick up the prize money.

All of that, plus more, is the burden of *Between Noon and Three.* The mildly salacious love affair with which the book begins is not titillation but a theological device. It takes an English professor named Paul, who is both a busy adulterer and an incurable romantic, and has him fall finally and for good in love with Laura, a thirty-five-year-old graduate student. He can see no way of ending his ongoing clutch of affairs, and accordingly he can see no way of living up to his vision of himself as the White Knight of exclusive romantic love that he now thinks he has to be in order for Laura to accept him. He is, in short, a dead duck by the Law of Romance. *And he admits it all to her. And she accepts him anyway, while he is still a sinner.* Hence the correspondence that makes my theological device work: Paul the professor, with his view of Romance as the holy, just, and good commandment he cannot keep — and which condemns him by its sheer gorgeousness — stands in nicely for Paul the apostle, with his insistence that by its very beauty, the Law of God condemns us all until, *while we are still sinners,* grace comes and liberates us from its curse without a single condition attached: no improvements demanded, no promises extorted — just the extravagant, outrageous, hilarious absurdity of free grace and dying love.

Needless to say, *Between Noon and Three* frightened a good many people — or so they thought when they were confronted with the use of an illicit love affair as a means of expounding the grace of God. What it really frightened, however, was not the people but the doctrinal and religious horses on which they were sitting when they read the book. Grace is wildly irreligious stuff. It's more than enough to get God kicked out of the God union that the theologians have formed to keep him on his divine toes so he won't let the riffraff off scot-free. Sensible people, of course, should need only about thirty seconds of careful thought to realize that getting off scot-free is the only way any of us is going to get off at all. But if all we can think of is God as the Eternal Bookkeeper putting down black marks against sinners — or God as the Celestial Mother-in-Law giving a crystal vase as a present and then inspecting it for chips every time she comes for a visit . . . well, any serious doctrine of grace is going to scare the rockers right off our little theological hobbyhorses.

I know. I wax irate. I could apologize but I won't, since I plan to fuss and fume all over again every time I see people who've been given a free, brand-new cream-and-gold Rolls Royce Corniche and who can't think of anything better to do than kick the tires, slam the doors, and complain about the color. Let me move on.

As I said, the third part of the earliest version of *Between Noon and Three* was almost completely rewritten and printed separately, but still under its original title, as *The Youngest Day.* In its published form, it turned out to be an eschatological ramble through the four seasons on Shelter Island, with Winter serving to get me to the subject of Death, Spring to Judgment, Summer to Hell, and Autumn to Heaven. As I first wrote it, however, I began it with a Mafia rub-out in order to provide myself with a corpse on which to do the eschatology of grace. The only nature-writing in that version was a description of the dirt road in a Long Island wood where the gangster's body was dumped. But since the Mafia types involved actually spoke like Mafiosi, my editor did not find it seemly enough to publish as overt theology — hence the conversion to wholesale nature-writing.

I have no regrets about the change; actually, I enjoyed making it. I even think the editor was materially, if not theologically, correct in insisting that separate publication required a more accessible presentation. Still, I would dearly love to see a publisher take the bit in his or her teeth some day and bring out the original version in one piece. It has quite a few hitherto unpublished goodies in it: a rollicking exegesis of the Latin of one of Augustine's choice passages; a dialogue between me and one of my characters in which the character gets the better of me, hands down; two sermons on the Pharisee and the Publican (one a piece of stand-up comedy and the other a takeoff on John Donne); and a rendition of the after-death experiences of the executed mobster based on William Golding's *Pincher Martin*. Hello? Hello?! Is anyone out there listening?

My three books on the parables of Jesus — *The Parables of the Kingdom, The Parables of Grace,* and *The Parables of Judgment* — had their origin in one of the many outtakes from *Between Noon and Three.* I was lecturing at Trinity College in Deerfield, Illinois; after two days of enthusiastic reception by the students, Valerie and I were sitting at breakfast in a motel. "They're with you a hundred percent," she said. "You have to stop hammering at them and end on an upbeat note. Why don't you read them the funny sermon on the Pharisee and the Publican that you originally put in *Between Noon and Three?*" I thought it was a good idea and said I'd do it. But Valerie, not being one to take a single opportunity to run my life when she can avail herself of two, had another idea. "You know, you really should write a book on all the parables. If James Beard can write *Beard on Bread,* why can't you write *Capon on the Parables?*"

Normally, my first reaction to suggestions from her about what I should or shouldn't do is to dig in my heels and give six reasons why my already-made plans for the season preclude taking her advice. But this time I grabbed a paper napkin, took out a pencil, and jotted down on the spot not only the way I would divide the parables but also the general outline of the entire work. With the exception that it turned out to be three books instead of one — and that it took several years longer than I thought it would to do the job right — that was all there was to it. The outline held from start to finish.

All three parable books have had a good measure of success, even to the point of producing some annual income that has covered more than one month's housing expenses. I have a theory about why their reception was as favorable as it has been. Most books on the parables of Jesus are written, naturally enough, by Scripture scholars. But the members of that fraternity, at least in my view, are a strange breed. For a long time — and especially at the present moment — they have been at pains to decide which of Jesus' words can actually be ascribed to Jesus and which must be reckoned as the work of the Gospel writers and of the communities of faith in which the Gospels were produced. Even when I myself was in seminary nearly fifty years ago, they were hard at this Sisyphean labor of developing critical gadgets by which the "real" words and deeds of Jesus could be sifted out from all the coarse lumps of ascribed utterance and action that made up, they seemed to imply, such a large proportion of the scriptural record. My fellow seminarians and I even composed a piece of doggerel about what would be left of the Gospels when the biblical critics got done with them. I can't remember any of it now except two lines:

The words of our Lord would no longer be dark,
And they'd all be contained in six verses of Mark.

That was back in the days of the "form critics." Now we have deconstructionists and assorted other literature hackers whose most recent bright idea has been the printing of the Gospel record in four colors to indicate the degree of authenticity they feel can be ascribed to the several passages. There is, of course, a certain legitimacy to all this. No one except a rabid fundamentalist can ever say we have the *ipsissima verba* of Jesus in their original form: even the "original" Greek of the Gospels is a rendering of the Aramaic of Jesus, of which we have no record at all. More than that, not even believers in the inspiration of Scripture can overlook the fact that the various communities of faith which the Spirit co-opted into the writing and acceptance of the Gospels were left quite free to put their individual (and sometimes wildly differing) stamps on the accounts we have.

But the quest for a "historical" Jesus lurking somewhere behind those accounts and discoverable only by critical diligence remains a supremely iffy pursuit. However brilliantly the biblical critics may reconstruct the "historical" Jesus, what they come up with is not history but postulation. For my money, the only historical Jesus there is, for better or worse, is the Jesus the Holy Spirit has disclosed to us on the pages of the New Testament — every word of which, one way or another, represents something the Spirit thought supremely worth mentioning about Jesus. If that view gives us problems, and difficulties, and even contradictions (and it does in many places), it simply enjoins upon us the labor of interpretation that all historical documents call for.

Jesus and Paul — and the New Testament in general — have the nasty but natural habit of talking out of both sides of their mouths on most important subjects. Jesus himself is sometimes easygoing, sometimes as hard as nails. Paul, when he speaks to responsible heirs of the Jewish tradition, is full of grace, freedom, and forgiveness; but when he writes to Greeks whose sexual mores, for example, make his pharisaic flesh creep, he sounds exactly like an Old Testament Jewish uncle. No one can read any long document (other than a lease or a will) without having to decide which of its insistences or stipulations he or she thinks central and which peripheral. And therefore no careful readers of Scripture — not even those (such as myself) who hold it to be the Word of God — can dispense themselves from the necessity of putting the arm on the peripheral in favor of the central.

Which means that it takes theologians and historians, not just literary critics, to do justice to the Bible. It is, after all, a theological and historical book; and it needs to be approached from inside those disciplines, not from outside them. It's that, I think, which accounts for the favorable reception of my books on the parables. By disposition and luck, I have never been much enamored of the biblical critics' approach to Scripture. My training and my interest have been in theology; and I think it is theology that both the writers and the readers of the Bible are rightfully interested in. Preachers of the Gospel need to proclaim something that is a responsibly theological approximation of the Good News to a world that has been giving itself nightmares for millennia with the bad news of innumerable dreadful theologies. They are called to reveal to their hearers not some putative one-fourth or one-tenth of the scriptural account that will withstand some current fad of critical scrutiny but the central thrust of Scripture that will pull the whole together — and that the church catholic has always held was there for the finding. And because my books on the parables try to do just that, they have found considerable acceptance among the troops in the front trenches who, week by week, are trying to do the same.

In those books, I do not attempt to rank the sayings of Jesus according to the likelihood of his having said them. Instead, I simply assume (as the Gospel writers do) that they are the words of the only Jesus we have — and then get on with the job of trying to make the best sense of them I can. And when you do that, you are in for a pleasant surprise: far from falling apart into a dozen different strands, they hang together nicely — just as the church, in reading them Sunday by Sunday, has always thought they did. There *is* a Gospel, and it is indeed Good Tidings, not the bad news that carping critics and tendentious religionists have made it out to be.

From Jesus' earliest parables of the kingdom, through his parables of grace, to his parables of judgment, I find not just a continuous thread but a seamless whole. I always respected Scripture; but after my rattletrap life taught me that I am nothing without grace, I loved it. It delights me as a theologian by its marvelous architecture, and it thrills me as a person because it is the happiest thing I ever came across. The catholicity, actuality, and mystery of the kingdom Jesus proclaimed are like wine in my mind. The grace he portrayed as working solely by death and resurrection lifts my heart because even if I have no goodness at all, my death is still good enough to get me home. And the judgment, the *krisis* he pronounces over the whole world he draws to himself on the cross, fills me not with shame or guilt but with rejoicing because it is a judgment of approval. I do not have to know or feel I am saved. I cannot do that. I do not have to sweat and strain to be saved. I cannot do that. I have only to trust that in him it is all handed to me on a silver platter. And *that* I can do, gladly: it's the only really fun thing in the world.

I wrote the parable books before 1988, toward the end of my first residence on Shelter Island. While they were still works in progress, however, I went back to employment in the church, being taken on as Assistant for Education at Saint Luke's Church, East Hampton, in 1984. But in 1988, when my landlord decided he wanted his house back, I moved to East Hampton — which has the reputation of being the home of the rich and famous, but which for me turned out to be famous mostly for the richness of its rents: I had to pay double what I had been paying on Shelter Island.

Before I left Shelter Island, though, I managed to write (in two bursts between the books on the parables) *The Man Who Met God in a Bar.* Of all my books, it was the one I most enjoyed writing. It's a transposition of the Gospel narrative into Cleveland. The narrator is the Saint Peter character, a New Yorker named Marvin Goodman who is in the women's wear business (hence the subtitle, *The Gospel According to Marvin*); the Jesus character, named Jerry, is a high-school dropout who is a cook in a Northern Italian restaurant. The novel, such as it is, follows principally the Gospels of Mark and John, but not slavishly: most of the action takes place in the spaces between the events of the Gospel narratives.

Naturally, it features the usual suspects, but they are updated. John the Baptist is Spencer, a big, gawking health-food nut who is Jerry's cousin. Spencer's mother is a doddering but mystical old lady named Elizabeth; Jerry's mother is Barbara, a beautiful forty-five-year-old political science major who is also an adept at yoga — a bit of a stretch, perhaps, for the Blessed Virgin, but not in this book; and Marvin's girlfriend-on-the-side in Cleveland is Jennifer, who stands in for Mary Magdalene. Marvin's wife in New York is Shirley, and his mother-in-law is Rhoda — who is healed of her diverticulitis, in Marvin's apartment on West End Avenue, by eating strawberry tarts that Jerry baked for a wedding in Cleveland. The Judas character, who is always a problem because you must inevitably make him a member of some group or other, is Curtis. To avoid offending any one minority, I arranged for him to be not only black but brilliant, gay, and a lawyer to boot. As I said, the book was fun to write — especially since, for all its clowning, it's a totally orthodox theological exercise.

There are also, of course, events corresponding to the major turning points in Jesus' ministry, likewise updated: a "baptism"; a feeding of the five thousand (done with an anchovy pizza); a raising of Lazarus; and a death, a resurrection, and an ascension (executed from a private plane). There is even a temptation — not in the wilderness but in the Cleveland airport just before Jerry's plane caper — conducted by Mr. Fosforos, Jerry's old high-school social studies teacher. As you can see, the book is as much Woody Allen as it is Mark and John; and as you will discover when you read it, it begins with the best bar routine in the world.

I still continued to write while in East Hampton (books and food pieces, as usual), and finally, after several years, I found a publisher willing to gamble on *Marvin* — for no advance at all. During that time, I began to contemplate two major changes in my life. Over the years, I had done a small amount of lecturing to groups brave enough to have me. It occurred to me that since I had no way of retiring on pension (my church pension was frozen in 1977 when the bishop let me go, and it hasn't thawed noticeably since), I might look forward to lecturing as a way of putting a net under my high-wire act after I was seventy-two (the Episcopal Church demands your resignation from whatever position you're holding at that point). Accordingly, through the kindness of my rector, Francis Creamer, I was able to take off pretty much all the time I could spare to fly around the country frightening the horses with my twin insistences that Christianity is not a religion and that grace is not a transaction. At the present time, I'm making about seven such jaunts a year; I figure that if I can inch that up to twenty or so by the time I'm out of church employment, I'll be able to survive (God willing and the crick don't rise).

The second change had to do with housing. Valerie and I had been pouring rent money down the tubes for seventeen years. The only houses I ever owned were the one I bought for my wife Margaret at the time of the divorce (my name was on the deed for less than two weeks) and the childhood home I inherited from my mother, which I lived in for three months until I sold it (at the bottom of the market) in 1977. At any rate, in 1993, when my East Hampton landlord was about to raise my rent yet again, Valerie and I began to shop around for another rental and to anticipate with dread the prospect of yet another in a series of moves that only a sudden interment seemed likely to put a stop to. And so, stumbling our way through the real estate scene like two innocents, we looked at some twenty-five possible rentals before it dawned on us (with a bit of advice from our friends) that maybe we could actually buy a house of our own.

To make a long story short, we did. Originally, we planned to begin looking seriously in late 1994, after I came back from a sabbatical and a visiting professorship at the University of Tulsa. But God, who takes care of drunks, children, and the occasional real estate novice, was kind. While bopping around Shelter Island (it's within commuting distance of East Hampton), we came upon the house we finally bought in January of 1994. The financing was a smoke-and-mirrors arrangement, and the mortgage took a seemingly endless eleven weeks to get, but we got it. I have a theory that the mortgage process has been designed to be the nearest thing to chemotherapy: you throw up a lot, your hair falls out, and you have chronic diarrhea. But now we are home-owners. We lucked out like bandits: we (and the bank) have a great house. Sure, shaping the place to our liking took almost two months of hard labor on both our parts and an inordinate amount of carpentry on my own (I called it a moving experience for our souls and a moving violation of my body). But as a result I now have the best kitchen I ever worked in and four huge "public" rooms that simply beg for parties to be held in them. In addition, the house has a deck, two baths, one commodious bedroom (overnight guests have to make shift in the living room), a terrific study for me, and a big, dry basement for my wines, my machine tools, my extra refrigerator and freezer, and my two perpetually unfinished harpsichords. It took two vans, six men, and eleven hours to move us thirty minutes away from East Hampton. Never again. If there ever threatens to be a next time, I'll move it all myself first — with dynamite.

Before I left East Hampton, though, I wrote two more books: *Health, Money, and Love* and *The Mystery of Christ*. As you already know, I have for a long time now been on two major theological kicks: an uncompromising insistence on grace alone through faith as God's way of dealing with the world, and a perpetual harping on the fact that Christianity is not a religion. In these next two books, I harped and insisted some more. *Health, Money, and Love* (I chose the title in the hope that its self-helpy tone would boost sales — it didn't) is a kind of multi-media exposé of the inveterate but futile religiosity of the human race. The Gospel isn't the only subject we religionize the stuffing out of; we do the same with food, money, sex — and any other subject we fail to put our hands on properly. We don't really like or trust all the gorgeous stuff God gives us: given half a chance, we fly from it as if it were the plague and take refuge instead in rituals, conjurations, and mumbo jumbo.

Take food, for example. These are hard times to be a food writer if you're actually a cook and not a devotee of the established religion of food. The list of God's creatures currently proscribed by the culinary temple police is so long that we are pretty much down to nothing but tofu and turnip greens. Salt, sugar, butter, eggs, cream, animal fats, tropical oils, chocolate, coffee, wine, liquor, tobacco — all are now sins whose punishments (excess weight, elevated sodium levels, bad cholesterol, heart trouble, and general bodily shipwreck) tarry not nor spare.

But why? Because those things are deadly? No: the human race has eaten them with gusto for centuries and survived, even to the point of living longer now than it used to. Or is it because they violate the integrity of the body? No again: we are omnivores; we have bodies specifically designed to digest such things, if they are taken in moderation. But alas, moderation is not nearly as much our cup of tea as religion is; so we learn our food catechism (even though it's revised every few months by the high priests of health), we keep the food commandments as if our life depended on them — and then we wonder why, if we are all such good boys and girls, our meals look and taste like prison fare.

Health, Money, and Love, after blasting a good many more such religions, finally takes aim at the worst one of all: the Christian *religion.* I call that the worst because it's an absolute contradiction in terms. There is no such thing as the Christian religion because Christianity, at its heart, is not a religion. Rather, it's the announcement by God in Christ that whatever it was that the religions of the world were trying to do and couldn't (make God think kindly of you, win wars, end poverty, get the crops to grow, stop your brother-in-law from drinking too much at your parties), the whole rigmarole has been canceled. In Jesus, God has put up a "Gone Fishing" sign on the religion shop. He has done the whole job in Jesus once and for all and simply invited us to believe it — to trust the bizarre, unprovable proposition that in him, every last person on earth is already home free without a single religious exertion: no fasting till your knees fold, no prayers you have to get right or else, no standing on your head with your right thumb in your left ear and reciting the correct creed — no nothing. All you need is faith that the entire show has been set to rights in the Mystery of Christ — even though nobody can see a single improvement. Yes, it's crazy. And yes, it's wild, and outrageous, and vulgar. And any God who would do such a thing is a God who has no taste. And worst of all, it doesn't sell worth beans. But it is Good News — the only permanently good news there is — and therefore I find it absolutely captivating.

Naturally enough, then, that was the burden of *The Mystery of Christ* as well. In it, I began to pull together everything I'd been trying to say over the years. The effort, as usual, was left-handed: the book took the form of a series of one-on-one pastoral counseling sessions, interrupted by group discussions of what I should or shouldn't have done with the person I was speaking to. But it was a perfectly serious effort. For a long time, it's seemed to me that the problems of modern theology could be solved more easily by a reworking of the notion of *sacramentality* than by the devices most modern theologians have come up with. The problems, of course, are real enough. Ever since the Middle Ages, the action of God in Christ has been expounded as if it were a *transaction,* an insertion into the world of some gimmick (the Incarnation, for example) that wasn't there before. But in the nineteenth and twentieth centuries, that transactional view ran into big trouble: doubts were raised as to whether the Jesus of Scripture actually did or said any of the things Christianity claimed. You know: Did he really claim to be the Messiah? Did he really heal the sick and cast out demons? Did he really rise from the dead?

For myself, though, I felt that the theological contraptions which modern theologians built to deal with these problems didn't so much solve them as give away the store that was supposed to have the solution in stock. For instance: they demythologized the Bible wholesale, leaving us with a Savior — a lifeguard, if you will — who, because he did not actually do the most important acts of rescuing that the Gospel said he did, seemed never to have gotten his feet wet.

Once again, there was a skin of reason on all this. The old, transactional view of how God works in the world was indeed discredited — though not so much by the galloping progress of modern thought as by plain common sense. The claim that God continually puts his finger in the terrestrial pie bears very little scrutiny. To any impartial observer, he doesn't seem to interfere much, if at all, with the general downhill slide of world affairs. If it was all so obvious that he was Mr. (or Ms.) Fixit, how come nothing got fixed?

But to answer that poser by implying that Jesus was no more than just another guy who put his pants on one leg at a time inevitably makes mischief. Unless you are a very careful theologian indeed, it comes perilously close to giving the impression that salvation hasn't really happened at all. Let me be quite clear about where I stand. For me, as for the church catholic, Jesus is both divine and human. As divine, he is one-hundred-percent God: all-knowing, all-powerful, and all-anything-else you care to make him. But as human — as the perfectly, utterly, simply, merely one-hundred-per-cent human being he is — he is precisely just a guy who (barring miracle, if you allow that sort of thing) can't stand upright with two feet off the floor. He is not Superman. Even orthodox theology has always said that.

So I came up with the bright idea of saving all of orthodox theology and solving all the problems of the modern critics in one fell swoop: *If God in Christ didn't do the job of saving the world in a way we can see, he did it in a way we can't see — in the Mystery of Christ.* And my device for effecting this solution was the standard catholic notion of *sacrament,* slightly reworked and extended.

For Christians, a sacrament is not a transaction — not an operation that produces an effect that wasn't there before. I am aware that the sacraments have frequently been expounded in a highly transactional way; but a minute's thought will show the wrongheadedness of such a notion. Take the Eucharist. And take the highest possible view of it: the bread and wine, at the beginning of the rite, are mere bread and wine; but when they are received by the faithful at the Communion, they are the body and blood of Christ — they are Jesus himself, really present in all of his divinity and all of his humanity, and in all the power of his death and resurrection. A question arises, however: Is this eucharistic "change of status" an ordinary, transactional alteration, like the change of flour into bread? Does the act of celebrating the Eucharist "mix up a batch of Jesus"? Does Jesus, during the service, show up in a room from which he was previously absent? Do benefits we were formerly without suddenly begin to flow our way in Communion?

The answer to those questions, I think, has to be a flat no. The faithful who gather in the church before the rite begins are already, Christians believe, the body of Christ. The forgiveness, the reconciliation, and the new life they have in Jesus are already and fully theirs. They do not, therefore, receive an *accretion* of Jesus. It's not that their tank was topped off with Jesus the previous Sunday but now needs a refill. They never lost a drop of him, because he never left them. They couldn't get any more of him than they already have. But if that's the case, do they really *receive* him? And if so, how do you go about theologizing that reception?

You refuse to make the Blessed Sacrament a transaction, that's how. You say it really is the presence of Jesus, but you don't make it out to be an *insertion* of Jesus. You say the eucharistic presence is a mirror held up to the church's face so it can see the Jesus it already has. You say it's a dinner with the Jesus who's already in the house. You say any non-transactional thing you can think of — just as long as you say it's a party the church is already at and not some limousine that brings Jesus to the church's door. And those same rules apply to the other sacraments as well.

Take sacramental confession to a priest, for example. On its surface, it looks for all the world like a transaction. A sinner, foundering in her sins, comes to the confessional box. The priest hears her sad tale of guilt and shame and then, with the magic zap of absolution, sends her home pure as the driven snow. But that won't wash. Every Sunday, in the Nicene Creed, she proclaims her acknowledgment of "one baptism for the forgiveness of sins." In her baptism, she was clothed with an irremovable suit of forgiveness. All the sins she ever committed were committed *inside* that suit: she was forgiven before, during, and after every last one of them. She does not "get" forgiveness from the priest; rather, the priest pronounces over her — really, authoritatively, *sacramentally* — the one forgiveness she already has. So it is indeed an absolution that she receives; but it is not a new absolution, or a retreading of an absolution that wore off — or, God forbid, a *handeling,* a bargaining with God for an absolution she has to earn by proper contrition. It's the same old free gift she never lost, but that she has finally, by renewed faith, woken up to yet again. The priest's words do indeed "convey" it to her faith in that dark box; but she in no substantive way *acquires* it.

There's an interesting historical sidebar to this. At the time of the Reformation, Romanists mostly went right on viewing priestly absolution as a transaction. But Protestants, having rediscovered salvation by grace alone through faith, were horrified at that. They felt that the only thing the ordained ministers of the church could possibly do — given the fact that Jesus had once and for all done all the absolving necessary on the cross — was to give *assurance* of a pardon already granted. Anglicans, however, with their perverse insistence on having everything both ways, decided to opt for a paradox. In the Book of Common Prayer, after the general confession in the Eucharist, they included not only the old, instrumental, transactional-sounding priestly absolution but also the "Comfortable Words" — a selection of New Testament passages that amounted to nothing more than an assurance of pardon possessed. Both/and, not either/or, was their watchword; and as a dyed-in-the-wool Anglican theologian, it's mine too — at every point in the theological enterprise.

To take just one more instance of what I think is the proper view of sacramentality, look at the sacrament of Holy Order — at ordination to the priesthood, to pick one of the orders. When the rite is over, the new priests possess, really and authoritatively, the priesthood of Christ. But have they *acquired* it *de novo* during the service? Have the newly ordained persons gotten for themselves a priesthood that the laity of the church don't have? No way. In baptism, the whole church is declared to have the priesthood of Jesus. So what are the church's priests, then, if they are not the exclusive holders of priesthood? Easy: they are mirrors in which the church sees the priesthood it already has.

Another historical sidebar. The "priesthood of all believers" was one of the great rediscoveries of the Reformation. But as Susan Sontag once pointed out, it got lost in the shuffle of Protestant history because the Reformers effectively abolished the ordained, sacramental priesthood. They took away the mirror and then forgot what they looked like: the priesthood of believers, as an operative truth in the lives of most Protestants, simply went begging. In their zeal to hold that priesthood was everybody's business, the Reformers tripped over the hard fact that what's everybody's business is nobody's unless you have somebody standing up in front of you actually doing the business — unless, in short, you have a real, sacramental presence to help you hang on to what you have.

Bear with me. This long, slow theological curve is about to curl in over the plate. In my reworking of the notion of sacramentality, the key insight into its wider applicability sprang from some questions that arose when I came to baptism itself. Was the great sacrament of Christian initiation an exception to the rule I'd been working out? The other sacraments might well be presences under certain signs of something that's already present under other signs; but wasn't baptism different? Wasn't it the *beginning* of a presence — the insertion, into a person who didn't have it before, of the redeeming work of Jesus? Was it not, in short, precisely a transaction? My answer to those questions, I felt, had to be no. While it is true that the church has often acted as if it conferred in baptism something that the world at large didn't have — as if we Christians in here were the saved "us" and the pagans out there were the great, gray-green, greasy, unwashed "them" who would never have Jesus unless we hooked them up to him by means of baptism — I found that impossible to hold.

Baptism, as I've come to work it out, is not an exception to the general rules for sacraments; it's the grand embodiment of them. The church doesn't take Jesus to the heathen: Jesus, because he is God, is already intimately and immediately present to the heathen before we arrive. And he's present in all his power, not only as Creator but as Redeemer. They've already got him, they're already home free, they're already saved — but they don't know it because they haven't heard it. What they need is not a dose of Jesus to cure them but some sacrament of the fact that they're already cured in Jesus. And baptism, as the constitutive sacrament of the church, is precisely that sign. F. D. Maurice said that when you baptize an infant, you baptize the whole world: if you can say all that wonderful stuff over some two-week-old who knows nothing, believes nothing, and has done nothing, you *ipso facto* say it over everybody. Jesus is the Light of the world, not the Lighting Company of the world. Neither he nor his church is an electricity supplier you have to get wired up to in order to have light in your life. He is the Sun, not a power utility; all you have to do is trust him enough to open your eyes and presto! You had light all along.

It was that insight that led to the ultimate extension of the doctrine of sacramentality. Because when you get baptism down right, the big question finally arises. *Is even Jesus in his humanity* an exception to God's non-transactional method of operation? *Is even the incarnation of God in Christ* an insertion of God's redeeming self into the world for the first time in the year 4 B.C.? *Or is Jesus simply the supreme sacrament, the real presence, under the sign of his humanity, of a redeeming presence that was in the world from the start?* In other words, is salvation through Christ a hole-and-corner transaction poked into the world late in the game, or is it the Grand Mystery underlying all of history?

My money, as you know perfectly well by now, goes on the Mystery — the *Mystery of Christ,* hidden for ages in the God who creates all things, but now made known by the Spirit in the Person of Jesus (Ephesians 3, *passim,* adapted). Jesus' words and deeds are not the actions of some *agent* who does a number on a world that hasn't had the benefit of his activity before. They are the actions of a God incarnate who has been around since before the foundation of the world and who now sacramentally reveals what he's been up to since square one. That's what I believe; and that's what, on balance, I think the Bible and the church have always said Christians believe. That we have far too often turned it into a transactional operation that took its own sweet time getting its act in gear is partly a pardonable error (God *did* take his time revealing it); but mostly, the transactional view of redemption has been a disaster.

And that's because it's unqualified bad news. If all we have to tell the world is that it can come home only if it goes through some series of performances that will enable it to latch on to God's acceptance of it, we might as well shut up. The world just won't respond to that in any numbers sufficient for salvation to be called catholic — and if you listen carefully to Paul, it not only won't do it, it *can't* do it. We will only have proclaimed salvation for the select few who are able to kid themselves into thinking they can meet a bunch of requirements that aren't there. (The predestination buffs, of course, got it right: people don't work themselves into salvation; God puts them there by his own inscrutable will. But the predestinarians blew it when they decided that God also put a whole bunch of people outside the reconciliation — just because he felt like it. They passed the course entitled Unmerited Grace 309 with flying colors; but they flunked Catholicity 101.)

As a matter of fact, it's precisely the way it keeps both the Gospel and the church catholic that's the thing I like best about my doctrine of sacramentality. *Nobody isn't saved:* Jesus takes away the sins of the *world,* not just of the cooperative. The church ceases to be an agency selling spiritual snake oil and becomes instead a party cruising the streets of the world trying to wake up all the deadheads and wallflowers to the fact that they're at the bash already. It invites not the world's cooperation but its faith. And therefore it's *Good News* — as nothing else in the world can ever be. The church is not catholic because it has everybody inside itself: it never has had them and it never will. The church is catholic because it's the sacrament of a catholic Jesus — of a Redeemer who already has everybody inside himself and who asks us only to trust him.

And that, Virginia, is what solves the problems of the arguments the modern theological debate has gotten us into. And it solves them the way all good theological solutions do: *by making an end run around the way the problems were posed in the first place.* Take any of the arguments you care to mention: the "war" between science and religion; higher criticism of the Bible versus fundamentalism; believers in miracles versus demythologizers of miracles; the resurrection of Jesus as literal event versus the resurrection as "Christ event"; conservative versus liberal — you name it. All of those stand-offs, as they originally developed, led to nothing but a hunkering down of opposing parties in entrenched positions. It wasn't that there weren't enough theological big guns and intellectual tacticians around to wage the war — there were plenty; it was just that nobody could see a way of breaking out of those positions.

But look what happens if you do my end run into sacramentality — if you go with a catholic, universal Mystery of Christ of which the Jesus of history is the great sacrament. It allows you, if you opt for "modern" views, to question or qualify any saying or action whatsoever ascribed to Jesus — anything except his historical existence and the totally unprovable (and therefore *un-disprovable*) faith-conclusion that he is the great sacrament of the Mystery of God incarnate. You don't have to say that his thirty-some years here are the only manifestation of that Mystery — there are plenty of others: the paschal lamb and the rock in the wilderness, to mention just two indisputable ones. And you certainly don't have to do a lot of theologizing to get non-Christians hooked up with him, because as I've expounded the sacraments, none of them works that way. All you need to concede is that he *died,* and that by blind faith you've decided to take that death as the central, reconciling fact of history. You can whip up any version of his resurrection you like, just as long as you don't refuse to keep the *Resurrection* at the heart of your faith. You can demythologize any miracle — any sign — just as long as you're willing to say that *Jesus* is the ultimate sign of what God has always been doing at all times, in all places, and for all people. You are in the snug harbor of your liberalism without having put even a scratch on the Good Ship Orthodoxy.

On the other hand, if you feel (as I do) that that's a bit much — if you feel, for example, that blasting your way through the back of the empty tomb with a critical jackhammer is unnecessary when the front door is already open (if, say, you are a conservative who has no difficulty with the reports that Jesus rose from the dead and sailed up into the sky) — then you are free to hold any or all of *that,* provided you remember that your salvation depends not on whether you can prove the reports but on the Mystery of the incarnate Word that lies beyond all proof. Just as long as you don't turn the work of God in Christ into a transaction — just as long as you don't make Jesus the Lighting Company of the world — you are in your old Kentucky home, rocked in the bosom of your conservatism.

But since I've said all that more than a few times in this preface — and at interminable length throughout my writings (especially in *The Mystery of Christ*) — let it go at that. Time now to turn at last to the three books in this volume.

An Offering of Uncles, the second of my published books, was my first deliberately theological work. Not that it didn't have more than its share of fables, imagery, and excursions — but then, that's the way I do theology. But since it came out in 1967, it predated the era of raised consciousness and contained (as I see it now) rather a lot of masculine references. For this edition, I've taken the opportunity to reword certain parts of the book (and of the other two as well) in order to eliminate such references — though I dare say not every feminist will think I've caught them all. It wasn't easy. Back in those days, *man* (and the pronoun *he* used relatively) stood not only for a male person but for humanity as such, male and female. (English is a cripple in this respect, having only one word, *man,* to refer to both notions. Many other languages have two: Latin has *vir/homo,* Greek has *anēr/anthropos,* German has *Mann/Mensch,* and — to the point in *An Offering of Uncles* — Hebrew has *ish/adam.*)

The subtitle, and the major theme of the book, is *The Priesthood of Adam and the Shape of the World.* The word *adam,* in the Hebrew of Genesis, does not in the first instance refer to a single male person. (See Genesis 1:26-27: "Let us make *adam* in our image. . . . So God created *the adam* in his image, in the image of God he created *them; male and female* he created *them.*") In the second and third chapters of Genesis, however, *Adam* gradually becomes the name of the first male human being — the first *ish.* Therefore the "priesthood of Adam," as I use the phrase, is intended to embody the primary meaning of *adam:* that is, to refer to a priesthood possessed by all men and women. *We* are *Adam.* Charles Williams even took to calling us *the Adam;* but I've always shied away from that usage because, unless you're a Charles Williams fan, it's a bit obscure. Bear it in mind, though, when and if you read the book.

An Offering of Uncles was written toward the end of the sixties, when all the apparently stable verities of the fifties were coming unstuck. Margaret and I had married in 1949 and promptly proceeded to bring forth the usual post–WWII gaggle of children. But in 1961, after four births, one late-term miscarriage, the death of twins (a stillborn girl and a boy who died at one day old), and two more births, we threw in the towel — just in time. Just in time, that is, to have teenagers on hand for the onset of adolescent rebellion, the sexual revolution, the drug culture, and the occasional visit from the police at 11:00 p.m. with one of our offspring in tow. It was hardly what we had in mind.

I was always struck by the fact that, in our role as the perpetrators of the baby boom, we were more old-fashioned than our own parents had been. We grew up, by and large, in small families; but we were unwilling to take that "modern" arrangement as our pattern. Instead, we renounced the family paradigms of the twenties and thirties and looked back to our grandparents' generation (if not farther) for what we took to be an older and better vision of family life. We immersed ourselves in "traditions" we had never known: teaching our children to read by phonics, recovering the ethnic roots of our grandmothers' cooking, setting our tables with faux Meissen china, drinking wine with our meals, and, of course, having all those children. In short, we were throwbacks — if you can call the invention *de novo* of such a pastiche of lifestyles the work of traditionalists.

But it didn't stop there. I for one was beginning to turn into the same kind of revisionist throwback in my theology. Having steeped myself in Aquinas, Andrewes, Laud, Pearson on the Creed, Newman, Pusey, and the like during my theological formation, I was equally unwilling to take as my example the several generations of twentieth-century theologians that immediately preceded me. The Fundamentalists, I felt, had rescued the Bible from the Evolutionists only to turn it into a straightjacket for thought. On the other hand, the Modernists and the Liberal Biblical Critics, in their eagerness to clean up the theological mess left by fundamentalism, seemed to me to have thrown out the church's doctrinal china along with the plate scrapings. Moreover, many of the attempts by neo-orthodox theologians to make some kind of peace between orthodoxy and modernity, while brilliant in some ways, left me wondering whether perhaps they were still a bit more neo- than orthodox. *An Offering of Uncles, The Third Peacock,* and *Hunting the Divine Fox* were my first passes at making an end run around the standoff.

An Offering of Uncles was an effort to take certain elements of the traditional concept of priesthood and, by broadening it to cover the whole human race, to use it as a touchstone for criticizing much of modern thought and life. Adam — humankind — was meant by

God to be the priest, the offerer who would lift creation into the City, the *civitas Dei,* the civilized whole that God longs for it to become. Jesus Christ is the Great High Priest not because he does some religious whammy on creation but precisely because he is the Word of God in *human flesh.* He does not do for us some priestly work that we, as *the Adam,* could never have done (we were made for the job, for heaven's sake!); rather, he does *in us* something we might have done but just didn't because we are *failed* priests. He saves our history by *undoing* the un-priestliness of the offerings by which we botched our history. When Jesus is lifted up on the cross and in the resurrection, *he draws all to himself:* by his renewal of the priesthood of Adam, he turns all of creation into the New Jerusalem that we, in the perversion of our priesthood, never have managed to achieve. And he does all that not by miraculously abolishing the shipwreck of history but by the alarming device of dying himself in the very thick of the shipwreck. He does not save us *from* failure but *in and by* failure. It is the mess of the world that is Christ's real *métier.* It is in the brokenness itself of our priesthood that he restores to us the priesthood of Adam.

In *The Third Peacock,* subtitled *The Problem of God and Evil,* I took a step further into the implications of the dreadful but saving fact that God saves us *in* evil, not from it. If you like, the book was an attempt at honest theology — at truth in Christian advertising. And for that reason, it was one of my earliest sallies against the notion that Christianity is a religion. Religion is the human race's vain attempt to perfect some series of transactions that will con God into doing something about its plight. But the prescriptions of religion never delivered on their promises: all the chicken sacrifices of history, all the fasts, all the nights of prayer, all the approved sexual behavior — none of it ever tidied up even the smallest corner of the mess of history. And therefore when God really does do something about the mess, he doesn't risk doing anything religious. Instead, he simply gets himself executed as a common criminal and then outrageously invites us to trust that everything religion ever tried to do has been accomplished precisely by that mindless piece of business.

It's a bizarre proposition, and *The Third Peacock* revels in its bizarreness. God is not some divine Mr. Goodwrench in a nice, clean shop (*pace* all the bumbling preachers who hold up such a God for our admiration); he is a disreputable Lover who makes all his important assignations with us in seedy and terrible places. When I wrote the book, I had not yet come as fully as I later did into the awareness of the loving awfulness of grace. But the seeds were there, waiting only for the rainy season to water them into life: I had to learn the hard way that God in his grace does not run away from my evils, nor does he tell me that he will come to me only after I have gotten rid of my evils. Even back then, though, the idea of a God with dirty hands — of a God who, while we were *still sinners,* could throw away his claim to be a respectable God and die for us — struck me as more on the mark when it came to the problem of God and evil than all the slick attempts of theologians to get God off the hook on the subject. Especially since it was God, on the cross, who put himself on the hook.

Accordingly, the book is indeed an exercise in theodicy — in the branch of theology that attempts, against the insuperable odds of a random world, to "justify God's ways to man." But as I said, it is an honest exercise. To my knowledge, it's the only work of theodicy that flat-footedly admits that God is an accomplice in the world's evil. To begin with, he made it possible. To continue, he did next to nothing about it when it happened. And to make an end, he claims to have solved all of its problems not by getting rid of it but by taking it into himself on the cross — and then inviting us to believe, against all evidence, that in Jesus his incarnate Word, everything is now hunky-dory. As I later came to put it, proclaiming the Good News of such a preposterous salvation is like trying to sell a pig in a poke — only worse. You might possibly trick some gullible soul into buying a three-legged pig if you talked fast and presented your merchandise in an attractive sack. But on any honest view of the Gospel, the poke that contains the pig of salvation is the ugly bag of all the world's derelictions — of all its lastness, leastness, lostness, littleness, and death. And even if, by great guile, you can actually get the customers past the repulsiveness of the poke, you still have a hard sell on your hands — because when they look inside, they discover you're asking them to buy an invisible pig.

Admittedly, that's hardly a winning sales pitch. But it has one huge advantage: it doesn't hold out a single false promise to anybody. Because evil, sickness, death — even sin — are here to stay. They are not options that religion or good behavior or clear thinking will enable us to decline. They are inevitabilities that even God in Christ gives himself no choice about. And that is the only Gospel we have to proclaim. If it is dreadful (and it is) — if the complicity of God in evil is an outrage to even the most elemental moral sense (and it is) — it nevertheless remains the only realism ever offered to the human race in the name of God. You may not like it. But by the very token of its awfulness, it does mean that you have a Lover who will never find *anything* about you unacceptable. And if you have the stomach to accept such a Lover . . . well then, you have a lot more than religion ever gave anybody.

I should add that *The Third Peacock* is a good deal more fun to read than the partial precis I've just given you. It begins with a piece of theological clowning in which I set up God's delight in creation as the root of the problem of evil; and it continues throughout with my usual mixture of serious thought and stand-up comedy. At any rate, it has been a favorite of many people: by my count, this is its fifth edition. (Incidentally, the prologue to the book, written for the third edition in 1986, is well worth reading — unless you are congenitally indisposed to introductions.)

Which brings us at last to *Hunting the Divine Fox: An Introduction to the Language of Theology.* Having gotten into the swing of writing offbeat theological treatises — and, in particular, having developed my lectures in first-year theology in the same vein — I decided to tackle a similar exposition of how theological language does and doesn't work. The first half or so of the book is simply the front end of my introductory course. For me, theology is not the explication of straight-line propositions about God but a word game in which analogies and images are tossed at a Mystery that lies beyond the reach of any ordinary human speech. Above all, the Mystery itself is not a transaction — not an insertion into the world of a divine fix — but rather a *universal, constitutive feature of creation* that has been operative from the start. The book takes off from the point where *An Offering of Uncles* left off, namely, from the priesthood of Adam — of the whole human race; and it claims that this priesthood was from the beginning nothing other than the priesthood of Christ, and vice versa.

The remainder of the book is simply my first shot at applying this non-transactional view of the Mystery to the notion of sacramentality. The sacraments of Penance, of the Eucharist, of Baptism, of Holy Order, and of Matrimony are reinterpreted in a way that, while it still allows for the highest possible view of their reality and effectiveness, nevertheless gets rid of the mechanical, religious interpretations of them that have muddied Christian waters for centuries. But I've already said quite enough about that; suffice it to add here only that my love affair with *Jerusalem,* with the image of the City that the world is meant to become, looms even larger in *Hunting the Divine Fox* than in any previous book — and breaks out like fireworks in an ending as good as any I ever wrote.

But enough, perhaps. I'm glad to see all three books in print again. It's been great fun doing what I've done over the years so far, and I have no intention of stopping now. I've put a good bit of labor into my writing, but I've never looked on any of it as work. In fact, I don't think I've ever *worked.* In my own mind, I've been neither a clergyman employed by the church nor a writer slaving away for fame and fortune. I look on myself as someone who, by the great good luck of a total skepticism about working for a living, has enjoyed the luxuries of a forty-five-year vacation to the priesthood and rather a lot of time in which to scribble. That I have been paid for any of it is just a bonus added to a career of doing what I pleased. I commend both the attitude and the books to you. You could do a lot worse.

Shelter Island, New York   ROBERT FARRAR CAPON
Autumn 1994

An Offering of Uncles

*The Priesthood of Adam
and the Shape of the World*

1. Prologue

AUCTOR: Well.

LECTOR: Well, what?

AUCTOR: Well, here we are.

LECTOR: But this is preposterous. An author is supposed to begin more surefootedly.

AUCTOR: Ah, but beginning is not that easy.

LECTOR: If you find it such a problem, why do you insist upon authoring?

AUCTOR: Because I have something to say.

LECTOR: Thank heaven for that. What is it?

AUCTOR: If I could tell you, I would have said it already.

LECTOR: Oh. And I suppose that since you have not said it, you cannot tell me?

AUCTOR: Precisely.

LECTOR: My congratulations. Your book is a model of brevity.

AUCTOR: Not quite. We are not yet ready to talk about a book, only a beginning. And my beginning is a model not of brevity but of honesty. The start of a book, you see, can be written either before or after the book itself. If before, it will be an honest but shakily written piece of business during which the author struggles to get his feet under him, and from which he escapes the first chance he gets. If afterward, it will be a piece of Fine Writing in which he ticks off briefly and with utterly fake aplomb all the things he has spent months trying to keep himself glued together long enough to say. In the first case it is a beginning, but not worth reading, and in the second it is readable, but no beginning. There is, therefore, no way to begin a book both honestly and successfully.

LECTOR: But that is obviously false. Many books begin well.

AUCTOR: You fail to distinguish. Books may begin well; authors do not. When an author sets out, he is only vaguely in possession of what he wants to say. He knows as much about his unwritten book as an architect knows about an unbuilt house: only, for example, how many rooms she wants, and whether the kitchen is to be central or auxiliary. The true work of composition must be done, hit or miss, from the ground up; to attempt it from the porch in will produce a monstrosity. The real beginning of a book, therefore, is always carefully suppressed. Not to do so would be an editorial sin comparable to leaving an excavation in front of a finished house.

LECTOR: I hope your editor has a firm grasp of all this. When will you ever begin?

AUCTOR: I already did. Two pages ago.

LECTOR: That is absurd. Give me something more definite, or I shall walk out.

AUCTOR: It is your privilege. These things take time. Would you be kind enough to ask me what I do for a living?

LECTOR: Very well, but it is my last exchange. What do you do for a living?

AUCTOR: I am a clergyman.

LECTOR: Is that all?

AUCTOR: No. I will make you a confession.

LECTOR: Good grief! Not one of those . . .

AUCTOR: Quiet! You have already had one exchange over your quota. You must listen or leave.

▼   ▼   ▼

I have a recurrent fantasy. The characters in it sometimes change, but the metaphysical substance is always the same. It began a few years ago when my wife looked up from her mending to remark that, for a man in my profession, it would be more seemly if something other than the seat of my pants wore out first. The comment, I felt, had an edge to it. She knew perfectly well that I say my prayers standing, since I invariably fall asleep when I kneel. I found myself taking umbrage. Perhaps I felt guilty at not being heroic enough to kneel without leaning on a chair, or perhaps I was just parrying; but, at any rate, I gave her a short disquisition on the sedentary age we live in, and I ended with the comment that she did ill to complain — that in all probability everyone in America was engaged in a ceaseless and noble struggle to close the wounds that civilization was inflicting upon our trousers.

It was the thought of that transcontinental concert of trouser seats being worn away that led to the metaphysical dimension. From the attrition of the pants it was only a step to the attrition of the persons inside the pants. I would look at people I knew with the strange feeling that, through the seats of their pants, they themselves were being worn away — a little bit every year — so that it was a race with death to see if there would be anything left of them to bury. I would wonder what could be done to stop the attrition — whether, for example, we would, as a race, have to give up sitting in the interest of self-preservation. But then I saw that the avoidance of sitting wouldn't help at all, because the wearing was being caused not by the places people sat in but by the fact that they were not sitting in places at all: they were set on top of a slowly grinding placelessness. Do you see what I mean? If the seats they sat in were *places,* they would destroy only cloth; but because they are *noplace,* they wear out people.

One of the characters in the fantasy may help to explain it: The Man on the Thruway. I would see him driving a late-model car from Buffalo to Albany. The inside of it was typically nowhere. It used to be that the driver's seat of an automobile was a recognizable place: the control room of a traveling machine. But no more. There are still knobs and gauges, but they have fewer and fewer necessary

connections with the inside of the car as *someplace.* Half of them
operate devices that could be anywhere: radios, cigarette lighters;
the rest control a machine that practically drives itself. And the
gauges. The old ammeters and manometers are gone. They have been
supplanted by apocalyptic little lights that give the driver no useful
information about the place he is in: they simply announce accomplished disasters. And the principal gauge of all, opulently central,
tells him only the speed at which he is missing other places. He sits
upon sleek vinyl covers; his feet touch deep carpet; acoustical ceilings
shelter him; music embraces him. It all whispers to him — tells
him, perhaps, that he is a tiger or a king, but in no known forest,
over no real kingdom. Nothing says where he is — and nothing can.
He is noplace.

He passes signs: Syracuse, Schenectady; he passes mileposts:
276; 189. They mean nothing to him. Place is irrelevant; distances
have become times. Albany is two more hours; food is fifteen
minutes. He passes scenery: trees, lawns. But it, too, is nowhere —
the same grass, endless from Buffalo to Albany. He looks ahead:
What is that? It is a bridge; but what bridge, in what place, he does
not know. He looks aside: What is this? It is a cloverleaf — anywhere, and therefore nowhere. It is all real; but it has ceased to *matter.*
The placelessness grinds into his soul. He grows thinner.

He stops to eat, stepping from nowhere into nowhere. The
thruway restaurant is another sacrament of his placelessness. The
same broadloom carpet stretches wall to wall; the same vinyl
upholstery bears him up. Music floats mindlessly in the dead room.
He orders. It is the same food he ate after Buffalo, served by the
same waitress. He pays and leaves, walking past familiar trash cans
full of french-fry bags and milkshake containers. The same flies buzz
over them in the heat. He struggles to find his car, tries several doors
until he finds one to fit his key, and drops with relief into nowhere
again. He feels thinner still, but he is headed home.

He races against the nothingness that wears him away. Home
at least may save him, build him up, stop the attrition. A singular
wife, a peculiar brood, local sandwiches, personal garbage. Places,
things; fragments to shore against his ruin; props to lift him from

the grindstone. He sits again and eats, and he begins ever so slightly to thicken. Unique and private voices speak to him, discrete and personal hands touch him. He struggles to place himself, to become some*thing,* some*where.* But the pain is too great. The voices make demands, and the hands will not be controlled. The grinding was easier to bear. He goes to his living room to relax.

Broadloom once more enfolds him; the vinyl enters into his soul. He sits again in noplace, and the last thin part of him wears down forever. He turns the knobs of the television. Sound swells from the dark oblong frame, the picture flickers on, and in the unechoing room he watches — and sleeps. Late at night his wife comes to switch off the set, but it is too late: Nowhere has done its work. The picture narrows to a point, burns for an instant, and disappears into the window on the void. In the chair are his clothes: worn trousers, worn shoes. Good enough, with a little mending, for his funeral; but the man himself is gone.

Nevertheless, at the end of the fantasy, I go through the motions of burying him — closed coffin to hide the tragedy. The funeral parlor proclaims his placelessness: broadloom and vinyl are his last country; men without faces bear him out. We drive down placeless roads to a cemetery laid with the grasses of the thruway. The grave is dug and waiting, but the coffin is lowered only slightly; it sways gently in the straps. The words are said, the mourners leave, and on a treeless plain he hangs forever in the air.

Men who have lived nowhere are buried nowhere.

No monument shall mark his head; no local roots clutch his breast.

Richmond and Kew have not undone him; Syracuse and Albany have not destroyed him.

No place wore him away, and nowhere receives him at last.

He shall return no more to his house; neither shall his place know him anymore.

2. *The Marsh Reed*

LECTOR: Well!
AUCTOR: Well, what?
LECTOR: Well — I never expected *that*.
AUCTOR: Neither did I. It is a chancy business.

▼　　　▼　　　▼

Proneness to fantasy is not the only effect of the sedentary life. A suburban parish priest, if he takes no steps to resist the pattern of his days, will find himself car-cursed and chairbound by the age of thirty-five. After eight years of driving everywhere and walking nowhere, I had arrived, short of wind and weak of limb, at the point of being unable to take a flight of steps without thinking of heart trouble. Exercise, of course, was the cure, but, as an unrepentant non-sportsman, my first concern was to find some form of it that would keep me out of the clutches of golf. It is, I suppose, the perfect clerical pastime, but it is just not my dish. For one thing, it can get expensive; for another, the exercise it provides is only intermittent; and, for the truth, I am no good at it. I am a duffer, and I am fit only for the duffer's part of the game. Once I had faced that fact, the rest was easy. I simply took up walking.

I have been delighted with it. It is free. It takes only reasonable amounts of time. It is always available. (It is essential to walk in all weathers. The fair-weather walker loses half the privileges of his sport: snow and rain, sunshine, fog, heat, and cold — no other exercise can match it for variety.) And it works. I have no facts to support it, but I have a theory that there must be a low incidence of heart disease among letter carriers. At any rate, the pounding heart is gone, the legs are usable again, and, doubtful blessing though it may be, I am much longer winded than before.

But walking has turned out to have intellectual as well as physical benefits. I am as much the victim of placelessness, as much the prisoner of canned environment as the next person. It has, therefore, been a delightful and metaphysical surprise to be introduced to *place* again. I have, for example, rediscovered what a hill is. The automobile is the great leveler. It not only annihilates distances; it irons all the prominences and eminences out of the world. I had lived in Port Jefferson for eight years as a parish priest, and I thought I knew it as a place, thought I understood pretty well how it gave itself out as *somewhere*. I was aware that it was hilly, and that that feature, on Long Island, automatically put it in select company: only the North Shore really rises and falls; the rest is mostly unrelieved outwash plain. But it wasn't until I walked up East Broadway for the first time that I, as a person, met the village as a place. It is a respectable hill. (The mark of a good hill, by the way, is the absence of sidewalk on its upper reaches. That is its letters patent of true prominence, the guarantee that only real walkers ever go all the way up: children, the poor, and the possessed. From the point of view of the municipality, such a motley crew as that can be left to walk in the gutter. Sidewalks are built for the sane.)

So I met my town on a hill, walking in the gutter for the last hundred yards, taking the land on its own terms, not mine. It was not an easy meeting — it never will be. It is physically impossible to take that hill at a normal walking pace and not be blown at the top. But it was a real meeting, and I am glad that the land can still leave me winded and refreshed.

It is another eight years now since I started walking; and up and down hills, past shacks and boatyards, along the waterfront, and through shaded streets I have found place again. In any other age it would not be much of an achievement, but in this one it is worth a little self-congratulation. I am part of a town, and I have not neglected the privileges of my membership.

Port Jefferson is just far enough away from New York City to have remained a small town, but it is also close enough to have felt the impact of the developers. More than half my parish lies outside the village proper. Sixteen years ago, the upland (and level) part of the countryside was rural: farms, woodlots, and scrub oak. Since then the housing developments have come in. It isn't Levittown yet, but the smell is in the wind. The better-looking ones, of course, have been left with a certain woodsiness about them, but even they are no place for a walker. The ones built on potato fields are just hopeless — great pieces of canned environment, dropped down in the middle of nowhere. It helps a little if the developers make the streets wind, but the repeating fronts of the five basic houses give it away: it is noplace.

Port Jefferson, on the other hand, is someplace — though, to tell the truth, it is not what it could be. It is untidy, distracted, and radically uncertain about just what place it is. But it is a place. There are a good many plans now to do it over, and heaven knows it needs it; but I don't look forward to the prospect. I don't trust the age to handle it properly.

The lower part of town, adjacent to the harbor, can be described with a little charity as a sprawling and indifferent sandlot: it was once a marsh, but it has been haphazardly filled in. Flowing across it, in a northeast path, is a creek that begins under the west hill and wanders toward the harbor. The creek is unavoidable and sempiternal; drainage demands it. Over the years, however, it has shrunk to the proportions of a glorified ditch. Along its length lies an assortment of junk: broken hulls, rusting metal — an anthology of seaside trash. I will trust any planner to see to it that it is cleaned up. But along its banks in places are great tall reeds with tasseled tops — the kind you can take home and make tiny whistle flutes of, if you spend a whole summer evening fooling with them. Do you think that the planners will leave those? What kind of odds will you give me that it will occur to any of them to make a park down there and encourage the reeds to grow the whole length of the creek? I wouldn't take your money. Not that the park wouldn't be worth it; it just will never happen. Or, if it does, they will pull up the reeds and plant marigolds. But I will give you two good reasons for making a park anyway.

The original name of Port Jefferson was Drown Meadow — a good, placey sort of name for a tidal swamp where men came to cut salt hay. In its wild state, it filled the space between wooded horse-shoe hills and sank slowly under the edges of one of the best natural harbors on Long Island. Through most of its civilized history, how-ever, it has been blessed (or cursed, if you don't like marine debris) with boatyards, gravel yards, and oil yards. The architecture of the village itself runs a poor second to the distinguished disarray of its waterfront. But, through it all, the creek with its stands of reed has remained: a part of the city of things that was here before men built a town. For me, that is reason enough for a park and for a bank of reeds in perpetuity. But I do not plan to hold my breath till it arrives.

The other reason is personal. I give it to you as a treasured secret. Marsh reeds, when full grown, vary from five to ten feet in height, and the tassels on the ends of the good ones are thicker than squirrels' tails. The next time you walk past a bank of reeds, try something. Pick out the tallest one you can reach, and cut it off with your penknife as close to the ground as possible. Ostensibly, perhaps even to yourself, it will seem that you are cutting it down to carry home to your children. No one will take serious exception. But in the carrying of it, you will make a discovery. Keep a record of your reactions: *It is impossible simply to carry a marsh reed.* For how will you hold it? Level? Fine. But it is ten feet long, and plumed in the bargain. Are you seriously ready to march up the main street of town as a knight with lance lowered? Perhaps it would be less embarrassing to hold it vertically. Good. It rests gracefully in the crook of your arm. But now it is ten feet tall and makes you the bearer of a fantastic mace. What can you do to keep it from making a fool of you? To grasp it with one hand and use it in your walking only turns you from a king into an apostle; to try to make light of it by holding it upside down is to become a deacon carrying the inverted crozier at an archbishop's requiem. Do you see what you have discovered? There is no way of bearing the thing home without becoming an august and sacred figure — without being yourself carried back to Adam, the first King and Priest. So much so that most people will never finish the experiment: the reed, if cut at all, will never reach home. Humankind cannot stand very much reality: the strongest doses of it are invariably dismissed as silliness. But silly is from *selig,* and *selig* means "blessed." If you ever want to walk your native ground in the sceptered fullness of the majesty of Adam, I commend the marsh reed to you. Whatever embarrassment it may cause you will be an *embarras des richesse.*

▼　　　▼　　　▼

My walking, therefore, has turned out to be money in my pocket — the recouping of an inheritance I had nearly been conned out of by a placeless age. But to walk through a village is not only to be restored to place. It is also to refresh the perception of the link between place and time, and so to come face to face with the fact of history. Place. Time. History. If I ask you whether you know what they mean, you will give me a confident Yes. You are sure you have grasped them for what they really are. But have you? Hasn't there been, since Adam's fall, a sharp and recurrent temptation to miss the point of them completely — to substitute plausible little mental diagrams for them? And isn't this the age of the triumph of that temptation? We like to believe that we see ourselves as living in *places,* as acting in *time,* as the protagonists of real *history.* But we seldom get near the realities: it is the abstract substitutes, the mental counters, that our minds fasten upon. Listen.

For place we substitute *space.* Think of the creek with its bank of reeds. It is a place. If it is to be saved, to be lifted up, to be kept as a part of the real history of this village, it must be saved as what it is, *for itself.* But that is hardly the most likely thing that will happen to it. The overwhelming temptation of the planners will be to bury it in a conduit and to plant macadam on its grave. And why? Because they will never have looked at it as a *place.* For them it will have been only an abstraction, something contained within coordinates on a civil engineer's map — a nice empty *space* which, once its natural intractabilities have been tamed, can be converted into their favorite kind of packaged *locale*.

They have their reward. I have a theory that the membership of the architectural committee for hell is being recruited on Long Island, with the best jobs going to the people who have run creeks through conduits and built laundromats, muffler graveyards, and motels along Route 25. I wish them no personal ill, but it would be against my principles to leave them without a curse: May ink run under their rulers forever, and their pencils break world without end.

And then there is time. And for time we substitute — well, that takes a little explaining. Words are sometimes a problem. *Time* in English is made to do far more work than should reasonably be expected of any one word. In Greek the labor of meaning is divided: there are two words for time. For abstract time — for time as a diagram, a system of coordinates — the Greeks had *chronos:* a solemn, unworldly notion they finally kicked upstairs and made a god. We have it with us still in chronometers, chronology, and chronicle. But for human time, for existential time — for the time that is to *chronos* as place is to abstract space — they had a word which, to the best of my knowledge, has not come into English at all: *kairos* — season, *high time,* opportunity. The distinction is not airtight, but it is solid enough to pass muster.

When I go for a walk in the morning, I notice the time at which I leave the house: 8:45, for example. That is *chronos.* Together with 9:10, it makes up the chronological coordinates of my walk. It is time as it can be plotted and drawn on a mental map. Once a person is trained to it, it is a comforting notion. It is pleasant to know what time, what *chronos,* it is, to be coordinated, to be on schedule. But real time, high time — *kairos,* season, opportunity, chance — is not trapped within the coordinates of the clock. It does not answer the minor question: What time is it? It goes straight to the major one: What is it time *for?*

Ever since Einstein, the impression has gotten about that somehow all our notions of time are inadequate. The advances of mathematics and physics are said to have proved that time is not absolute but relative, and that, worse yet, it can run at different rates for different people. For some years now the philosophical composure of the person in the street has periodically been sent sprawling by articles about what is called "the twin paradox." It seems to be a physical and mathematical certainty that if you sufficiently accelerate one of a pair of twins, you will start doing tricks with his time. When he gets back from his trip at something like the speed of light, he will find not only that he thought he had been gone less time than his brother reckoned, but that he *really had been.* Time would have gone slower for the traveler. His beard, if you please, would actually be shorter than his brother's.

To almost everyone, this is upsetting. We are used to conceiving of time as an absolute and unchanging continuum through which everyone passes at the eternally valid rate of sixty seconds per minute. But our consternation is based on a failure to distinguish *chronos* from *kairos. Chronos* never has been anything but relative. It seemed absolute only — precisely — because it was *cut off,* abstracted — because it had been turned into a god. *Chronos* seems constant only because all the clocks we can read — sun clocks, water clocks, escapement clocks, electric clocks, radioactive clocks, biological clocks, all clocks, down to the clock that makes my beard grow at the rate it does — are locked in the same relative velocity. It is a simple case of conspiracy. The answer to the question "What time is it?" has always been a put-up job.

But *kairos* is different. With our customary skill, you see, we have gotten the whole thing exactly backwards. We think *chronos* is absolute and *kairos* is relative. We imagine that we will always be able to be sure what time it is, but that we have to take potluck with what it is time *for.* As it turns out, however, what it is time *for* is the only thing that is not relative. Take the twin who left his brother at nearly the speed of light, but consider not the physical conditions of his being but the man *himself.* Use your imagination. Call him Cain. Assume that his hasty departure was due to his having murdered his brother, and behold! You have broken the trap of time.

You can let his *chronos,* his clock time, his biological time, do all the tricks it wants, but through all that relative *chronos* it will only be high time, *kairos,* for him to repent. And when he — young, radiant, and unrepentant — climbs out of his capsule, the old, unchanging law will be waiting for him. It will be a *kairos* for the assessment of his guilt and the payment of his debt. No matter what his *chronos* does — let him come back a thousand years too late for any living person to remember his crime — he will still come back in the same *kairos:* in time to hear the voice of his brother's blood crying from the ground.

Kairos, therefore, is the real thing, and *chronos* only a kind of game that a relative world is content to play. *Kairos* is the time of human beings, of events, of history; and *kairos,* not *chronos,* is the time I enter when I step out of my doorway at 8:45 A.M. For, as I walk, *chronos* ceases to matter. What counts is not what time it is, but what it is time for. And therein lies the true glory of walking.

The wind blows down the harbor, and it is high time — a *kairos* rarer than inlanders think — for the smelling of the salt air. Or the hedges are in bud, and it is a season, a *kairos,* for the chewing of privet leaves, for the relishing of green and bitter tastes. *Chronos* cannot find such things; he lives too high in the sky. These are events in the time of human beings. Their coordinates are found not on clocks but in the conjunctions of the web of history, in the mutual confrontations of real beings.

If you want to prove all this to yourself, notice what happens the next time you go for a walk (a walk of refreshment, of course, not of necessity). First of all, you will, insofar as you give yourself to walking, cease to pay any serious attention to the clock. Your time spent in walking is time spent outside the coordinates of *chronos.* If you should happen to pass a clock during your walk, you will not know quite what to make of it. It will seem to have lost its connection with the time at which you set out. You know, of course, that it is in the same system — that even if, *per impossibile,* the lighting company took leave of its senses and started supplying 50-cycle current instead of 60, all the little synchronous motors in all the electric clocks would still keep perfect step and conspire to present *chronos* as the changeless god he is. But the clock in the middle of your walk is irrelevant because you have, by walking, immersed yourself in historic time, in *kairos,* in the time of due season and of singular conjunctions. You have entered a time in which *now* is not a dimensionless point at the end of the second hand, but a *kairos* as wide and as high as all history.

For *now* is when the gull sits on the piling and the world is still. And *now* is when he leaves, dropping lazily before he glides and rises. And *now* is when the sun goes for good behind the growing overcast, and the bright day that began at some other *now* is gone forever. Do you see? Do you see how little it matters that the gull flew away at 8:53 or that the sun went in at 9:01? *Chronos* has his uses, but he can never tell you what it is time for.

The second experience is similar. As you lose track of other people's time during a walk, other people will lose track of you. Even if they know your usual path and pace, they will be hard put to guess where you are at any given moment of their measured time. This is partly because their private assessment of *chronos* will be based on the automobile, and they will have no working knowledge of the speed at which a walker proceeds. But it is also because they will generally be unprepared to imagine you as caught up in real *kairos.* They cannot assess the time of the watching of gulls, of the tasting of privet leaves, of the detour to catch the smell of creosote as it blows downwind from three new pilings baking in the sun. To the degree that they have a sense of their own *kairos,* they may be able to make allowances for your wanderings; but, if they are blind to everything except chronology, they will figure you wrong every time.

▼   ▼   ▼

Place, therefore, not *space. Kairos,* not *chronos.* Less preoccupation with what time it is, and more questions about what it is time *for.*

But the worst error, the deadliest substitution of the abstract for the concrete, of the essential for the existential, has yet to be mentioned. It is the substitution of *legend* and *chronicle* for history. And it is deadly because it is a compound of the other substitutions and has twice the power of perversion. History (to make a start on its definition) is the shape, the meaning of events. It is the direction, the gist, of things that happen in high times at real places. It is not simply the written or verbal record of events — that is only historiography, history as known, history as a science; nor is it the foisting of interpretations on fundamentally pointless and random happenings — that describes only bad historiography, non-history, history as missed. It is not the making of a point, but the catching of a point; not the assignment of meaning, but the discovery of meaning; not the fabrication of legends about a mythical beast, but the snaring of a real one. History — existential history — *is* the beast. What people have had to say about it is only the joyful or desperate record of the chase.

It is the very wiliness of the beast — his love of peculiar dens and his fierce impatience with cages — that so often brings us home from the hunt with something other than the beast himself. It is much easier to make up legends about him than to find him; much simpler to draw abstract diagrams of where he ought to be than to grasp where he really is. And there is always a flourishing market for the legends and diagrams. The crowd around the tavern fire is quite willing to sit and listen while the theoreticians explain how all the beast's wanderings through the trackless forest are regulated by economics, or fate, or the class struggle, or the principle of evolutionary progress. And there are always plenty of woodsmen willing to give out long and detailed accounts of every inch of the forest, without ever once showing you the beast himself. If you accept the theoretician's word for it, you will end up with *legend;* if you accept the woodsman's, you will have only *chronicle.* Only a real hunter can show you history.

About the legends and the diagrams, and about what I think is the real shape of history, I intend to say something by and by. Whether I am a hunter or a theoretician will be yours to decide when the time comes. Right now I want to take the easier subject first and explain what is wrong with *chronicle* as a substitute for history.

If I were to give you an exhaustive list of everything I did today, together with precise spatial and chronological coordinates for where and when I did it, you would, in one sense, know everything about my day. But what is more important, you would, by the same token, also know nothing about it. That I brushed my teeth at 5:47, for example, and saw a gull on a piling at 8:53 tells you nothing. Either of those events could be central to my history — or both of them irrelevant. The gull could be the lifting of a decade of despair or just another bird; the brushing of my teeth, an event unnoticed even by myself, or the first morbid suggestion of cancer. History cares which; chronicle does not. History is concerned with shape, direction, gist, singularity; chronicle jams everything into a mold. Chronicle tries to sound like history, but it never makes it. It is too abstract, too egalitarian, too ready to treat 5:47 as the equal of 8:53, and therefore too stupid to discover meaning.

Furthermore, chronicle, as it is actually practiced, is only the handmaid of history. Pure chronicle is endless and insufferable. Having no sense of judgment, no principle on which to choose among the things it is able to coordinate, it either drowns in its own data or else asks history to choose for it. The actual chronicles people compose, therefore, are really histories whose authors have ceased to think historically for themselves — who have bought a historical bill of goods without knowing it.

You have no doubt read history written like that; but what is more important, you have also *heard* history — personal history — that was written like that. Take a marriage that is almost on the rocks. Whatever attempts at a common history there may have been at the start, whatever agreements there once were about the gist and direction of their relationship, they have long since failed. Husband and wife have withdrawn into separate meanings; their marriage has ceased to have a history of its own. For a while, of course, they may manage to keep a common chronicle going: they may still be able to agree that last Monday he left his socks in the sink or that yesterday she did tell him she was going shopping. But only for a while. History is the mistress of chronicle; if husband and wife live separate histories long enough, they will end up with separate and irreconcilable chronicles.

One of the things a parish priest learns early is that there are three sides to every marital disaster: his, hers, and the truth. Somewhat later in the game he comes to realize that this doesn't necessarily mean that anybody is lying, at least not consciously. He becomes accustomed to finding the couple completely unable to agree on even a single item of chronicle. The truth is not suppressed; it is undiscoverable. The priest never does find out who put the socks in the sink or who picked up the carving knife first. The events are assigned to two different people in two equally authoritative chronicles. Nobody is lying; it is just that history has fallen apart and chronicle has followed suit.

History, therefore, is anything but academic: the grasping of it is the central business of human existence. First of all, because events — the singular conjunctions of people, places, and high times — either have a shape or they do not. If they do, it will make all the difference in the world to us to find out what that shape is — to get it right instead of wrong. If they do not, then life is not only a vapor but a deception, and we are all kidding ourselves by pretending to shape even a single word. The human race, of course, does not hesitate much between the alternatives. Most of us choose to think that history exists, and all of us *act* as if it does. So much so, in fact, that we spend most of our days doing something about it. We deny it, we rewrite it, we claim the only true understanding of it; we read it any way we like. But we read it as if possessed.

Every person I meet has a history that threatens or promises involvement in my history. Every thing, every place, every time is a mysterious conjunction, a sign to be interpreted. This book, therefore, is about the deciphering of a sacred stone — about the riddle of history. It is about our peculiar obsession with shape, with direction, with meaning. About why we bothered to invent marriage beyond sex, and friendship beyond advantage. About why we make towns and join lodges; about why we paint and whittle; about why we write poems and fugues. About peculiar creatures who would rather sing than shout, and who, from the first day they learned to use words, have never ceased to love to make them scan. Accordingly, I intend to define humankind — Adam — as the historical animal, as the being with a strange thirst for the *gist* of things. I want to refresh the sense of the priesthood of Adam, to lift up once more the idea of human beings as the priests of creation, as the offerers, the interceders, the seizers of its shape and the agents of its history. And there is no better place to begin than where history itself began. Listen.

And the Lord God planted a garden eastward in Eden, and there he put the man whom he had formed. Why? Why not be content to let Adam range through the open and random places of the world? Why this garden, this park, this *arrangement,* this shaping of creation? What on earth was God getting at? Mightn't it be that Eden was to be the sacrament, the sign, the effective hint of history? Of course. The placing of the first human being in paradise (the word meant "park," and *Eden* meant "pleasure") was the hint that Adam was to be nothing less than the priest of creation, the beholder and offerer of its meaning.

And the Lord God took the man and put him into the garden of Eden to dress it and to keep it. Look, Adam, he says. Look closely. This is no jungle; this is a park. It is not random, but shaped. I have laid it out for you this year, but you are its Lord from now on. The leaves will fall after the summer, and the bulbs will have to be split. You may want to put a hedge over there, and you might think about a gazebo down by the river — but do what you like; it's yours. Only look at its real shape, love it for itself, and lift it into the exchanges you and I shall have. You will make a garden that will be the envy of the angels.

As it turned out, Adam has — and Adam hasn't. We have missed the point of creation twice for every time we have caught it once; and hovels, ruins, and wars are the record of our failures. But it is the *point* that remains our preoccupation; the catching of the hint of the park is still the heart of our calling. For 75,000 years, give or take what you like, we have raked leaves and split bulbs, and we have built ourselves some pretty fancy gazebos. Culture — civilization — is the sum of our priestly successes, the evidence of the fulfillment of our vocation. The life of Adam — of every human being — is parks and plazas, and houses worthy of our priesthood;

it is falling in love with the hinted garden in the world and lifting it into a paradise indeed. Though unjust kings and queens, we are royalty still; though we have failed our priesthood, we remain priests forever. History has been our glory, and history has been our shame, but the shaping of creation into the City of God remains our obsession. The Mystical Body is the point of our being.

My creek with its reeds, therefore, is not far from the truth; my walking by it is a natural exercise of my calling. I long to see it a park because Adam grew up in one. I carry my marsh reed not only with pleasure, but by right.

3. The Bench Mark

Set in the sidewalk at the southeast corner of Port Jefferson harbor, halfway between the gravel yard and the icehouse, is a round bronze marker about four inches in diameter. I shall give you full particulars. In its center is a plain circle inscribed with a short line running north and south. Around this are three concentric bands of lettering. The innermost reads: $250 fine or imprisonment for disturbing this mark; the next: For elevation write to the Director, Washington, D.C.; and the last: BENCH MARK U.S. COAST & GEODETIC SURVEY.

It is some comfort to know that the powers that be are concerned to tell me where I am, but I am afraid they are too spiritual for my tastes. I am told that, if you write the Director (a grim and forbidding title: Who is he? Has he ever carried a marsh reed?), you will receive, accurate to several decimal places, the precise elevation of the plaque above mean low water. It is the old penchant for defining place in terms of space. Mean low water is like the man in the street: a handy abstraction you will never find anywhere. Look, instead, over here.

Due north from the mark is the dockside edge of the gravel yard. The harbor is calm now, and the tide is out, but I have stood on this spot at other seasons. I have come here with a crowd of my fellow townspeople — a fool among fools, but one with them as never before — during the last hours of a hurricane. It was a town meeting such as never happens in the time of clocks: we were called to stand in the howling wind and watch with morbid fascination while yacht after yacht was torn from its mooring, pushed drunkenly before the storm, and pounded to pieces against the bulkheads. Later on you could hear men entertaining each other with guesses about how far above mean high water the harbor had risen; but, while the storm lasted, space and *chronos* were forgotten. This was a *place* then, a conjunction of persons and things in high time and high wind. The next morning would be time enough for the engineers and the bankers to assess the damage; then and there we were too much in history to think in their terms. I am sure that no one bothered to notice how long we watched. Small boys raced up and down the stone heaps; men tried, foolishly and bravely, to board a boat and start its engine; and women with children hung back and talked about whatever it is that women talk about at such seasons. The bench mark has its coordinates and its uses, but the place of that conjunction was beyond its competence. Now come over here.

Walk up East Main with me. At one time it was actually the principal street of the village, but, when the shipyards left the center of town, another street usurped its title, and it had to be content with merely adjectival distinction. Perhaps out of disappointment the area around it became a backwater; for a long time it was considered a rough neighborhood. (There was a tavern at the lower end of the street which was still open when I first went to Port Jefferson. I can't remember its real name, but locally it was always referred to as "Bucket of Blood.") The roughness is pretty much gone now, and, as far as I am concerned, the street is priceless. It is the only part of the center of the village that still qualifies as a *place*. Though it has been cleaned up considerably, it still has buildings that follow the lay of the land and speak with voices of their own. I hope the planners take a good look at it before they turn themselves loose.

If you start from its lower end and walk on the west side of the street, you pass the following places: a fish market; something that looks like a foundation (actually it is the ruin of a truck garage cut into the side of the hill — the roof used to be level with the sidewalk, but it was torn off a few years back); an overgrown side yard with a rock garden and three mysterious gravestones (after sixteen years I still know nothing about them, and I don't know anybody who does — a real *place* is full of mystery); an old, narrow, two-story shingle house, now empty of people; an old, wide, two-story shingle house, now full of junk; and a space where a building used to be. Far enough. This is what I wanted you to see.

When I first started walking, the building, though ramshackle, was still there, and people lived in it. It was made of brick and wood — a firetrap of unquestionable orthodoxy. By and by, however, nobody lived in it at all, and it began to fall apart in earnest. A couple of years ago the property was bought by a neighbor, the building was torn down, and the foundation filled and seeded. It was an improvement.

But before it came down, it was gradually pierced and disemboweled; through the broken brickwork and gaping windows you could see into the second story. There, perched in the middle of a collapsing floor, was an old iron-frame bed, painted, as it should have been, in chipped and dirty ivory. When the house went, it went too; but when I pass the place now, I imagine I still see it perched there in the air, a lost piece of history — a place that was once a place, and now is nowhere. I come upon it daily as upon a scene of singular conjunctions (were they gracious or violent? were they faithful or promiscuous?); a bed of local joys and pains, a thing of high times, due seasons, last chances. Where is it now? Has it simply gone whistling down the wind into nothing?

It may be foolish of me, but I rebel at that: history so perishable, meaning so meaningless, seems hardly worth the bother. It makes our priesthood inane. The whole point of our liaisons is the weaving of a greater web; what we have in mind is always vaster than what we have in hand. Whoever they were who entered that bed, they entered it because, somewhere in their meeting, they caught a glimpse of the web, felt a twinge of priestliness. They acted, when they most acted, because they saw themselves as ministers, as builders of a city larger and longer than themselves. It does not much matter what kind of city they willed — it may well have been a city of unreality and perversion. The point remains that, simply as human beings, as priestly agents, they could not help making history: they could not even slip between the sheets without having something in mind. Historic triumph or historic blunder, theirs was a conjunction of historic animals; if the history they made is now gone completely, it can never really have been there at all.

If all our cities go to ruin, if all our webs break and ravel, if friendship, family, law, and justice survive only as long as the floorboards hold up — if the shape of the world simply flakes away like the paint on the bedstead — then our wound is incurable. We are not sick of some alien disease that destroys our history; we are sick of history itself. It is not that the corruption of our best is our worst; it is that our very best is poison. Our deepest desire, in every one of our conjunctions, is to weave with longer threads than we can hold, to make the tapestry of history reach from East to West. But if change and decay reign supreme, the length of the threads and the vastness of the tissue are delusions. We are not weaving at all. We are only crocheting little squares for a crazy quilt that no one will last long enough to put together.

Any attempt to speak meaningfully about history, therefore, must come to grips with *change.* On the one hand, growth and transition, birth and corruption are obviously the raw material of history: in a world where nothing changed, the imposition of newer and higher shapes would not only be idle; it would be patently impossible. But, on the other hand, it is equally obvious that change is the very thing that wrecks the shapes which we in our priestliness try to impose: all our beds fall down. We have arrived, therefore, at a paradox. From here we go straight up or straight down; it is time to walk carefully.

As any reader of old tales knows, the only solution to a paradox is a *mystery:* the apparent either/or is the door by which the deeper magic enters the story. Unfortunately, however, the wisdom of old tales has not always been around when it was needed. True, human beings, elves, and hobbits may set their traps for mystery as soon as they smell a paradox, but a good many philosophers of history have insisted on hunting simplicities instead. Their attempts to account for the relationship between history and change have produced legends and chronicles galore, but the results have been somewhat less than satisfactory. Some of them have ended up denying change, some of them have abolished history, and almost all of them have, one way or another, taken the true agency of history away from real beings — from *things* and *persons* — and have handed it over to gods, or ghosts, or fancy mystiques.

Accordingly, the problem raised by the vanished bed on East Main Street cannot be skirted. As I promised, I shall eventually tell you more of what I think is the nature of the mystery that solves the paradox. (As a matter of fact, as evidence of good faith, I shall tip my hand right now and give it to you in code: history is saved from destruction by change because the priesthood of Adam has been renewed through the Passion and Resurrection of Jesus as the High Priesthood of Christ. See, for example, Hebrews 7:24 and 25. But no more. All things in their seasons.) For the present, I want to spend a little more time on some of the solutions to the paradox which, I think, make more problems than they solve. If you do not like philosophy at all, skip to the next chapter. On the other hand, if you like your philosophy done to a fare-thee-well, you had better do the same: what follows here will be too random for your taste. But, if you have the patience for it, I propose to divert you briefly, not with a complete natural history of historical errors, but with a little portfolio of philosophical field sketches. Herewith, therefore, a homemade, hand-lettered Bestiary of Unhistoric Monsters.

Occasionalism

*(presumed extinct, but still flourishing;
specimens frequently found among the pious)*

Occasionalism is the doctrine that denies what is called secondary causation. It is a very pious-sounding proposition indeed. It says that God alone is the real actor in all events — that *things* are not true causes at all, but only fronts for God. According to occasionalism, it is God who makes the eggs hatch and the leaves fall. And not simply in the sense that God made a world full of substantial beings which are then capable of acting in their own right, but in the sense that nothing except God really acts at all: only the Prime Cause *matters*. Bach did not write the *Fugue in D Minor*; God did. Bach was only the occasion, the front. And I have not written this book, or blown my nose, or, to push it all the way, told my wife a lie. God did. If an occasionalist wants to make room in his system for freedom, he has to do unwarranted and illogical tricks with it. If he is consistent, he simply makes God the author of evil.

What is right about occasionalism is the clarity with which it sees the *ultimate* responsibility of God for everything. What is all wrong about it is the way it abolishes the *proximate* responsibility of individual things for everything else. It honors God by dishonoring what he made. Bach did so write the fugue — Bach himself: a real, acting, two-fisted, feet-on-the-ground *substance;* and I blew my own nose — I: a true *secondary cause,* standing gloriously *extra nihil* and *extra causas.* Occasionalism makes the world meaningless. If only God matters, if nothing on earth really changes anything, then nothing on earth makes any difference. History is a put-up job.

Essentialism

(rare and unpopular; largely driven off by existentialisms of various sorts; formerly the favorite household pet of high and dry scholasticism)

The error of essentialism is to make too much of the abstractive power of the intellect. The mind indeed knows by grasping essences: *cat, pineapple, player piano, horse;* but essentialism, in a rapture over its ability to pickle *horse* in the juices of the mind, forgets that only existing horses are real beings. The essence *horse* has logical being: it exists in the mind; but it does not exist in reality or in any Platonic realm of pure ideas. There is, to be sure, something about actual horses that jibes nicely with it, but, for all that, *horse* is not horses. They are solid and changeable; it is immaterial and unvarying. The essentialist's world, therefore, is a world without drama and without history. It has no room for real change. It is only a stylized pageant in which changeless symbols make formal bows to each other as they pass. It is all neat and dainty; but it is a world without meetings, unfit for human habitation. It is a universe in which nothing will ever lurch toward you in love or anger, a world in which nothing *stinks* — a world in which you will never have to scrape horse manure off your shoe: the essentialist variety is odorless and remains politely in the vicinity of the horse.

Essentialism inevitably leads to a static view of reality. History is the shape of change; deny change, and you will never even begin to get near history. Yet, in the name of history, essentialism has produced some of the most changeless and non-historical monuments in the world. Disneyland. Freedomland. Places that are no-place. Places where nobody lives. Places where you can see, in all its pickled Platonic beauty, the true essence of an American town in the 1890s or a frontier stockade in the Old West. Diagrams! Enclaves! Abstract forts where the siege of change can be resisted as long as the admissions roll in and the banks are happy with the mortgage. And the so-called restorations of colonial villages are no better. Restorations to what? Not to history. In the worst of them, no one is allowed to live at all. Employees in costume come in from 10:00 to 6:30 to tend the images. In the rest — in the ones that have not insulated themselves by excluding people — the real inhabitants live lives that have nothing to do with the essentialist tourist trade. Behind the abstract, early Federal façade of Stony Brook lies the changing and real life of a Levittown or a Rollingwood. Such towns may not have a very wise view of their true history — they may have none at all — but at least they have sense enough to keep their distance from the essentialist pretense in their midst.

Chance

(common, but little understood; the name is applied
to many specimens, some harmful, some not)

Chance is the doctrine that change occurs only at random and that meaning, therefore, is only apparent, not real. I am not happy to have to use *chance* to describe it. I do so only because it is the common word, and the substitutes for it are sometimes misleading. But *chance* has such a glorious history, such a richness and viability, that I think I shall switch to *accident* right now. In mathematics, for example, chance has a long, meaningful, and respectable pedigree: it is not vague or accidental; it is precisely predictable. Insurance companies make money. And behind chance, in Latin, is *fortuna,* fortune, that which occurs in the nick of time. Next to it, in English, is *luck.* Noble company! A Roman goddess and an English lady. And nice people! Not distant proto-proto-proto-fathers like *chronos,* but charming, available women who can make real history if they set their minds to it. And, finally, there is ordinary usage, where we speak of first chances, second chances, and last chances — all of them gorgeously, solidly historical. I have made up my mind. I will not sully the word. *Accident* must do its work.

The doctrine of *accidental change,* then, destroys history. And it destroys it from the ground up. So much so that nobody can write anything about a world of pure randomness, a world in which everything is an accident. The first attempts at it failed, and so have all their successors. Take Lucretius. In a treatise called *De rerum natura* he set out to define the world in terms of the random motion of atoms. He did very well and wrote a long book, but he gave the whole thing away at the start. In the beginning, he said, there was a perfect and parallel rain of atoms all falling in straight lines and never colliding with each other. So far, so good. But where in that world does change come from? Ah, said Lucretius, what happened was that one of the atoms swerved and bumped its neighbor, and the resulting *mêlée* set the whole world of change in motion. From there on, the system worked beautifully. With enough bumps and rattles you get elephants, mushrooms, and kumquats. Behold a world built by accident! Elephants are as good as mushrooms are as good as kumquats are as good as people; lies are as good as truth, and senselessness as good as shape. It is all just bumps. There is no meaning and no history.

Ah, but did you watch his left hand closely? Did you see where that first bump came from? Of course you didn't. He couldn't show you without ruining the act. Because that bump was not random. It was unique. No matter that all the other things in his world have no explanation but accident, that one at least had a *history;* it caused some thing, it acted some where, it moved in *high time.* Lucretius produced a historyless system by the shabby trick of palming a real piece of history.

Eventually, as I recall, he faced up to it. He raised the question of where the first bump came from and said he just didn't know the answer. He should have stopped right then. But he didn't; and neither do the rest of his accident-mongering brethren. As I said, it would ruin the act. For the accidental view of history has to be *faked* somewhere. No one can consistently, from the ground up, present accident as the explanation of change. Somewhere they have to insert an "I don't know" — a disclaimer that the beginning simply was what it was: different. But if the beginning was different, why not the rest? If you have to import a historical gimmick to get started, why not try historical gimmicks all the way through? If you have to excuse the beginning by saying that's just the way things were, why not excuse the whole order by saying that's just the way things are, and get on with it — on with the serious business of facing history instead of dabbling with diagrams? *Vale, Lucreti;* you are no help at all.

Fatalism and Determinism

(commonly supposed to be two distinct species; on examination, however, found to be the front and hind ends of the same beast)

Fatalism and determinism both offer the same magical key to the riddle of change: everything is predetermined. Every change that has ever occurred has been the result of an already completed shape. For the fatalist, it is an unnatural, immaterial shape, a power of air and darkness against which mere things struggle in vain. For the determinist, it is a natural and material shape, working irresistibly within things from the beginning. Nothing occurs that was not built in from the start.

They are both very close to the truth, so close that it is a case of not seeing woods for trees or towns for houses. There *is* a shape. And it is not just the result of accidental collisions between things. And it *is* in some sense superior to things — outside and pulling, or inside and pushing. But there they lose it. Because the shape is not, in any simple sense, irresistible — the pulling and the pushing are more mysterious than that. And it is not just inside or just outside — it is strangely both. The occasionalist was wrong when he made God the only actor; how much more are these two, when they make fate or mechanism the only actor. They have misread the play. Fate and mechanism are not actors at all. Fate will be lucky if he can get a job as prompter, and mechanism should be happy he is a stagehand. God, of course, is an actor, but not the way the occasionalist thinks. Apart from his role as author and producer — in which he takes exceptional care to stay out of the play and let his creatures stand proudly on whatever feet he gave them — he shows up as a protagonist only mysteriously, as a *thing* among other things: among the children of Israel, for example, or, supremely, in the *humanity* of Christ. He appears to insist that the drama of history be played out by creatures themselves — by men and women, wood and steel, mountains, rivers, rain, and sand. He will not allow them to be fronts for anybody.

The error of fatalism and determinism, therefore, is that they do just what God refuses to do: they take the responsibility for history away from things and park it somewhere else. They invent outside forces or built-in mystiques and make them the real actors in the play. They claim to have discovered a formula which, if it could have been known, would infallibly have predicted all things. They can write you the recipe for history without having to look at history at all.

That, of course, is just thinly veiled occasionalism. They may posit mystiques where occasionalism posits God, but the end result is the same. In place of sly little trapdoors between the inside of God's mind and the inside of things, they run hidden wires to every existing being — economic wires, physical wires, fatalistic wires, psychological wires — and then insist that it is the current in the wires, and not the things themselves, that make history. But that is to make an even worse shipwreck than before. Bad enough that occasionalism should make things a front for God; worse ten times over that they should be turned into patsies for a lot of abstract and mindless forces.

Out with all the occasionalisms, then, whether divine, fatalistic, or deterministic. It is *things* that make history, not forces, not mystiques — not even God in any simple sense. Just real beings acting for themselves within the real but mysterious purpose of a graceful and competent creator; things solid enough to act out of their own natures, and a God sure enough of his power to give them their head. Mysterious? Of course. If the occasionalisms had been willing to admit mystery, they would not have run afoul of mystique.

Pantheism

(a monster; rare in its pure state, but widespread in hybrid forms; sometimes attractive, always dangerous)

One word only. Pantheism is occasionalism without God. If occasionalism *with* God makes nonsense of history, how much more pantheism, whose god is only the sum total of all the occasions — a kind of cosmic chronicle that omits nothing, prefers nothing, loves nothing, and hates nothing. It is a diagram of indifference, a dark and illegible legend. Out with it! Ugh!

Evolutionary Supersession

(the most commonly domesticated of all the beasts; the sacred cow of modern times)

Evolutionary Supersession is my own fancy name for the extension of the biological hypothesis of evolution to every other subject under the sun: history, art, science, language, architecture. In stigmatizing it, I have no intention of attacking the biological hypothesis itself. The history — and the idiocies — of the nineteenth-century clerical sport of Darwin-baiting are still too fresh in people's minds to give me any hope of being understood if I did. About evolution itself, therefore, I offer no criticisms, only a caution: evolution is not the same thing as destiny; it is, at best, only a description of one of the ways in which *things* make history. The mystery of the shaping of the world cannot safely be reduced to *any* mystique — especially not to a transformist one. Evolution may indeed be crucial to the mystery — may be the left and right legs on which it runs and leaps; but in a sane definition it will be seen only as the body of the mystery, not as its soul and substance.

The caution is, I think, necessary. The modern world is so used to equating evolution with history that it quickly misreads even the most expert handling of the subject. It assumes almost automatically that the final destiny of the world is a matter of the mere working out of built-in transformist processes. Take, for example, Teilhard de Chardin's concept of the Omega Point. It is frequently assumed to be a kind of glorious last stop on the railroad of creation — someplace that the world will arrive at quite on its own steam. Yet, as far as I can see, the Omega Point is simply Teilhard's evolutionary way of talking about what I have referred to as the fullness of the mystery of the City. As a matter of fact, on a fair view of all his writing, it turns out to be none other than Christ the Incarnate Word mightily and sweetly ordering all things: Teilhard is as far from mere mystique as the Bible is. But such is the fascination of the transformist epic that his commentators, as often as not, set him forth as the supreme vindicator of evolution as the key to history.

My point is that he isn't; and that evolution simply can't do the work they set for it. What it really accomplishes is a good deal of mischief. The habit of equating history with evolution makes disastrous alterations in the way we look at the world. Just allow evolution as a mystique to become the interpretive principle in any field, and, in proportion to the extent of its application, the true shape and history of the subject will vanish from sight.

For what does it do? It offers itself as a master key for discovering the shape of change. Once we adopt it, we promptly acquire a penchant for thinking not about the real history of things but about the evolutionary shape they are supposed to have. We begin by seeing what comes earlier as a provisional, a transitional version of what comes later. Then we find ourselves looking on the earlier as explainable only in the light of the later. And finally we discover we are unable to assign any intrinsic and abiding importance to the earlier, since its truest function was to be superseded by the later. One disclaimer. I am by no means ruling out the fact of change, or the possibility of a legitimate doctrine of development. I am only saying that evolutionary supersession makes things in themselves meaningless, and that it makes real history indecipherable. It is a key, all right, but it does not fit the lock of the actual world.

More than that, it contains the seed of its own destruction. By its constant insistence that the meaning of the earlier is discoverable only in the later, it effectively cuts itself off from discovering any meaning at all. It is all very well to say that the earlier phases of a science or an art are important chiefly because they can be seen in the light of today's syntheses; but only the shortest-sighted among us can fail to see that the evolutionary saw that thus fells Thomas Aquinas, Telemann, Newton, and the harpsichord also cuts off the branch we are sitting on. If the past is important only as a transition to the present, then the present is important only as a transition to the future: the much-touted evolutionary meaning of history turns out to be one that never arrives. As a matter of fact, the evolutionary view of history never does come up with *meaning*. It starts with a *mystique* of improvement, and, thousands of years later, it makes an end, with the mystique still beautifully intact, but with no way of allowing anything but the contemporary to matter. Mercifully, few people apply it consistently: while they are tearing down old buildings with one hand, they are holding an old novel with the other. But, insofar as it is applied at all, it plays hob with history. For it is not an approach to history. It is a mystique of the modern, a cult of the contemporaneous. For all its devices, it never escapes from the purblindness that leads people to think today's hemlines the only right ones.

Here is a quick and exceedingly partial list of instances in which it has done its damnedest: the facile economic evolutionism that sees property only as an institution to be superseded; the glib assertion, mostly by non-scientists, that Newtonian physics is dead; the prejudice, among cellists and flutists, against gambists and recorderists; silly things said about the lute by people who have never heard Dowland played by Julian Bream; idiocies uttered about Giotto being transitional to Masaccio and Masaccio an unevolved Michelangelo, by people who apparently can't see that Giotto thought he was a painter in his own right.

The past stood for itself; if you take it as transitional, you preclude the discovery of its meaning. Its history escapes as you write it. If the evolutionary supercessionists would only content themselves with working up a good doctrine of development, they might have a chance of discovering something about politics or painting or music or the history of science. But they insist on evolution, and as a result they massacre the past. Their watchword is: No prisoners!

One other instance. The history of language, seriously and factually contemplated, defies evolutionary explanation. To be sure, the drugstore encyclopedias and the little (and not so little) school science texts still hand out the grunt-and-groan theory of the origin of language. They leap from the *oogle umph* of the savage to the prose of John Donne with scarcely a strain. Evolution accounts for it all.

What they never seem to see is that no known savage has ever been caught with a vocabulary limited to *oogle umph;* that it is precisely in the early stages of a language that you are likely to find more complicated accidence; and that most historical languages, if they can be ascertained to run in any direction at all, seem actually to run downhill.

Language, almost more clearly than anything else in the world, refuses to have even its poorest specimens written off as of transitional importance only. Every known instance of it, from the best to the worst, looks more like a game played for its own sake, like something that would matter even if never another word were said. The real growth of English, for example, is not evolutionary but developmental: not the endless succession of transitional forms, but the slow and continuous building of a city of speech, the age-long addition of monument after monument to the real and enduring fabric of the metropolis of the English tongue.

What is needed is a moratorium on evolutionary explanations and an honest attempt at another, and more merciful, doctrine of development. The evolutionary interpretation of history is gratuitous: *post hoc* is not necessarily *propter hoc;* it could just as well be *propter* something else of vastly greater mysteriousness. The successions of history make more sense when understood in a way that does not destroy the past. The early and the late are better seen as the spreading suburbs of an old and growing city than as discrete and transitional individuals which ceaselessly replace each other. For what it is worth, therefore, I give you the doctrine of the Mystery of the City as my contribution to a sane concept of development.

Take the whole tissue of any science. Take theology, for example. We have our share of the evolution-mongers. They keep howling for a modern theology to suit the modern world. They are quite prepared to discard the theological past as so much useless baggage. But they are wrong. The former and latter theologians of the church are, all of them, more intelligible if they are taken not as each other's precursors and successors, but as earlier and later builders, each of whom did his work, left his monument, and went to his reward. True enough, some of those monuments — Arius's, for example, or

Novatian's — have been submitted to the wrecker's ball, and better structures built in their places. But others have been left to stand as seemly and useful buildings. On the evolutionary theory this is unintelligible — only the latest suburb is fit for modern habitation. But on a sound doctrine of development the whole city of theology remains our rightful territory. The real history of theology, therefore, is not an endless supersession of opinions but the slow disclosing of the true shape of a city.

Or take the history of the natural sciences. The hint of the fundamental formula for relativity turns out to have been buried all along in one of the oldest buildings in mathematics: the Pythagorean theorem. Einstein does not supersede Pythagoras; he is his fellow citizen — and in no mean city. At the age of ten, Einstein rejoiced when he heard the theorem and proved it on his own; as for Pythagoras himself, he sacrificed one hundred oxen the day he discovered it. That is history. It carves change into useful shapes. Evolutionary supersession is a dull tool. It simply butchers meaning.

Or, finally, take Port Jefferson. It sits by its harbor like the woman at the well — it has had many shapes, and the shape it now has is not its own. Bounded by hills, set down on its salt marsh, it has failed to be a city more often than it has succeeded. But its failures have been always — have been precisely — failures to become *itself*, to find Port Jefferson in Port Jefferson. Its history has consisted largely of the missing of its history; but it has never stopped trying. And it cannot: it has eyes. If it will only keep them open, they will tell it all it needs to know. They will tell it, of course, that it has not found its history — anyone with eyes can see that; but they will also tell it that its history is still waiting to be found, and anyone with eyes can see that too. Home is where we start from. If the day ever comes when we get it right, we will rejoice in the discovery of something that was there all along. With Pythagoras we shall sacrifice one hundred oxen.

Do you see what that means? It means that history is not simply the building of the City or the finding of the City; it is *the growth of the City in a high mystery.* It means that there are no shortcuts. No neat little mystiques that will make it pop up automatically; no fancy fates that will drop it down, ready-to-install, from the realm of pure ideas; not even a God who will push it down your throat willy-nilly. It will indeed grow up from the earth, but not by a mystique; and it will indeed in some sense come down from heaven, but not by miracle. It will grow up in the mystery of the real and substantial interactions of things that can act for themselves; and it will come down in the mystery of an omnipotence that rules by grace and not by force. When it comes for the first time, it will have been here long since; when it comes for the last, it will be, astonishingly, the same thing.

Have I given my whole case away? Have I locked the mystiques out of the front door only to let them in at the back? I don't think so. It is *mystery* that saves me. But mystery in earnest, not just puzzle. Mystery as God's inscrutable way of doing business. Mystery as the way he steers the bicycle of history with his hands in his pockets. Nobody is shoved, nothing is jimmied; nothing need ever be anything but true to itself. *He never even touches the handlebars!* Pilate is Pilate, and Caiaphas is Caiaphas; Peter is Peter, and John is John; the soldiers are soldiers, and the women are themselves; the nails are iron, and the cross is wood. All in their own natures, all acting for themselves: the creatures of a God powerful enough not to have to use inside mystiques or outside clubs; of a God who can afford *anything;* of a God who can do nothing but hang there and still ride history home no-hands.

4. The Renegade Priest

Very well, then: mystery as the key to change. And mystery *neat* — not mystery and water. Not the diluted kind that solves the case by saying it was only the butler that did it, but the full-strength solution whose last unnerving word is that the butler was really an archangel in disguise.

But is that a fair answer? Does it give even the sympathetic listener any smallest crust to gnaw on? Do you not have a right to wonder whether it is being used to excuse mere mystification? Granted that the heart of mystery must by nature remain within the veil, may you not still reasonably ask to finger the cloth a little? If you are told you cannot hope to see the mystery face to face, is there not at least some cleft in the rock where you can hide as it passes and catch a glimpse of its back parts — of the angle of its hat or the style of its walking?

There is. And you have seen it already: the space left by the demolished building on East Main Street.

The bed in the air, you recall, was a piece of history that had been lost from sight; and it was, by that very fact, a challenge to the possibility of any history whatsoever. If things that once were thought to matter supremely can, by the simple process of physical change, cease to matter at all, then something is wrong somewhere. Either we were mistaken about the mattering or we were mistaken about its disappearance; but one half of the dilemma has got to give. My own bias, of course, is clear, and I propose to follow it: we were right the first time. Things do matter, they do *mean;* the inveterate human assumption that we have something to *do* with history is no delusion. When we write, when we sing, when we tell children not to leave juice glasses on the piano; when we flirt, when we cry, when we marry, when we burn — we are not just kidding ourselves. We were meant to mean: shape and history are our native air.

But how do you prove it? What do you look at to see it? The question comes back stronger than ever: If that history is saved, where is it? And this time the answer, though still a mystery, begins at least to show the sleeves of its shirt. In the emptiness between two buildings we brush against a singular bit of weaving, a piece of cloth with a strange and exciting *hand:* the bed in the air was one of the conjunctions of the City. It may now be gone, but its connections run forward and backward into the web of history. And not only that. The couple who lay in it were priestly beings: if they still exist, the offering they made of each other still stands, for good or ill. Two facts, therefore: the fact of the material existence of the web, and the fact of the continued being of the priestly creatures who wove it. A left sleeve and a right. Not the mystery itself, of course, but at least some solid vestiges of its clothing. *Presences,* not just hopes. Two contacts with something that demands more than a shrug in reply — something to which the only possible answer is: *Who's there?*

Consider first the left sleeve: the *web* left by the mystery of change. Individuals replace each other constantly, but the City remains with us. The bed in the air has long since vanished, but the history of that bed persists: it is extended beyond itself in the fabric of the City — it has continued to *mean,* to make a difference. And it has continued in a way that is very plain and old-fashioned: it has had physical and moral consequences; biologically and personally it remains the source of blessings and curses. Perhaps, for example, the marriage in that bed was fruitful. Children went from it into histories of their own. But they went endowed by *its* history. Bright or dull, kind or cruel, rich or poor, sick or whole, they proceeded forth as all things must: from other things — the heirs or victims of their origin. The bed from which they sprang was a conjunction of the web of history; the threads that met there crossed, joined, and continued on into the tissue of their lives. Their IQ's, their blood types, their pigmentation, their accent — all came to them trailing long warps from a past that does not even need to be known to be received.

What is all this but the City? To say it is a very primitive aspect of the City is to leave it a city nonetheless. But to say that it is nothing but itself is to miss the point altogether. The very fact of physical change is the first hint of something beyond physical change: continuity. Nothing moves itself. The threads are precisely the threads of a web; relationship is an intimation of the City. And it defies reduction to meaninglessness. Even the biological and geological stones of the City will not keep their peace at that. The fact of physical causation will not let itself be taken for granted. The whole will not be reduced to its parts. To say that IQ is only genes, or eye color only Mendel's law, is impossible. Why *only?* Cloth is not only threads; it is weaving. The real issue is why are there genes at all, why Mendel's law? The ultimate question is: *Who's there?* To let it go at genes is like being kissed in the dark and saying it was only a kiss in the dark. People who can do that should be suspect. They have found a lipstick-stained cigarette on an uninhabited island and have gone back to counting clam shells.

Or take it up a notch. The people who lay in that bed either grew in love or shrank in hate, and their love or their hate went forth with power. They grew up in the shadow of the beds that preceded them, and their own bed cast its shadow on their children's history. Again, long warps. Shuttles that cross and recross the loom. Blessings. Curses. Real gifts — gracious or sinister. How many generations of mishandling did it take to leave him unable to love a woman, or her unwilling to hold her tongue? Or how far down the web will the thread of her pity run, and where will his patience not extend its rule?

The first hint of the City, therefore, lies in the real transmissions that occur between things — in the *exchanges* that make up the tissue of history. We stand in a world of discrete individuals, but in all that world no individual is separate from the rest. Genetically, morally, legally, and economically, we are members one of another.

Even the left sleeve of the mystery is a marvel of weaving, a tissue of coinherence.

And if the physical web of being is such, how much more the other sleeve, the web formed by our priestly oblation of the world? For beyond the concrete transmissions — well past the comparative simplicity of the blessings and the curses — lie the vast complexities of the City as it is lifted up by the priesthood of Adam and held within the tissue of the mind. Having picked my bone with essentialism, I have no further argument with knowledge. In its true place it can hardly be exalted too much. It is the glory of humankind, the chief vessel of our priesthood. Our disasters are due to its perversion, not its use.

I have a black-and-tan hound who walks with me every day. He answers, when he likes, to the name of Tom. It is now illegal, even in Port Jefferson, to walk a dog without a leash, but I do it anyway. As a matter of fact, I consider walking a dog an outrage — on man and beast. Dogs are creatures in their own right; they must act for themselves, not be operated by people. They must walk, not *be walked.* Tom and I proceed through our village in an equality. It is his as much as it is mine. And it is his in a way that cannot be mine except through my priesthood as a human being. Sometimes, when we come to the foot of town, he leaves me, and I do not see him again for hours. My path and his diverge; we follow separate threads through the tissue of the city. My way lies along streets, but his along tracks that even boys cannot follow. Across yards, past hedges, over the sandlots, and through the creek he traces the pattern of his going; and in the wonder of his animal knowledge, he sees and remembers, and learns the way. (There are days on which, my children tell me, he hangs around the school — a good mile from the house — just before the buses leave. Even when my wife has driven the children home herself, he invariably arrives before them.)

My reaction to all this is wonder and delight. There is a Port Jefferson about which I know nothing except through Tom. It is a city of another size and shape, a set of unimaginable vistas and detours. And my wonder and delight are only heightened by the fact that Tom himself knows so little about what he knows. He can beat an automobile home — he is master of this city as few people are — and yet he does not know it as a *city*. He can navigate the web, but he will never *think* of it. That is my office — mine as Adam, the priest of creation. The meeting of his threads and mine are mine alone to see. If the City grows because of Tom, it will be because Tom's knowledge has been taken up in mine.

And from there it is only a step to other threads, and to conjunctions like the sand of the sea.

At one of the gravel docks, huge stones are currently being lifted from barges and loaded on flatbed trucks. No one here now seems to know much about them. They are a subject for speculation. Where do they come from? Where are they going? A city of men and women, in its natural and casual approach to mysteries, chats idly about them. But it chats by necessity; for the paths of those stones are more lines in the web, more tracings of city upon city. The inquiry is a priestly quest, the search for a handhold on the shuttle by which the stones are woven into the fabric of history.

As a matter of fact, my own knowledge of them is slightly more extensive. They were quarried, I presume, somewhere up the Hudson, hewn from their ancient places in a city of hills, and floated downriver through the Sound to this harbor. The trucks, I understand, take them to Montauk, or Westhampton, or someplace out east to be set down on the edge of the land in an attempt to achieve the shaping of still another city. There they will lie in great stone groins built out into the sea. From the ribbing of their first city into the groins of a second, and only I — Adam — know it. The web is built ceaselessly, but it is we alone who see it and lift it up. The City comes to fruition only by our priesthood.

It is vast beyond dreams. Even in the fibers of one man's being, it extends to the corners of creation. What do I hold within me for lifting, for oblation? The passing smell of coffee roasters on a dark day in lower Manhattan. Sunlight on Lake Michigan, and the waves lapping at still other groins. Rain on the tenement-lined streets off First Avenue, where Stuyvesant Town has since reared its head. The forever vanished slashes of sunlight shining down through the tracks of the old Third Avenue El.

We were meant to love the City and to lift its exchanges beyond themselves; to grasp its weaving and to feel its *hand.* Not simply to be the lovers of beauty, but the lovers of *being,* just because it *is.* For it is *ens inquantum ens* that is the root of beauty, goodness, and truth, and of the oneness that is the raw silk of the tissue of the city. But it is Adam the priest who alone can see its threads for what they are and weave them, through their crossings and conjunctions, into history.

▼　　　▼　　　▼

Two hints so far, therefore, of the outline of the mystery: its operation in things by the mute but eloquent fact of change, and its operation in human beings by the lifting of the web into their knowledge as history. It is a beginning. But it is no place to stop. It raises as many questions as it solves. Granted that the mystery seems present in things and in us, how do we know it is not just an appearance? First of all, what of the misshapings of history, what of our endless years of wrong history and bad history? If we love shape so well, why do we wreck it so often? Should we not expect so great a mystery to be somewhat more successful? And, secondly, what about the fact that the priests of the mystery — human beings — can hold the City together only as long as they can hold themselves together? Our knowledge is as wide as all history, but it goes out when our brains go out. We die. The marvelous devices that held the city in the conjunctions of their wires go into the ground — are disconnected, disassembled, and junked. Where is meaning *then?* Have we discovered the marks of the mystery only to lose them again in a darker forest? Have we built a dike against unmeaning only to have it destroyed by the pressure of the waters it contains?

It is important not to give too fast a reply. There are so many cheap answers in circulation, and so many trite and inadequate versions of the expensive one, that it is more helpful to try to state the problems in detail before delivering any — even the best — precut solution. The problems, of course, are the old riddles of Sin and Death: the twin results of Adam's fall, and the immemorial destroyers of the history we always seek and so seldom get right. Consider death first.

Even if the web of being actually exists in the mute changing of the physical world, it does not really *matter* — enter history — until it is grasped by our priesthood and lifted up beyond itself. If there is not a mind around capable of taking in its meaning, there is very little sense in talking about meaning at all. But if each of the minds that grasp history is capable only of a temporary grip, if shape and meaning can be blown out, as they are, in death after death around the clock and world without end, what good is the grasp of history in the first place?

Ah, you say, but things are not that bad. Individual minds may die, but the succession of minds goes on. The tissue of history lives by its wits. With a little agility, it will manage, by written word or spoken, to find itself new minds, new houses, before the old ones cave in. But be careful. You are on the verge of a cheap answer.

In the first place, it is hardly even a half-truth. Only the smallest part of anyone's grasp of history can be transmitted. We may, by dint of a lifetime of talk, communicate some of what we have grasped to other minds; we may even, in the farthest reaches of poetry, succeed in transmitting much of it. But *all?* Never. The determinative flashes of sunlight on cobblestones, the instants of anger and minutes of tenderness that are integral to the shape we know the world to have — the thousand impressions that have flowered into meaning for us — remain radically incommunicable. On the day we die, a hundred chapters will go into the rubbish for every one we leave on someone else's desk. History — grasped history — can indeed be transmitted; but not enough of it to take the edge off the horror of unmeaning. My history's survival in others' minds is carrion comfort. It is peace with oppression, consenting to the destruction of a city at the price of the preservation of a bungalow. The consolation is too small for such a loss.

Nevertheless, when a John Kennedy dies — when any famous person falls under the sentence — the editorial writers trot out merely mental survival as the principal string of their bow. He may be gone from us, they mourn, but his words and works will live as long as humanity itself draws breath. They mean well; but it simply will not do. Of all that was disconnected by the assassin's bullet, far too little remains. John Kennedy was a priest offering the world in the sanctuary of his mind. And so are Nathan Cohen and you and I. The enormity of the destruction of such temples is hardly lessened by the knowledge that four stones and two third-class relics of a priest are on view in some foreign country. It helps a little, but not much.

Furthermore, the survival of history in the minds of successive generations is unacceptable from our own point of view as priests. It is not only that so much of the history I have lifted up will go into the discard with my body; far worse is the fact that it is *my* oblation that will be lost. What I have seen and loved has been lifted up for *it*self and for *my*self, not for entombment in an abstract racial consciousness. I have run my own fingers over the fabric of the world; my offering has been precisely mine: the oblation of my own heart's astonishment. If that goes for good, I can hardly be blamed for looking down my nose on the consolation that someone else will offer in my stead. Death is the unfrocking of Adam the priest. That is why we cry at funerals: because poor old Sarah will never in this world be allowed to say Mass again, never again lift up the beings around her table, never be permitted to run her own hands across the silk of her friendships or the burlap of her pains. Small comfort that there are still other priests to offer; *her* offering is gone, and the loss is inconsolable.

The cheap answer, therefore, will not do. If there is any hope for history, it will not lie in books or other minds. If there is ever to be an answer to the problem of Death, it will have to deal with death itself. Meaning can be saved only by the lifting of the sentence under which Adam stands.

And the same is true of the problem of Sin. Either the mis-shaping of history will be seen as a remediable perversion of our natural love of shape, or it will destroy shape altogether. But again, before any attempt at presenting the answer to sin must come an effort to understand how sin entered in the first place.

When you have lost an idea, a hint of meaning, you can

sometimes find it by retracing your steps. You get up in the morning, perhaps, you brush your teeth, you wash, you dress; and, as you do, you arrive at the formulation of a brilliant gambit for attacking a problem. Downstairs then, and to breakfast. But over your second cup of coffee, you discover that the flash of insight has escaped you: *that* you thought of it, you are sure; *what* it was you thought of, you cannot remember at all. The only thing for it is to go back, to walk once again through the rooms in which it first occurred. And you do. And somewhere between the toothpaste and the mouthwash, between the socks and the shoes, the meaning returns as good as new.

So also here. If the first hint of history was given by the placing of Adam and Eve in a *park,* a paradise, an Eden, that is the place to walk through again to find it.

The park, then, was theirs to behold, to lift, and to offer. It was in the garden that they first saw shape; and it is in the garden also that the first hint of the misshaping rears its head. *But the serpent was more subtil than any beast of the field.* Ah! And he said, *Yea, hath God said, Ye shall not eat of every tree of the garden?* Ah! Yes. That was it.

God says to Adam and Eve: See what I have made you. Behold a creation with a shape that cries out for shaping, with a meaning waiting to be meant by somebody. I challenge you to a game of oblation. My serve first. Watch now! Watch trees and grass, watch earth and mountains and hills; watch wells, seas, and floods, and whales and all that move in the water. Catch! Catch beasts and cattle and men and women; catch winter and summer and frost and cold; catch nights and days and lightnings and clouds; catch *omnia opera Domini* — catch them, and return the service!

And Adam and Eve say to God: Wait a minute; I didn't hear you mention that tree over there. And God's jaw drops.

Look, God says, that's only the foul line. Forget it; it's just a rule. I have my reasons for it, but it's in a good place, believe me. If I can provide the court and the game, trust me to make the rules to play it by. After all, you haven't even returned the service yet. Try it again — my serve.

And once more, across the net of the world, come ice and snow and light and darkness, fire and heat and dews and frosts, winds of God and fowls of the air, and *omnia germinantia in tetra.* And this time Adam and Eve throw down their racquets, and with an edge to their voices say: But what about that tree?

Do you see? The wrath of God is only his exasperation at players who will not watch, at partners who will not return the service. It is the divine *good grief!* over the purblindness of creatures who would rather argue about the foul line than play the game. There is your answer to why the game of history has gone so badly: we are *in* the game, but not *with* it. We could play if we wanted, but we would rather score debating points of our own. We are priests who will not return the service.

Mercifully, it has not turned out quite as badly as it might have. Sin is strong enough to spoil history, but not strong enough to wreck it altogether. There is just too much shape in the world, and too much love of shape in us, for history to fail completely. Even as carping Adams and Eves we have had our moments. The glory that was Greece and the grandeur that was Rome and the joys of open-eyed courtship and the delights of the city of the sciences have not altogether gone begging. Culture is the record of what priestly success we have had. That it is a tarnished record is sad; but that it exists at all is the proof of our priesthood.

And more. Even our failures are priestly. The slavery upon which the ancient world was built was a wrong oblation within the city. The building of the Third Reich upon the extermination of the Jews was a wicked offering, the perversion of a priesthood that should have held them for themselves and lifted them into the City. Such things prove history in the very act of destroying it. The sins by which we have ruined the shape of the world are precisely the acts of spoiled priests: resentment, prejudice, envy, hate; lust, greed, sloth, pride. Sin is not accidental or irrelevant: it is the oblation of the right things in the wrong way. It is the very best in us that wrecks the world. The riddle of a misshapen creation must be solved not by despairing of that best but by the healing of it in the renewal of the priesthood of Adam.

▼   ▼   ▼

There is, admittedly, one part of the mystery that will remain a mystery forever: Why did God make us priests in the first place? The only honest answer is as mysterious as the mystery itself: he was pleased to have us so. Beyond that no one can go. But even that is a hint at which the heart leaps up. *He was pleased!* We are what we are not out of necessity but out of delight. For all the disasters of its history, the world is still a *lark,* a game into which we are invited by God. That the game has gone badly can never finally count as long as the invitation still stands. And if, beyond the mere invitation, God has actually promised someday to restore us to our true priest-hood . . . well, that is a hope worth any waiting: a day not only for you and me, but for Tom and the marsh reeds and all the beds of our conjunctions; a day for the triumphant proclamation of the web, and for the building of Jerusalem in a green and pleasant land.

5. *Interlude in the Garden*

You are free to receive with joy or reject with horror what comes next. I accept, sight unseen and with equanimity, whatever theological or philosophical stickers you see fit to fasten on me. Whether I am a fundamentalist or a liberal, or both, or neither, is mine to know and yours to find out — and, having found out, to ease me in or out of your scheme of things accordingly. I am in your hands.

Since the garden, Adam and Eve have worked at their priesthood by whatever fits and starts they could manage. There is very little in creation they haven't taken a notion to do something about. They have done things up, done things over, and done things in; but, well or badly, they have done. And their doing has been a *historical* pursuit. The definition of human beings as historical animals is not only as good as any; it is better than most. We are the priests of the world, the beings whose lives are a search for shape, an obsession to draw what we love *into* our history and to cast what we loathe *out* of it. I propose, therefore, to take a closer look at the details of our oblation. But since the scope of our priesthood is so vast — since we are so regularly more staggered than settled by it — I shall do the job by halves. In subsequent chapters I shall dwell first on our lifting of *things* into history; then, a little later, I shall come to the way in which we lift up more complicated beings: *persons*.

But first I want to make a detour — to draw a longish line under something I think makes a difference. I have talked about the creation of Adam and Eve as the introduction of priestly — of historical — beings into the world; and I have talked about the fall of Adam and Eve as our failure to exercise our priesthood — as a disaster in the history department of creation. What needs to be added now is an insistence that the priesthood of Adam and Eve cannot be just a historical principle: Adam and Eve themselves, in their creation and in their fall, have to have been a historical fact. No matter how many fine and fancy meanings we may be able to draw out of their historicity, it must also have a plain meaning: somewhere along the line, some people had to have shown up at a real time and place as the first of a race of priestly beings.

I feel I am about to lose my audience. I shall give you one disclaimer. I am not at all concerned here with whether those people were a lonely he and she, or a crowd, or whether they were made in one shot or gradually pasted up over millions of years. The only point I want to make is that if you seriously intend to see history as a real web, then the web itself must have a beginning, *and that beginning must be discussed historically.* No one should be exempted from the attempt to write Genesis; and no one ever is. Admittedly, neither scientists nor theologians have reporters' notes on the event, so everybody has to do the job imaginatively; but it is precisely that job that everyone has to do, scientists as well as theologians. There is no real choice about Adam and Eve. The only open question is whether we will do them, and the rest of history that follows from them, justice.

I bring this up because a great deal of solemn nonsense has been bandied about on the subject. In the interest of making a hasty accommodation between a stale biblical chronology and a half-baked theory of universal evolution, all kinds of things were said by all kinds of people. On the one hand, biblical obscurantists made a frantic attempt to salvage the chronology by sweeping scientific knowledge under the rug. On the other, modernist theologians retreated so hurriedly before the specter of evolutionary supersession that they abandoned wholesale the theology and horse sense of the Scriptures. The first have, mercifully, met the fate they deserved; but the second are still with us. They have such a fear of sounding like Genesis that they end up sounding like gibberish. They are so afraid of making

Adam and Eve particular human beings that they forget that, if history is real, some particular people will have to turn out to have been Adam and Eve. In the day of judgment we may find out that they called each other Oscar and Enid and that they lived on a Norwegian fjord; but those will be only details. They themselves will have existed. And the essential historical fact about them will be not simply that our biological inheritance came from them but that *all* the threads of the web began with them. It is precisely the rest of history that you lose if you unload Adam and Eve.

You think I am tilting at windmills. But consider. Do you really think that the objection to the Adam of Genesis was based on a scholarly unwillingness to accept Bishop Ussher's word that human beings first appeared on a Friday morning in 4004 B.C.? I do not. That was only the particular sandbar on which the scholars finally ran aground. If it had not been that, it would have been something else. Their real trouble lay in the fact that they (and we) had been sailing for several centuries in the shoal waters of a non-historical view of history.

Under the influence of what they conceived to be the demands of evolution, they took to expounding both the creation story and the narrative of the Fall as myths. And by *myth* they meant something quite specific: a fundamentally nonhistorical truth, presented under the guise of fictitious history. (There is, admittedly, a historical way of using myth — it can also mean an imaginative, but not unlikely, reconstruction of an event that really happened but went unrecorded at the time — but that is not what they had in mind.) The story in Genesis became, in their hands, only a diagram of the spiritual state of Everyman; they lived in mortal terror of ever allowing Adam to be anyone's grandfather.

And yet, that is the critical point. Adam has *got* to be somebody's grandfather — and Eve, somebody's grandmother — or history is nonsense. The human race is precisely a web: times without number, good science has done nothing but confirm that. If I got my flat-footed walk or my love of caviare from my own grandfather, the case is closed. History is by that fact real; and all real *things* have beginnings. My grandfather himself had a grandfather. And if you rummage around long enough, somewhere in the web you are going to run into a fellow who had no human grandfather at all and who, therefore, is the real granddaddy of history. That gentleman is Adam.

Why, then, were the theologians so afraid of talking theologically about the beginning of the web? Why were they so scared of Adam? For two reasons. First, because they had an exaggerated view of the apologetic value of intellectual fashionableness; but secondly, and chiefly, because they had long since ceased to think seriously about the tissue of history. Evolution, as a built-in mystique, had conned them out of it. They were so awed by the supposed extent to which human beings had changed that they felt guilty about saying anything definite about their origin. And so they invented one of the most insidious distinctions in the history of anthropology: the division of humankind into historic and pre-historic. Admittedly, it has a legitimate meaning: humanity after historiography as opposed to humanity before historiography. But in the popular mind the effect of it was to divorce *us* (human beings) from *them* (missing links) and, by leaving us without any theological estimation of our actual beginning, to rob us of a true view of the rest of the web of history.

My fuss about the historicity of Adam and Eve, therefore, is essential. The human race has lived under the compulsion of history for as long as it can remember: it has been obsessed with shape and meaning from the start. No theory of the origin of humanity is worth a plugged nickel unless it can make room for meaning *at the start*.

Adam and Eve are inseparable from the web. We are the priests of creation, the agents of the mystery of the City. There is not a man or woman in the world who doesn't grapple with meaning all their lives. To omit the discussion of meaning from the account of their origin, therefore — to allow it to wander in the middle of the piece like an orphan of the storm — is to leave it an orphan forever. If meaning arrived late, it never arrived at all; you cannot derive something from nothing. It would have been better not to talk about the subject at all than to dodge the issue by beating up on Genesis. Whoever wrote it was a theologian and historian of the first magnitude. If you don't like the way it was done, you are welcome to try making up your own version. But don't think you can just sit on the sidelines and throw stones. You can't write history without talking about beginnings.

But the insistence upon the historicity of Adam and Eve is not justified simply by the necessity of a historical account of the creation of the human race. It becomes supremely important in the narrative of the Fall. The Scriptures, you recall, make no bones about the historicity of *that,* either. God made man and woman and set them in a garden; and for a short while at least, they lived in a state of goodness before they went sour. Modern theologians, however, almost all of them, throw up their hands at that. The evolutionary notion that humanity has slowly risen out of meaningless savagery into meaningful history has so captured their minds that they find the notion of a historical time of innocence simply unthinkable. If they comment at all on the story of the temptation, they do it by trotting out their Adam-is-Everyman fowling piece and blasting the history out of it. But two can play that game. I have here an Adam-has-got-to-be-Somebody squirrel rifle, and I intend to use it. History must not go undefended. Stand back.

There is only one person you can blame (or thank) for putting meaning into the world: God is the only possible author of history; we didn't make ourselves any kind of animal, let alone a priestly one. But there are two agents you might blame for taking meaning out of the world: God — *and human beings.* Of those two, however, only human beings can sensibly be faulted. For if the confusions of history are God's doing — if God raised up meaning on a Friday and kicked the stuffing out of it a week later, smiling an unruffled, inscrutable smile all the while — then meaning simply has no meaning. Shape is nice, and so is shapelessness; gardens are nice and so are tangles, and life is nice and so is death; and history is non-history and good is evil; and nobody is to blame for anything — and away we go into the great Oriental Nothing, or All, or Whatever that doesn't give a damn. I don't know about you, but I can't buy that. It doesn't sound like much of a God to me; and it certainly doesn't sound like the God of Abraham, Isaac, and Jacob.

Accordingly, the biblical insistence on blaming the human race for the shipwreck of history is a stroke of historical genius. It is the only way of accounting for unmeaning without having meaning fly straight out the window. And yet modern theologians rattle blithely on about how the story of the fall of Adam and Eve is just a historicized version of a nonhistorical truth (which, since this is just a plain old historical world, is simply a six-bit way of saying that it was never really true at all). But that breaks all the warps in the web right on the spot. For if, from the minute we showed up, things were the way they are now — if we have always been the kind of creatures that wreck the shape of the world faster than we form it — then three unpleasant consequences are inevitable. First: the mess is God's fault, not ours. Second: it is, to say the least, disingenuous of God to go around throwing people out of gardens as a punishment for not avoiding the unavoidable. And third: it is a little surprising that we still think shape is better than shapelessness. If it's such a toss-up between meaning and unmeaning, why do we go on feeling it's a bad idea to burn libraries?

What makes the theologians go on so? Something quite simple: they have been frightened by their own prehistoric men. Their heads are so full of missing links, flesh-eating apes, and caveloads of cracked skulls that there is no room for the real tools of their trade. They will not touch the crucial, history-saving, theological concept. The only thing that can keep meaning from destruction by sin is a doctrine of original righteousness — some insistence that for a time at least (however short), in some place (however small), the human race (Adam and Eve) was good and not bad. If history never had a real chance, then there is no real history. Meaning cannot arrive late; either it comes for the first course, or it does not make the party at all.

The author of the book of Genesis, therefore, is not to be sneezed at. He was a theologian who knew his trade. He provided a real beginning for the web, and he provided a way of distinguishing the building of it from the rending of it. He may need a little scientific updating now, but until someone comes along who can match him for historical sense, I hope you will excuse my not jumping on any of the bandwagons I have seen so far.

And having said that, I have done. Here endeth the longish line.

[89]

6. *The Oblation of Things*

I shall tell you now why I made that detour. I am going to talk about our oblation of things; and in doing so, I am going to try to distinguish right oblations from wrong oblations in terms of history. I have a notion, for example, that good art is historical: a lifting, if you will, of genuine things into genuine history; and conversely, that bad art is nonhistorical: a lifting of fake things into non-history. But in order to make that distinction work, I had to posit it as valid for every person who ever lived — for T. S. Eliot, J. S. Bach, Michelangelo, and Jane Austen, for Smith, Jones, Pincus, and Casey, for the artist who did the drawings of bison in the old French caves, and finally for Adam and Eve themselves, whoever they were and whatever they did. Nobody can be left out. Even a single truly *prehistoric man* will wreck the whole tissue of history.

For if we are not all in the same game, there is no point in making much of the way you and I happen to be playing it now. We are just members of a crowd of discrete individuals following our own noses and achieving, at best, our own amusement. If, however, we are all together in the oblation, then it becomes something more than amusement — it becomes *culture*. Drawing, music, and poetry become not simply private diversions but cities in themselves, joint ventures in the offering of specific kinds of oblations. And if that is true, our habitual assumptions about art are justified: culture exists, standards are possible, and good and bad are not meaningless noises. To put it all tightly: if Adam and Eve were truly prehistoric, culture is only a fad, a Johnny-come-lately in the history of the race. But if culture is not a fad, then Adam and Eve cannot be prehistoric; they must be right in the act with the rest of us.

On, then, with the act. Here beginneth art, culture, and the oblation of things.

▼   ▼   ▼

I take my children to the beach. On the north shore of Long Island it is a pretty stony proposition. The mills of the gods grind coarsely here; but, in exchange for bruised feet and a sore coccyx, they provide gravel for the foundation of the arts. Every year we hunt for perfect stones: ovals, spheroids, lozenges, eggs. By the end of the summer there are pebbles all over the house. They have no apparent use other than the delight that they provide to us, but that is the whole point of the collection. The very act of hunting them is an introduction to the oblation of things. Look at this one! Do you think it will split evenly enough for arrowheads? What color is that one when it's wet? Lick it and see. Daddy wants a big flat round one to hold the sauerkraut under the brine. Will this one do? We walk down the beach lifting stones into our history: we are collectors, ingatherers of being. Humankind is the lover of textures, colors, and shapes — the only creature in the whole world that knows a good pickling stone when it sees one. The arts go way beyond that; but that is where they begin.

The child who runs the satin binding of her blanket between her fingers, the boy who carefully oils his collection of ball bearings so they will not rust, the woman who loves to handle thick braids, the man who opens his pocketknife just to hear the satisfying click with which it closes — all these are priestly builders. It is in our simplest oblations that we are at our historical best. When we rise higher, we make more mistakes — we diagram and spiritualize what should have been loved and offered as things; but at these low levels we are successes. The world has seen few badly offered blanket bindings, few profaned ball bearings. As long as we can hunt stones, we will know that the fire of our priesthood has not gone out.

But the oblation of things goes far beyond such simplicities. It is in the arts and the crafts that we most display our priestliness and historicity. It is in them that Adam proceeds to successes and failures so vast as to defy comprehension; and it is precisely in the attempt to see them as priestly and historical that they are best understood.

It is a common error to suppose that the artist does what she does for herself — that she is a peculiar being who loves certain things in a way not open to others. It is also common to dismiss the craftsman as a fellow who does things for money. To some degree, of course, that is all true. Artists are usually a little odd; the laborer commonly, and legitimately, looks forward to his hire. But after that it falls short. For each is engaged in an offering of things not simply for personal benefit but for the sake of the things themselves — and for the sake of other people. The painter paints because she loves the way things look and wants to offer her sight of them to others. The poet speaks because he loves words and longs for them to be heard as he hears them. And the cabinetmaker fashions and the joiner joins and the chef cooks and the vintner toils because they love the conjunctions of things and will them to be moved into the weaving of the web. All arts come from having open eyes; and all arts are performing arts. Even the solitary artist in the cave draws to be seen, offers up what he looks at as a priest for others. It is only in bad drawing, bad writing, and bad woodwork that motives other than priestly ones become primary. It is when we stop loving what we do — and stop caring whether others see — that we become guilty of artistry that is not art and of craftsmanship that is only shoddy.

I shall give you some instances. I must choose them, of course, from such arts and crafts as I myself possess. They will have all the drawbacks of my own limited and imperfect oblation; but if they have even a crude integrity about them, they will do for illustrations. I give you language, music, and cooking.

▼   ▼   ▼

If speech is the crowning gift of humankind, then the arts of language probably qualify as the most nearly universal. Not all people can draw, many cannot sing, and the world is full of cooks who ought to be allowed to rise no higher than the scullery; but all human beings speak, and practically no one is immune to the delights of rhyme and reason. The child, as soon as he learns words, *plays* with words. The teenager, with her stock of current clichés and her mercurial pattern of jargon, is a poet. She may recite only commercial slogans and comparable idiocies; but she recites them, at least partly, because she loves the way the words rattle. And somewhere along the line she will, unless she is starved to death, come to love some very grand rattles indeed.

I remember the first time I read Shakespeare's sonnets. "Lilies that fester smell far worse than weeds" stuck in my head for weeks — not so much for its meaning as for its marvelous *wordiness*. The city of speech is old and new, and rich beyond counting.

Fortunatus:

Flecte ramos, arbor alta, tensa laxa viscera;
Et rigor lentescat ille quem dedit nativitas;
Ut superni membra regis mite tendas stipite.

Andrewes:

A cold coming they had of it. . . . The ways deep, the weather sharp, the days short, the sun farthest off, *in solstitio brumali,* in the very dead of winter.

Eliot:

And all shall be well and
All manner of thing shall be well
When the tongues of flame are in-folded
Into the crowned knot of fire
And the fire and the rose are one.

Cummings:

All in green went my love riding. . . .

That only a few have the craft to forge such words takes nothing off the edge of the marvel by which we can sense the priestliness of their oblation. And it is not only the grand and gorgeous words that qualify. The world is full of jokesters, punsters, and phrase-coiners; an endless noonday mass of badinage and repartee is offered across the lunch tables and water coolers of the world. The *bon mot* is as old as history. And there is the phrase we want: the *good word,* the word in due season, like an apple of gold in a picture of silver. The delight of talk. A highly placed cynic once said that speech was given to us to conceal thought. He was, of course, wrong. But the negative of it is almost as far from the truth. Speech is no mere tool of communication; it is a joy in itself. To bring it into history only for communication, to teach college courses in the art of communication, to refer antiseptically to the press and radio as media of communication is to lift up only the smallest corner of speech for oblation. Speech should indeed inform, as food should indeed nourish, but what sane person will let either subject go at that? Unfortunately, much of what passes for prose only goes to prove that sanity is in short supply.

And what a crime it is, what a sacrilege! In an age when words are more available than ever, the *bon mot* is harder and harder to find. This is the era of the non-book, of the *pastiche,* of the work that labors only to make a point — of a literary spirituality that wants meaning but will not fondle the words which are its body. This is the era of talks, of reports, of analyses that are unbearable because the talkers and the writers are insufferably bad lovers. And, to throw a stone at my own trade, it is the era of sermons — words about the Word! — that have no taste at all, because the preachers do not see that words themselves are lovely.

Nothing has brought us to such poverty except the neglect of our own priesthood. Even television cannot be blamed. It was a brilliant device. It might have been one of the chief builders of the city of speech. That it has spewed forth only slogans and jingles — that it has, by and large, not only failed to lift speech but profaned the language as well — is due not to its nature but to its use in unpriestly and unhistorical ways. It is the triumph of art as diversion as opposed to art as oblation. Week after week, at the cost of vast sums and heroic efforts, hopeless plots are served up with featureless characters stuck into them like so many raisins in a pudding. At their best they sometimes manage to make a *point,* but they seldom reach delight — and they threaten constantly to become pointless altogether. To aim at communication is to aim too low. It is the old story that, if you will not try for the best, you will lose even the mediocre. Adam the priest cannot say the Mass of language for any other reason than the oblation of language. It will not allow itself to be used. If it is not offered, it will be lost.

▼   ▼   ▼

And then there is music. We sing and drum and stamp our feet. Our children chant by nature. Nobody can resist shouting into a barrel. We are mad about sound. Even the dreadful, bleating records my teenagers listen to are minor priestly delights. The pounding beat, the socking repetitions of the tonic-subdominant chord progression — all the things they will someday come to look upon as vulgarities — are not as bad as all that. They should indeed be urged to pass beyond them, but they are nonetheless their first lessons in the seminary of sound. Left to their own devices and given a chance to play — almost anything — they are on their way to a real love of music. Think of what is in store for them. The delight of the discovery that the progression I-ii has a flavor that I-IV cannot match — that the F chord with a d in it lifts the guitar and themselves and the song into another dimension. And Tchaikovsky. I have not deliberately listened to him for ages, but there was a time when I thought that the Fifth Symphony was the height of music. And from there, where will it not go? My own children's tastes used to give me pause. I felt that uplift should be the order of the day. But I was wrong. They listen to trash, but it doesn't bother me anymore. If, on even a single evening of the year, just one of them will put scratches in Uncle Hobart's record of

Julian Bream — if they wear out, in the course of their stay with me, only the oboe solo in the Violin Concerto in D Major by Brahms — the musical priesthood of Adam is safe for at least another generation.

Safe, but hardly triumphant. For our failure in music is like our failure in all the arts — a failure to make them truly priestly, a penchant for nonhistorical and irrelevant forms. Far too much of the music we now have is only heard, not played or sung. It makes no demands, does not ask to be lifted; it just hangs around. We have canned music, background music, and music to do everything but listen to music by. But music cannot be only entertainment any more than speech can be only communication. We aim too low. Both are major oblations, and they will settle for nothing less. Neither can be merely used: they must be *played*.

Thank God for wine. Without it we would have almost no singing at all. Practically the only place where people now sing when they are cold sober is in church; and, to tell the truth, it sounds like it. As a professional religionist, I wish I could make a more glowing report; but, by and large, the singing is wretched. It is a triumph of use, not play. And for every person in church who sings, there are five who stand aloof from the whole business as if it were faintly disreputable.

Why? Because they are embarrassed by the sound of their own voices: they are ashamed of their priesthood. The city of music, which fairly cries out for lifting into their history, is firmly and permanently locked out. I think that secretly, in their heart of hearts, perhaps, they envy people who play. But they do not show it often. If only they would. It isn't a matter of working themselves into miniature Isaac Sterns; the harmonica will do if it comes to that — or even tenth-rate four-part harmony. They underestimate the power of the arts. A child can practice for weeks on the strength of a single chord progression. Even the smallest oblation will lift the priest as she makes it; even a little attention to what is really there will be a historical triumph.

▼   ▼   ▼

Lastly, take food and the art of cooking. Once again it is a matter of the priestly lifting of things into history, a preoccupation with what really *is*. Consider the egg.

Set aside at once, for oblation at another time, all the biological and physiological marvels of it. Forget for the moment the fantastic intricacy of the mechanism from which all the higher forms of life spring. Disregard, too, the wonder of its parts, its divisions, and its tremendous *complications*. Omit, finally, all other eggs but one: no frogs' eggs, ducks' eggs, robins' eggs, or goose eggs; no snake eggs, no dinosaur eggs, no platypus eggs, no roe; no *ova* of any sort or kind but the eggs of the common hen. And what have you done? You have renounced a whole world only to gain a dozen in its place.

For in our priestly attention to the fruit of the barnyard — by our lifting of the egg into history — we have discovered what no other animal will ever know. What will the egg not do? It will scramble, boil, bake, or fry — or go down raw if you have the stomach for it — and sustain and delight you in the bargain. And that is only the start of the prologue of the introduction. It will thicken sauces, raise dough, explode into a soufflé, or garnish your soup. It can be taken with sugar and whisky, or with salt and red pepper; and still you have hardly begun. Omelets are more numerous than the generations of the human race: Soubise, Boulestin, Paysanne, or Espagnol; French, Italian, au Rhum, aux Fines Herbes; Sausage, Kidney, Lobster, or Ham; and even Plain, if you like the taste of eggs. And Sauces. Mayonnaise, Hollandaise, Béarnaise, and Figaro; Sabayon, Custard, Brandy, and Zabaglione.

But enough. The case is closed already. What on earth is going on here if it is not the historicizing of the egg by Adam? And, beyond the egg, of all foods as well. We cook. Oh my! how we cook. The variety of our offerings goes so far beyond necessity, so magnificently past nourishment as to prove our priesthood without even leaving the breakfast table. Alas for cheese and wine and mushrooms! You will not make this book. Too much evidence is the mark of a weak case.

▼　　　▼　　　▼

I conclude on an adjacent note. We eat as well as we cook. Food enters not only the tissue of our history but the tissue of our bodies, too. And sometimes it shows. We become fat and well-liking priests; we acquire an amplitude that befits the dignity of our ministry. And yet in this silly age we insist upon making a problem of weight. I give you, therefore, a little omnibus on Food and Fat, a *divertimento* on Dieting and History.

The root of the Hebrew word for *glory* means "weight." In English, *girth* rhymes with *mirth* and *worth*. Everyone loves a fat uncle.

I remember as a child going to the beach with my uncles and my father. I can still see, glistening in the sun and surf, handsome padded expanses of *back*. I can still smell the unforgettable reek of salt, sweat, and olive oil as I hung on great shoulders and rode fearlessly over the waves. But I am sure that now, if there are any such paragons left in the world, they are troubled about their weight — that their wives, their physicians, and their friends are engaged in a vast and successful conspiracy to worry it off them.

It is the nonhistorical approach run rampant. I remember my uncles as sacred groves, as *places* in my history, as anointed stones of the city of my being. But the diet-mongers see them only as abstract spaces. They inquire after their height — a dreadful irrelevancy to begin with — and, after consultation with a table, they arrive at what they think should be their weight. They refuse the men themselves; they insist upon a diagram of humanity instead. They dwell only upon what they would like a man to conform to; they never come within a hundred miles of knowing what a man *is*. A curse on them all! If they had their way, there would not be an uncle in all the world worth having.

Ah, you say, but surely you are not about to allow the world to be overrun by fat? Does not even a love of the human body for itself — does not even a priestly and historical offering of uncles — impose some canons, some standards? Of course it does. I have nothing against reasonable efforts to remain in human shape. I object to only two things: abstract definitions of that shape, and dieting as the means of achieving it.

The abstractions are wrong because, nine times out of ten, they are based only on fads, social or medical. No chart can tell you how fat my uncles should be. You must spend some time with them before you attempt so delicate an estimate. You must see them swim and dance and carry children on their backs; you must look at them for months of Sunday-night suppers, behold them at plates of *braunschweiger* and steins of beer, before you dare to decide anything as intimate to their history as their weight.

And the dieting is wrong because it is not priestly. It is a way of using food without using it, of bringing it into your history without letting it get involved with your history. It is nonhistorical eating. And it is pure fraud. Bring it down to cases. Take an uncle with an embarrassingly low metabolic rate: if he gets more than 1,800 calories a day, his weight goes up out of control. He puts himself in the hands of dietary experts. They oblige him with a program. It works. At 900 calories per diem he becomes an up-to-date, low-budget uncle. But, if you see him in a year, he will have put it all back on again. And why? Because no sane human being can stand living on 1,800 calories every day till the clap of doom. So he nibbles away for a while, and then in desperation surrenders himself to creamed lobster, mashed potatoes, and a proper string of double scotches. He is lost, and he knows it. He just gives up.

The only thing that can save him is *historical* eating — eating worthy of the priesthood of Adam — eating that alternates as it should between feast and fast. The dieter is a condemned man. Every feast is, *ipso facto,* a sin. He apologizes for eating my *pâté;* he abjectly acknowledges his guilt over my wife's Cake à la Bennich. Good is evil to him, and bounty a burden. But if he would fast! If he would take *no* food on Wednesday — and none on Tuesday too, if he wills to reign like a king — what prodigies might he not perform at Thursday's dinner; how, like a giant, go running from course to course?

What a poor, benighted age we live in. How we deny ourselves all sauces but the best. How little of what surrounds us is ever offered either by use or abstinence. And there is the secret. Fasting is an offering, too. The dieter says: Sweets are bad; I cannot have them ever. The faster says: Sweets are good; I will not take them now. The dieter is condemned to bitter bondage, to a life that dares not let food in. But the faster is someone preparing for a feast. His Lent leads to an Easter, and to mirth and weight of Glory.

7. *The Main Thing*

Between the oblation of things and the oblation of persons, there is a great gulf fixed. When I lift an egg into my history, the egg is, for all practical purposes, passive. It is content to come on my terms. To be sure, it will come on its own terms too — it will be fresh or rotten, large or small, single- or double-yolked, as it chooses — but its concern for itself is of a fairly undemanding sort. As far as history is concerned, my use of the egg is pretty much a one-way street: *it* becomes involved in my history; I do not, in any important sense, become involved in its. Indeed, on the definition of humankind as the historical animal, the egg does not really have any history to involve me in.

There are, of course, creatures other than ourselves that can draw us into their works. To a dramatic extent. There are rivers in flood and there are hurricanes and tornadoes. And, if you like individual attention, there are army ants and man-eating sharks. But even in such cases we hardly see ourselves as being invited into someone else's history; we feel more put upon than asked, more consumed than offered. By an exceedingly charitable stretch of the imagination, we might find some small satisfaction in the knowledge that the shark will be fatter and more well-liking for having digested us: the process *is* a part of the web. But charity like that is rare. Commonly — and justifiably — we like our meanings a little more meaningful. The histories involved are so disparate that we prefer to save the name "history" for the human side of the operation.

Adam's oblation of *things,* therefore, for all its complexities, remains fairly tractable. It is our offering of *persons* that is the really difficult work. For when we offer up other human beings — when we invite, or are invited by, other persons into the exchanges of the City — we step into a two-way street. Or an eight-lane expressway! While we offer them, they are just as busy offering us: we receive invitations not by return mail but in the same post. As far as eggs and wine and dogs and violins are concerned, I am more or less in command of the situation. I am, within tolerable limits, the master of my fate. But as far as John or Harry or *that girl with the marvelous green eyes!* are concerned, they are just as much masters as I am. They, of their fate, and I of mine — most likely — but all of us masters of each other's, too; and there's the historic rub. As long as history is only a question of how an "I" will handle an "it," the achievement of decent — of fitting — oblations is at least imaginable. But as soon as it becomes a matter of two "I's" offering each other simultaneously, we have entered the realm of outsized offerings, of oblations 9½ AAAA and 6 EEE. The salutary "I-Thou" relationship is also the world's principal source of blisters and corns.

The job of taking two independent persons, two historic animals — two histories — and bringing them together in love or friendship, in marriage or business, has always been ticklish. Men and women can usually manage to be clear in their minds about what they take to be their own meaning — their personal view of the shape of things; and most of us can make reasonable allowances for the fact that other people see different meanings and different shapes. But for two such beings to undertake a *joint* meaning! To attempt to make room in *my* history for *your* history, without slighting either or wrecking both! Why, it's a wonder we even dare ask anyone the time of day, let alone think of inviting someone's friendship, devotion, or love. That we so commonly do, of course, is the most convincing of all the proofs of the existence of the City — of history. That anything with such odds against it should be attempted with such unabashed regularity can only mean that we were built for nothing else. It is as if every human being in the world chose daily to go over Niagara Falls in a barrel. It proves something about human nature. If an animal plays dangerously, we conclude it is built for danger; when we go through the world with our eyes open for friendships, for alliances, for love — when we are so continually *on the make,* morally or immorally, inviting whole other histories into our history — it can only mean that history is our native air.

By and by I shall have something to say about the leonine, the tigerish, the fierce and wild way in which, for ill and for good, we play the game of history with other persons. First, however, one last item from the realm of things still demands attention. It is the human body.

Trumpets, towels, tripe, and teapots; razors, Rembrandts, radios, and rattlesnakes; the world is full of a number of things. Isaiah, Jeremiah, Ezekiel, Daniel; Merrill Lynch, Pierce and Smith; it is more than equally full of persons. But lying on the borderline between the two is the flesh of which we are compounded. It is a *thing,* to be sure, but in a class by itself. Pierce could be Pierce without his desk, his coat, or his debentures; but without his body, he is not Pierce at all. The body is not a thing that *belongs to* us; it is something that is inseparable from us. Of all the things that can or will be involved in our history, our body is the foremost. As long as we are, it is. We have no choice about it.

But that does not mean we have no choices. History is precisely the conscious and voluntary oblation of the world. Accordingly, our bodies, of all things, must be consciously and voluntarily offered. And not only *my* body, but others' too. My wife, my children, my friends, my collaborators — all come to me as bodies, as *things* that are, at the same time, *persons;* and as persons who are, to an alarming degree, things. Behold, therefore, a historical world — a world of uplifted grandfathers and offered uncles, and of innumerable ministers who hold each other's bodies in their priestly hands.

▼   ▼   ▼

One might think that the very "bodyness" — the corporality — of human nature would be proof against the grosser forms of unreality. It seems only reasonable to hope that the fact that we are *things* would keep us from wandering off into the more monumental historical irrelevancies. But that is not necessarily the case here any more than it is in the realm of arts and crafts. As a matter of fact, it is probably safe to say that since the human body is the *main thing* in the world, it will be the subject of the principal perversions, of the most un-historic oblations. And it is.

Take, first of all, the notion that the body is, by its very nature, evil — unworthy of, or inimical to, the real nature of a human being. Oriental religions, of course, have made the most of that idea, but there is hardly a thinking part of the world that hasn't had an attack of it at one time or another. No doubt most modern people — misreading Saint Paul on the subject of the warfare between the flesh (fallen nature) and the Spirit (God the Holy Ghost) — think that the Christian religion takes a dim view of the body in all its parts and passions. Puritanism (or, to give it its proper name, Manichaeism) is commonly looked upon not as a Christian heresy, which it is, but as the genuinely Christian view, which it is not by a long shot.

Set down here, therefore, the fact that orthodox Christianity has nothing against the body, and everything for it. First, God made it. Second, God loves it. Third, God took it to himself in the womb of Mary. Fourth, he walked the earth in it, not with disdain but with enough obvious pleasure to acquire a bad reputation in the eyes of fussy people. And finally, he died, rose, ascended into heaven, and reigns forever as the *incarnate* Lord — in a body — with *flesh, bones, and all things appertaining to the perfection of Man's nature.* The problems raised by orthodox Christianity are anything but Oriental. They are embarrassingly — shockingly — *fleshly.* The current age, if it hears the true doctrine at all, finds it not too spiritual but too *material* for its tastes. It is not God who is too refined for us. It is we who find God's announced way of doing business slightly . . . vulgar.

Or take the long and peculiar history of sexual fetishes. There are few places in the world where we have been content to leave the glorious normality of the human body — male or female — alone for long. Not satisfied with offering up lips that looked like lips, or skin that looked like skin, or feet that looked like feet . . . *tacet* the rest . . .

we have resorted to doing tricks with them. Usually, rather sordid tricks; and, almost as often, grim, solemn, quasi-religious tricks. Only the prurient find them entertaining. We easily see the un-historical offerings of other nations as un-historical; but at home, in our own backyards, we are not always so clear. We grow used to our fetishes; they become second nature. One man's meat is another man's perversion. The nearly universal penchant of the human race for shying away from the real shape of the body and fastening its desires on irrelevancies ought to be a giveaway that something radically un-historical is going on. When the body has to be pinched, stretched, or reprocessed before we can get enthusiastic about it, there is a good case to be made that it is not being loved or offered *as a body*.

The history of fashions in dress fits nicely into that case. In spite of the fact that the Scriptures mention clothes only *after* the Fall, I do not think that clothing can be dismissed simply as the attempt of Adam and Eve to hide their sexual shame. Dress is as much an art as is cooking. If you are allowed to put chives on top of rice, it must be equally lawful to put lamb's wool on top of a woman — provided only that you do the job historically. Both the chives and the rice, both the wool and the woman must come through the operation enhanced, lifted, *offered*. The true materialities involved must be respected, and the conjunctions between them must be appropriate. But, given that, clothing is one of the glories of human beings.

In heaven we shall wear white robes — no doubt something more stylish than flour sacks, too. The picture of Christ in majesty at the beginning of the Revelation of St. John the Divine is not only majestic; it has about it a hint of sartorial elegance. The golden girdle is not a necessary piece of equipment; it is a stunning and gracious touch. Clothing is with us for good; nudism, it would seem, is only another wrong turn. It is like restricting yourself to raw vegetables. The unadorned body is indeed a glorious thing, like the unadorned apple. But the diet fanatics who will rob me of my pie, my strudel, my turnovers, and my sauce are un-historical and mad. I will have no truck with them. An apple vested with pastry is not less, but more, an apple. It is an apple displayed and regnant.

The arts of embellishment. Perhaps that is the phrase. We *dress* our meat, we *vest* our tables, we *drape* our windows — and we *clothe* our bodies. That the decorative arts are not as grand as the creative arts says nothing against them. They are still an oblation, and, as such, they enter the web. The idiocies of the history of tailoring must not disenchant us about the sanity of the subject itself. Bad baroque is only the failure to embellish germanely; euphuistic prose is only speech offered up without real respect for language. And foolish fashion is the same. Whatever the human race does often, it will also do badly, with alarming frequency; but it must not be stopped for all that.

To walk through New York City is to see everything at once, especially in the matter of clothing. Much of what meets the eye is, of course, dreadful. For every Daughter of Eve whose clothing is a compliment to her body, there are five who walk wrapped in insults. I offer, therefore, three categories — three glittering, but not entirely useless, generalities — in terms of which a woman may judge the priestliness of her own dressing: by her clothing, she may turn herself into a Frump, or a Tomato, or a *Woman*.

The Frump is the woman who, by either ignorance or choice, does not really dress at all: she simply puts things on. Poverty has nothing to do with it. You can find Frumps in the fanciest parts of the city. And you can see real women in the poorest. Dress depends, as do all the arts, on taste and craft and talent more than on resources. Money helps, but it helps only the artist. For the bungler, it only insures more stately monstrosities. The Frump might as well not have a body at all, for all the good her dressing does her. If only she would hold herself in more priestly hands!

The Tomato, on the other hand, is another breed. As far as she is concerned, her chief concern is to display her body. But alas! The clothes she selects display only her unpriestliness, her inattention to what her body really looks like. She has, poor girl, accepted the fetishes as the truth: she has poured her body into a shape it does not fit, set it upon heels on which it cannot walk, and decorated it with whatever irrelevancies happen to have caught the current fancy. She draws, no doubt, the lioness's share of looks and whistles, but only because the crowd is as blind as she is. She always makes me a little sad: I see her as living evidence of the way we waste ourselves. If she is young, I am sad because she could be so much more stunning than she is. And if she is old, she breaks my heart. At 55, Tomatoes should not be out on the stand at all.

But then there are *Women*. And New York, since it has lots of everything, has Women on practically every street. Real pieces of history moving graciously past my history as I walk! Rich and poor, old and young, tailored and casual; how they *strike*, how they *stun*, how they *ravish!* All praise to their tailors, uptown or down. And greater praise to themselves, for they have exalted their bodies and put on robes of glory. If there is a sartorial section of purgatory, they will, no doubt, pass through it in an instant, while their poor sisters have to spend ages unlearning all the things they thought they knew. Nevertheless, I judge them not. I leave all such divisions to wiser and purer eyes than mine. Here at least is one fool who will not rush in. Let Women only remember their royal priesthood, and vest themselves accordingly.

And men? Well, I think we will all have to do some time for the way we dress. That a Son of Adam, created to play Lord of the world to Eve's Lady of the world, should walk his native land clad almost invariably in a collection of cloth tubes hitched together with a leather thong can be tolerable only to a people who have clean forgotten what a man's body looks like. What have we done to ourselves? Where was it we forgot that a man's legs alone are so delightful that the psalmist felt obliged to insist the Lord is not influenced by them? Why no kilts, no hose? Or if you like conceal-ment and majesty in your decoration, why no togas, no robes? Go and stand at the U.N. Watch an African chieftain glide by. Then walk through Brooks Brothers, if you dare.

As a priest, I have a privilege reserved to only a few in this dull age. Along with judges and academic dignitaries, I wear mean-ingful robes. It is an enviable distinction. And the envy can be felt. Most men will gladly put on a cassock, if only they can manage to set aside what the world has so foolishly taught them about skirts. And they will even more gladly put on a real cloak.

While not actually a vestment, the heavy black melton cloak is a standard item of the priest's wardrobe. When properly made, it is a vast semicircular garment, reaching from shoulder to heel and capable of keeping out any wind that ever blew. The ordinary name for it is a "cemetery cloak," after the most notable place of its use. The vestment houses, however, sensing that they are dealing with greatness, give it a grander name — *Cappa Nigra* or *Cappa Magna* — and they frequently give it a deep hood to crown the mystery. If you hand it to an ordinary man and tell him to put it on, he will always hesitate. It is like the marsh reed: it threatens to make too much of him. But let him wear it once, and you may have a candidate for Orders on your hands. Humankind cannot stand very much reality; but it loves the smell of it just the same.

▼   ▼   ▼

Clothes, however, vest only the least part of the body. The seven-eighths of us from the neck down are no match for the crown which sits above it: our *faces*. For it is in the face that the body most clearly ceases to *belong to* a person and becomes what we *are*. Face is the physical counterpart of *name*, and both are easy synonyms for *person:* if my name *and* my face are forgotten, I am nobody indeed. It is, therefore, the oblation of face — the using, the shaping, the adornment of the human countenance — that, of all physical offerings, lies nearest to the lifting of persons into history. If our bodies are the *main thing*, then our faces must be the mainmost — thing of thing, image of image, very thing of very thing.

And the subway is the place to behold it, to see the glory of it when offered historically — or to feel it escape you completely when it is not. Look at the women! A real face is worth all the weeks of waiting you have to go through to find it. At any age — and in an incredible variety of shapes — it speaks, and is heard, as a précis of history: *There goes somebody!* The offering is rich beyond measure. But it is also rare. There is a frump face to go with slatternly clothes, and there is a tomato face to match the tomato suit. Makeup is indeed allowable — even an art. But, in the hands of such women, faces are not made up — they are made down, made over, belittled, *unmade.* They take the most personal thing in the world, the ultimate sacrament of uniqueness, and recast it as the millionth extrusion of a common mold. Though it is worn by fifty women, it makes no difference between them. They are not persons, they are a class; and an unthinking class at that.

Their hair is set with no respect to their faces. Their eyebrows are applied at random, like incomprehensible italics. Their lips are irrelevant parentheses, wrecking the very context they were designed to clarify. Behind the makeup, there is indeed something personal and singular, but it has all but slipped away through unpriestly oblation. Faces? Hardly. Defacings. Estranged faces! The women who wear them are so far from looking like anybody in particular that only a man as far removed from reality as they are could possibly behold them gladly. Unfortunately for us all, however, there are plenty of both, and the pointless masque goes on and on. A woman's face is a rare thing.

To the credit of men, the same cannot fairly be said of most of them. The subway teems with individuals. There is nothing in the world like the unadorned variety of men's faces. It is entirely possible to make an airtight case for the reality of history from their noses alone. That anything so modest should be capable of such *effect* — and that such minor changes in it should so transform an entire countenance — can only mean that the primary function of the nose is to *mean,* to signify, to declare. Smelling is merely a faculty that occupies a closet somewhere inside the head; it is the nose itself that is . . . well, everything Cyrano said it was, and then some.

And if, on top of that, you receive into evidence the rest of the wonder of men's faces — the diversity of their outlines (long and thin, round and beaming, squarish, oval, even, odd), the multitude of their jaws (Lantern, Milquetoast, English Bull), and the endless peculiarities of their eyes, their ears, their hairlines, and their cheekbones — you drown yourself in an ocean of proof for personality. Faces are the chiefest things of history. One man's face by itself is a whole sea of matter, uplifted, and for oblation; a single subway car contains the raw materials of a universe of men, every one of whom will be an uncle worthy of offering. And were you to take a trainful, a stationload . . .

LECTOR: Ahem!

AUCTOR: Yes?

LECTOR: I wonder if I might ask you a personal question.

AUCTOR: Yes?

LECTOR: Your own face. It is . . . well, half-hidden behind your beard.

AUCTOR: Yes?

LECTOR: Am I to assume that you find this consistent with a historical oblation of faces?

AUCTOR: You are.

LECTOR: I have a feeling you are avoiding the issue.

AUCTOR: I am.

LECTOR: This is not at all like you. Why will you not speak out? Why not say plainly how beards are historical?

AUCTOR: I was trying to spare you. The beard is even more meaningful than the nose — its historicity would require volumes to do it justice.

LECTOR: Can you not possibly be brief?

AUCTOR: You are like all the others. You are unworthy of even an outline of the outline. But you have piqued me. I shall speak.

To the question "Why do you have a beard?" seventeen answers are possible. They are as follows:

(Simple): I like it.
(Taciturn): I just do.
(Sheepish): Lots of men have beards.
(Rude): None of your business.
(Cowardly): Oh? Don't you like it?
(Confident): It is manly.
(Overconfident): It keeps women away.
(Practical, *in respectu causae efficientis*): Because I don't shave.

(Agnostic): I don't know; I stopped shaving and it grew.

(Theological, but cautious): You will have to ask God.

(Practical, *propter incommoditatem rasurarum*): I was tired of cutting myself every morning.

(Devout): It is a gift of God.

(Practical, *pro bono prolis*): I look more paternal with one.

(Meditative): It would be ungrateful to die without having seen it.

(Practical, *sed propter vanitatem*): It hides my weak chin.

(Theological, *propter causam finalem*): God meant man to have one.

(Practical, *ad placendam uxorem*): It tickles my wife.

In deference to your impatience, I now skip whole tractates — their titles, in part: Of the Colors of Beards; Of the Shapes of Beards; Of the Lawfulness of Trimming Beards; Of the Optimum Length of Beards; Of the Classes of Men Who May Rightly Choose to Go Beardless — and out of the whole of the *magnum opus* I give you only a digest of the abstract of Tractate XIV: Of the Historicity and Priestliness of Beards.

History is the shape of change; and change, to be noticeable, must be neither too fast nor too slow. A man's face, however, principal though it may be among the things of the world, sacrament of history though it is, does not, for the most part, change at a *convenient* pace: its smiles and winks are too fleeting for record, and its growth and aging too slow for continuous attention. What is needed is something that will move slowly enough so that its motion will go unnoticed, but still change quickly enough to constitute a daily or weekly reminder of history. God, therefore, to give human beings a perpetual memorial of the fact that their changing must be shaped — that their faces must make history — gave them *hair*. To women, hair upon the crown, to grow long with the addition of days, and to require shaping and formation. And to men, hair upon cheek and jowl, hair to lend suitable majesty to the oracle of their mouths, so that even the greatest fool might swear by the beard of the prophet.

For most of the animals, God provided only *reasonable* tegument, hair that grew to a convenient length and then stopped, hair that needed no historicizing. But the hair he gave to men was a gift *in excess,* a deliberate inconvenience, an awkwardness that could become majestic only by oblation. The choicest ages of the world have been precisely those in which men's hair has been offered historically. And, conversely, the most benighted ages have been the eras in which the razor has been rampant. A short beard, a curled beard, a braided beard, even — if it must be — a moustache, is hair historicized. But a clean-shaven face is hair obliterated. It is evidence not of oblation but of history washed down the sink. What might have been a daily offering is only a loss; the morning sacrifice of men turns out to be only murder.

▼　　▼　　▼

But I give you no more. You have served to bring me to an end. Our bodies, lovely in eyes and lovely in limbs, cry out for oblation. Even a light lifting of them lifts us as we offer. No thing, let alone the main thing, is evil: *Ens inquantum ens est bonum.* The body is not the solemn burden that we have made it, not the grim totem the world takes it to be: it is a noble animal, a fabulous steed, whom God has appointed to keep us company and to bear us home. Brother Ass was made to carry the king into history. What a pity we do not show the beast more love.

8. *The Courting Dance*

When it comes to the oblation of persons, there is a loose but tempting connection waiting to be picked up. In English, the words *person, parson,* and *priest* are near neighbors: they share some footage of fence in the backyard of usage. Enough, at any rate, to suggest that somebody has already caught the hint that both parson and person are up to the same thing — that both are priests, offerers. The definition of a human being as a person, and of persons as priestly agents within history, turns out to be not altogether whimsical.

But for all that, it still does not turn out to be the common one. We assume, of course, that it is. We take it for granted that the concept of person is so firmly built into our philosophies and institutions that we hardly need give it a thought. Yet, for the past hundred years or so, it has had a hard time maintaining itself. Most modern definitions of humanity are non-personal or impersonal. At their best, they ignore the concept; at their worst, they positively destroy it. It is another case of illegible legends. I shall not spend any more time on them than it takes to note what is perhaps their principal feature: a penchant for the words *only* and *nothing but*.

The human race, we are told, is *only* the product of biological evolution. A human being, the announcements proclaim, is *simply* so many dollars' worth of chemical elements. Thought, they insist, is *nothing but* electromagnetic impulses in the brain. There is a name for this line of argument. It is called the reductionist fallacy. It takes something that is a complex whole and defines it only in terms of its parts. It reduces what a thing *is* to what a thing is *made of*. It will allow only operational definitions, not metaphysical ones.

For example. A biomedical engineer, in the course of his experiments, comes up with some amazing facts. He finds that the electrical stimulation of certain centers of the brain, or the minute adjustment of certain aspects of body chemistry, will produce the subjective sensation of, say, stark terror, complete serenity, or philosophical omnicompetence. It is a remarkable discovery; and it is one in which anyone can take legitimate intellectual delight. To know anything real is indeed good. Unfortunately, however, the engineer usually goes a step further. Not content with having arrived at positive knowledge, he feels compelled to insist that his physical discoveries are the only valid positive knowledge available. As a result, he comes up with a statement that catapults him abruptly out of the physical and into the metaphysical realm. He proclaims that terror, serenity, or philosophy are nothing but physical phenomena. He becomes a reductionist. For him, the fact that young love and mild indigestion use the same physical equipment constitutes an all but overwhelming temptation to refuse to see any real difference between them.

If he would confine himself to his own physical researches, it is quite possible that he might do some good — at least as far as advancing knowledge within his own field is concerned. But when he turns himself loose in law or politics, in love or marriage, he becomes a menace. He will quickly insist, of course, that he intends to speak only about physical reality; he will usually disown any metaphysical designs. But the disclaimer comes too late. The minute someone employs the reductionist argument, he is already waist-deep in metaphysics, with the water rising around him like a river in flood. For what he has really said is that metaphysics is either an impossibility or a merely subjective exercise. In any case, he has reached the dangerous point of having gone to work on metaphysical concepts without a single truly metaphysical tool in his kit.

That is why the concept of person has to be kept alive. In an age when all kinds of experts are more than ready to tell us that only our parts really count, we need to retain a firm grip on the notion that the whole of us is what matters; that our *names,* our identities as persons — who we are as distinct from what we are — are the most important thing about us. We need a metaphysical grasp of humankind. The law, of course, and politics as practiced in a democracy still act as if the metaphysical notion of person were the key concept in anthropology. But most lawyers and politicians have long since fallen short of it. They have, along with the rest of us, been sold a merely physical — an engineering — view of human nature. Human beings, in their hands, are always imminently in danger of being used, operated, manipulated rather than respected.

To illustrate. From time to time, the question of euthanasia manages to become one of the features of the press. It is argued that if someone, by accident of fate or birth, has reached the state at which he is "only a vegetable," we should be allowed to dispatch him, quietly and painlessly, from life. The contention is that so much of his equipment is gone that he no longer qualifies as human, anyway. The law, until recently, refused to have any truck with this: it went right on treating him as a person and insisting that nobody has a right to do him in. But the euthanasia enthusiasts, in their readiness to lobby for a change, may be moving at a speed that is hazardous to our philosophical health.

The flaw in their argument lies under that little qualifier about guaranteeing the painlessness of the *coup de grâce.* They seem always to feel obliged to pretty it up. But on their reasoning, that is totally unnecessary. It is only a sop thrown to the human consensus they are about to evict from the halls of justice. If the poor "basket case" (even their words are impersonal and grim) is no longer human, why don't they simply add some cement blocks to the basket and drown him like a cat? Why the expense, why the ritual of disposing of him as if he still mattered?

The answer, of course, is that even in abolishing the notion of person, they can never cut all of their ties with it. They will, when the time comes, duly bury their own dead. Aunt Suzie's body, even after it is less than a vegetable, will be ceremoniously laid away. And, after the funeral, they will — destroying their whole case in the process — go and sit in a lawyer's office for the reading of a piece of paper that will inform them, the living, of the present, and sometimes devastatingly effective, *Will* of the deceased. Not only does the law treat Aunt Suzie as a person in life; it allows her to go on making history after death.

I propose, therefore, to ignore the engineers and their enthusiasms. But I also propose that, at the same time, we all keep one eye very carefully glued on them. Someday, no doubt, they will reach such heights of refinement that they will be able to duplicate all of the physical components of a man or a woman; and the day after that they will probably find a way of pasting them together so that they will be able to announce triumphantly that they have manufactured a human being. When that time comes, we must all be ready to explain patiently to them that they have done no such thing. We must tell them that they have only foolishly succeeded in conferring real being on something which the race, so far, has been wise enough to confine to fairy tales. They will have made a Troll, a Goblin, an Orc. They will have brought forth to the light of day something which can *do* everything a person does without being what a person *is*. They will have made an *it*, not a *person*. And if they insist, as they will, on bringing it to tea or to Mass, let us hope and pray that somewhere in Christendom there will still be a bishop wise enough to instruct the faithful to throw stones at it *ad majorem Dei gloriam*.

Out, then, with the reductionists and their trolls! And up with human beings as persons — with history's parsons, meaning's priests. We have neglected them far too long already. There are vast technologies waiting anxiously in the wings. Unless we are ready with a clear defense of person, we shall all be shoved offstage by the goblins. Remember I told you so. *Hora novissima, tempora pessima sunt, vigilemus!*

▼　　　▼　　　▼

To work then. The first thing to be insisted upon is the fact that every personal offering of history must be precisely a priestly one. It is not enough simply to obtrude histories upon one another.

We affect those around us in many ways. Because history is a shaping, a selection, of the events that chronicle hands us, history necessarily involves chronicle. Accordingly, if I can manage to intrude, by main force or stupidity, into somebody else's chronicle, I will, to some degree at least, have become a possible candidate for inclusion in his history. If my car crumples my neighbor's fender, if my dog chases his cat, if my fist lands in his face, we are already on the edge of affecting each other's histories. If he is a wise man, of course, he will certainly ignore the first two, and probably ignore the third. But wise men are rare; an incredible amount of meaning is commonly read into such events. And if I go further — if I water his stock, foreclose his mortgage, or slander his name — well, I am in his history almost willy-nilly. We are, by one leap, in a position to make or break each other.

Whether two persons come together in an oblation that makes history, however, will depend on more than common chronicle. It will depend not only on what they do *to* each other but on what they do *with* each other — on the priestly or unpriestly offerings they make of what has happened. And that means that no truly personal relationship can be left to fend for itself. It must be seen, in advance, as an imminent oblation, and it must be shaped accordingly. The approach of person to person is precisely a dance, and a courting dance at that. None of my meetings with human beings is a mere event, either in their lives or in mine. Every introduction is an invitation into each other's meaning, a *terrible* opening of one history to another. In friendship, love, or any other alliance, we enter inexorable exchanges, rendering death and forever at each breathing.

Needless to say, we do not commonly see the kind of care we should expect in such meetings. Even in the most deliberate invitations — when we invite love, when we propose marriage — we act frighteningly off the cuff. We come at each other as casually as we approach watermelons. We hold each other in careless, calloused hands. We see those we should offer only as beings to be used. We grasp them, but we watch ourselves.

One of the appalling aspects of the pastoral ministry is the gradual discovery of how badly people deal with other people. Wives, husbands, parents, children — so many of them are only handled, not offered. Yet, even in the worst cases there was always a time at which the note of *courtship* — of gracious invitation, of courteous oblation — was not only present but predominant. The utterly broken marriage, the relationship in which the partners can now see nothing but misused advantage, was once a priestly thing in which they gave themselves as each other's ministers.

That is the first key to the mystery of courtship. I do not want at this point to narrow the notion too much. Romantic love will come in soon enough. Here I want only to use the word to describe the inveterate desire we conceive, at certain times and toward certain persons, to open ourselves to them and to invite them into our history. I want to keep its definition broad enough to include not only the approach of man to maid, but also the motion of Smith toward the fellow on the next barstool or of a clerk in bookkeeping toward a typist in public relations.

Why do we do it at all, when we so commonly do it badly? Why this perpetual mating ritual in such a monumentally frustrating world? What does it mean, except that we were built for courting, for courtesy, and that, God help us, we can do no other. But if that is true, then our real work becomes at least a little clearer. It is not to find a way around the courting, but to find a way through it. Not to avoid it, but to understand it and to try to see that we do it courteously, personally, in ways worthy of the priesthood of Adam.

When I take up with someone else (the phrase is solid, and priestly too), I enter into a transaction which, if it does not involve oblation, will necessarily mean disaster. When I behold a dog or offer a cat, I must take care that I behold it for *itself,* not just for *myself.* Even things cannot simply be used. But when I behold Henry or Mary, I step off the deep end of oblation; for I am inviting into my history beings that cannot — that must not — allow themselves to be used. Unless I undertake to lift them for themselves, they will begin to snarl at my concern; unless my invitation evokes an invitation in return, we are in for trouble.

For themselves. The ultimate mystery of personality — of personhood — is that no person exists for his or her own sake. As a matter of fact, it is precisely my own welfare that is the last thing in the world I am to be concerned with. Priests are to spend their days offering for others: the Good Shepherd gives his life for the sheep. The beholding, the loving — the adoration, if you will — of my own being is somebody else's business, not mine. Persons were meant to enter into a dance of mutual oblation, a simultaneous offering of each other. The City, the web, history itself, is the tissue woven by such priestly acts. That it has not been formed well in this fallen world goes to prove only that the world is indeed fallen — that the exchanges which were ordained to weave the web are the very ones which, by perversion, have been its destruction. But in all the long and disastrous history of their courting, Adam and Eve have never ceased to court. The only trouble is that they court themselves first. Pride, self-love, egotism are only — are precisely — the right oblation offered by the wrong priest. Like all classic perversions, they are just a whisker away from the truth.

We were meant, therefore, to do easily and courteously for each other what we must under no circumstances attempt to do for ourselves. Narcissus perished for looking at himself; had he done exactly the same thing for another, he would have thrived. The mirror is a tricky proposition. A priest, when he or she goes to say Mass, puts on the vestments in a side room. Every proper sacristy has a mirror, often a full-length one. So far, so good. There is no excuse for slovenliness at the altar of God; anything that will help the priest go to the sanctuary properly hitched and neatly girded is a help. But I think that most priests have some misgivings about their sacristy mirrors. True persons who are about to offer up all things in loving adoration perceive the impropriety of spending even a second looking at themselves. It is disconcerting; it is imminently . . . perverse. I always feel better when it is an altar server or a fellow priest who casts the final approving glance at the gathering of my alb or the set of my chasuble.

Our fellow priests. There is the word. The offerers who make sacred for us what we ourselves would only profane. And how we need them! How we cry day and night for those priestly others who

will love our faces, our bodies, and the marvelously odd twists of
our minds! Not, God forbid, so we can be appreciated, accepted, or
gratified. Not for any of the dreadful psychological reasons for which
the world tells us we need them. But in order that we may be
delivered from the horrible burden of trying to appreciate ourselves
— so we can be about the business of saying our own Mass for
somebody else, free in the knowledge that others have already taken
care of us. Self-preservation may be the law of the jungle, but only
mutual and priestly oblation can build the City.

▼　　　▼　　　▼

Courting *in genere,* however — courting in the wide sense, courting
as the way of men and women with each other, courting as the
priestly invitation of all other persons for offering — holds only a
small candle to courting *in specie.* The first is a loose and general
diagram of the oblation; the second is the rich and detailed picture.
It goes no better than the former, of course; indeed, it goes worse:
it is an invitation to more intricate involvements and to vastly greater
inexorabilities. But it goes — and goes and goes — just the same.

Nowhere else is the priestly approach to other persons quite so
clearly drawn as in the first motions of courtly, of romantic, love.
The whole desire of the *courteous* lover is to sing the praises of the
beloved and to hold her up for adoration. It is precisely the priesthood of Adam and Eve that is the root of romance; not sexual desire
or rational analysis. They come in soon enough, of course, but in
the first instance they are palpable irrelevancies. They may well be
the cause of eighty percent of the affairs in the world, and of one
hundred percent of the hanky-panky: sex and logic are indeed heady
draughts. But the recognizable rightness of the romantic oblation
remains the overpowering elixir. It is the *courtliness* of the offering
of the beloved that intoxicates: the joy, the ease, the elation with
which we become each other's ministers is the straight 100-proof
marvel.

But there is more. The priesthood of Adam and Eve is the
instrument of meaning as well as the spring of joy; romantic love

makes history just as necessarily as it sings praises. How well do you remember? There is a small and entirely common English word that will prove it to you. You have used it all your life — easily, almost meaninglessly. If someone asked you, as a child, to select the ten most thrilling words in the world, you would not have thought of this one in a million tries. And yet there was a day — when? at sixteen? at eighteen? — on which it became the bearer of an overwhelming freight of joy. You stood next to someone with whom you had entered into mutual oblation, and in the casual utterance of it you came face to face with an unexpected burst of meaning. One or the other of you spoke the blessed word: *us.*

History is made in moments, in decisive instants of transition. And the creation of an *us* from what was only an *I* and a *Thou* is one of them. Nothing is a clearer proof of the historical nature of humankind than the thrill of meaning, of shape — of history — which invariably accompanies it. Even if it is forgotten forever ten minutes after it was spoken, the mere occurrence of it remains a monumental giveaway that history is our meat — that the achievement of meaning, the weaving of the web, is the real reason for our ceaseless courting of one another. If we came together only to use or to gratify — if we met only to blow hot-breathed I-need-you's or greedy I-want-you's at each other — no little word like *us* could matter the way it does. If our courting were only flirtation — only a dabbling with history, only a toying with persons — the discovery that I have suddenly become involved in *us* would be a nuisance, not a thrill.

Indeed, unless our courting is deliberately pursued as historic, it will be not only a nuisance but a menace. There is no middle ground between use and oblation. Once the word *us* has been uttered, a new and common history has been created by fiat of adoration. It can make us or break us, but there is no easy turning from it. It is precisely the new historical entity *we* that must now become not only a new object for oblation but a priestly agent in its own right. As I and Thou became *we* by mutual oblation, so *we* now must walk into history to make a joint offering of other things and other persons.

Oblations multiply. John Smith courts Mary Jones. He becomes her lover, her offerer, her priest. Courteously, she returns the oblation and obliges him with her love. Two priests; two oblations. But now they are John-and-Mary — the Smiths — and that makes a third priest who must offer and a third history that must be lifted up. Where does it stop? It doesn't. John must now offer *us,* and we must offer John; and John-and-Mary together must become the offerers of the Davises next door and of all the intractable in-laws and relatives who present themselves for oblation. All this, mind you, and they have hardly even begun to offer. Allow them, in addition, only a modest number of children and only the few years it takes for the children they beget and the family they constitute to become priestly agents themselves — and what have you? A web? A tissue? The words are too poor. You have a brocade, a tapestry of mutual oblation. Even in one small corner of the world, the shuttles fly so fast and the warps come so thick upon each other that the mind staggers to comprehend the weaving.

And if the making of history is so, how complex, how snarled, how tangled beyond all possibility of grasp or unraveling must be the *unmaking,* the failure to offer. The loom on which we weave cannot be stopped short: it produces triumphs or disasters, but nothing in between. *Corruptio optimi pessima.* Lilies that fester smell far worse than weeds. If, with our friends, we allow use to replace oblation; if into our marriages we admit competitive, exclusive oblations; if toward our children we extend only surly tolerance where there should be priestly lifting, what wreckage must we not expect? The really appalling thing about us is that we are so regularly appalled by the way things go wrong. If we knew our nature and our failings better, there would be much less room for surprise and perhaps a little more seriousness about the necessity of oblation all across the board.

For if no *single* priestly agent can safely act for himself or herself — if every individual man and woman must say Mass for another, lest they perish by pride — then the same is true of a compound priestly agent, of an I and a Thou who by mutual oblation have made themselves an *us.* They entered a common history by opening their eyes upon each other and by lifting each other in love. But now that they are in it, they must take care to act in their new priesthood: to look out, not in; to offer not themselves, but others. Friend and friend, man and wife, enter a joint — a *collegial* — priesthood. If they insist upon looking only at themselves, if they think that the meaning of their romantic meeting can be saved by celebrating only the original and private rituals of courtship, they will wreck everything. When a friendship or a marriage degenerates into a discussion of what it means to the individuals involved, it is already lost. We cannot safely look at each other beyond the initial courting. I and Thou must, to a large degree, be replaced by *us;* we must stand in our new history, not facing each other, but side by side. Courtship is the invitation not to a life of private Masses but to a joint Mass in a new and common priesthood — to a concelebration, if you please — for the lifting up of all that is not ourselves. It is just because we are priests that no one can afford the mistake of Narcissus. God has not willed us to offer alone; he has called us into an almost endless succession of priesthoods: into histories that themselves become agents of history, into twinings that are themselves elements of a fantastic brocade, and into ministries that move continually outward and homeward into the high Priesthood of the Mystical Body itself.

9. *The Historic Bind*

There are no doubt many forests through which the complexities of our oblation of fellow human beings may be hunted. To enter them all would be more exhausting than rewarding. Accordingly, I choose to explore only one: the family. At its edges I may touch briefly on friendship, but the family is, I think, a dense enough wood to keep us all busy for at least as long as we have energy and time.

The wood, the forest, the *apeiron* — the place where you are so crowded by detail that you cannot see the horizon, cannot grasp shape, direction, meaning. It makes a good first metaphor for the family. We enter marriage as we enter a wood: with purpose, with hope, with direction. We continue in marriage as we continue in a wood: confused, haunted, and imminently lost. And we survive marriage as we survive a wood: by a combination of dumb luck, faulty knowledge, and helpless goodwill — and at the price of coming through with no thinnest skin left upon a single tooth in our heads. It's a great hike when it's over, but the campfires at which its praises are sung are seldom the ones we light in the forest.

You have read far enough in this book to be, if not convinced of, perhaps used to the idea that the marriage of two persons is a deliberate and priestly attempt to make history. That much has at least a certain clarity, a simple elegance about it that delights the mind. But if any couple expects elegance like that after they have slipped between the sheets of the marriage bed, they should be instructed to pray for patience while they wait. It is a long time coming back. Therefore, if the concept of the priesthood of Adam can strike even a spark in the thick darkness of family life — if the idea of person as the agent of history can explain even inelegantly what on earth is going on around our beds and boards — let us by all means see what it has to offer. We have precious little time to lose.

▼　　▼　　▼

Take John Smith. Add Mary Jones. Mix with a *soupçon* of benefit of clergy, and you have, as already indicated, Smiths. Better than that. You have *the* Smiths: like *the* Bronx, they are an entity arthrous and articulated, a singular and historic city.

Next, take your Smiths and tuck firmly in bed. Set aside for a while to let the initial leaven of their historic choice work. When nearly doubled in bulk, remove, bake, and cool under weights. It is a recipe that will make enough history to serve a regiment.

Consider, first of all, the children a marriage brings into being. In the act of conception, through the months of gestation, during the hours of birth, and for a fair number of years after that, children are really beings without a history of their own. The child in the womb may be a historic being, but the only history she is involved in is her mother's. And the child in the cradle, the toddler in the pen, is not much different. The portrait of a young couple with their first baby is still an elegant one. But the snapshot of a pair of beaten forty-five-year-olds surrounded, overshadowed, and stymied by a handful of teenagers and a clutch of elementary-school pupils has less to recommend it on the level of intelligibility. Somewhere in between, elegance left by the back door. Around the end of the first child's toddling and the beginning of talking, a second and unnoticed pregnancy began; another and quite painless delivery was accomplished. A *person* was born. A piece of history began to distinguish itself and quietly proceeded to start a history of its own. A new priest was ordained *sub rosa* and sent back to his old haunts, with no collar and no letters of ordination, but with all the powers of the priesthood of Adam.

From there on, the story of a child is the classic story of the unrecognized prince in his rightful kingdom. His poor parents are totally unprepared for his claim. With immense goodwill, they struggle like peasants and villagers to find out what is going on, but they are always several episodes behind in the story. The pains of childhood — the agonies of the teens — are due precisely to the emergence of a priestly agent among beings who are not ready to have one arrive so soon. The common phrase for the process — "cutting the apron strings" — is dull and unenlightening. It provides no reason for the event; it describes it only by means of an external analogy. And, worse yet, it leaves parents with no consolation whatsoever. After all, they provided the best apron strings they knew how to make; and they tied them for the best of all possible reasons — the child's safety and profit; and they know for certain that, at the age of thirteen or fourteen, this fractious string-chopping beast in their midst is still a good six or sixteen years away from being able to manage his or her own affairs with either safety *or* profit.

But if they would see that rebellion not as a destructive cutting but as a legitimate (if misunderstood) request by one priest to another to be allowed to say his own Mass — well, that would soften the blow a bit. The apparent rejection then becomes a step *toward* history, not away from it. Mind you, I do not think teenagers see it that way; but I do think that's what they are up to, even if none of us understands it. Take my teenagers, for example. They are trying to get clear enough of my priestly grasp so that they can come back at me with a historic grip of their own. They began, you see, with no history but mine; in order for that history to become theirs, it has to be freely lifted up by them. They cannot simply accept my first city with them — from their point of view, that was too much like necessity. If our last city together is to be built at all, it will not be enough that I invited *them;* they must, somewhere, somehow, invite *me.*

And to do that — to make their invitation recognizable to us both — there must sometime come a refusal of invitation. A tentative rejection preliminary to a voluntary acceptance. It is not a case of doing evil that good may come. What I am talking about is not an evil; it is only a move in the game of oblation. That it is, in a fallen world, commonly accompanied by — even drowned in — attendant evils argues nothing against the fundamental sanity and reasonableness of the game. And this is only what wise parents have always known and what foolish parents, in rare moments of wisdom, have always suspected: that if you take children lightly, they will love you sooner. Slap them down as a mother cat does her bumptious kittens, but never do less than the cat. Forget it all till the next time; bear them no grudges. We are not making scores here; we are making history. New priests are always obnoxious. Don't stifle the one thing that can save them.

Needless to say, however, such advice is hard to follow. The marvel is that any parents manage to act on it at all. They are thrust, by their parenthood, into a position of almost crippling disadvantage: there is no such thing as cumulative experience in the home. Each of the budding priests in their household begins to offer at his own surprising time and in her own startling way. That my first son does not reject me this year is no guarantee that he will not reject me the next — or that my third daughter will not rebel with a vengeance when she turns twelve. We are called to no rehearsals, only public performances. The pieces we so carefully practice are the very ones we will never be asked to play again. Everything that matters has to be read at sight.

To her father or his mother, a newborn baby is only a marvelous *it: child* is commonly a neuter word. Parents know, of course, that their child will soon be more than that, but the full weight of their knowledge does not press upon them at first: children become priestly agents only slowly. For a long time they remain more pets than persons; and through all those lovely years, parents practice offering them *as* pets. But by the time they are able to do it really well, they discover, to their pain and confusion, that such treatment is the one thing in the world that the children, in their newfound historicity, cannot possibly put up with. As the curtain rises on the crucial performance, they open their assigned parts as parents of teenagers and find, to their horror, that the music does not contain a single passage in which their hard-won expertise in scales and arpeggios is needed at all. The entire piece is a long-breathed *adagio* — a problem not in fast passage work, but in artistry, phrasing, and articulation. They are no better off than rank beginners. To stumble through it at all is no small success; and if they should be able to grasp even a hint of the outline of its shape, its meaning, in the one awful first and last reading they are allowed — well, that would be a triumph indeed.

▼   ▼   ▼

Children, however, are related to more than their parents. Their oblations of other members of their families may be different, but they are no less complexly historical. Brothers, sisters, close cousins stand in an equality. They do not arise out of each other's history; they begin their lives as historyless *its* thrown together in the web of a family. There is between them not the clear, elegant, all-or-nothing distinction that exists between parents and infants; there is only the physical distinction of pups in a litter. To be sure, the farther apart they are in age, the more their relationship will tend to approximate that of parent to child. The boy of fourteen is at least a half-trained priest: his often gracious offering of a five-year-old sister proves it handsomely. But his offering of a big brother of sixteen is harder to interpret. The only thing it seems obviously to prove is original sin.

That is why the priestly work of brothers and sisters is in some ways even more exacting than that of parents. They begin without history, without oblation, but somewhere along the line they must step back far enough from all that surrounds them to behold it and offer it freely. They start their life in the midst of a concelebration to which they were only dragged by the hair of their heads — in a Mass which they know so well that it is practically the last thing in the world they will recognize as a Mass. If they are ever to hold their brethren up in priestly hands, they must, with those same priestly hands, first put their brethren down, off, and out, just so that they can then pick them up freely. Their first fellowship with them was an imprisonment about which they had no choice. If there is to be a second fellowship, it must be based not on the serving of a common sentence but on the acceptance of mutual invitations. Only someone who is really *out* can be invited *in*.

The beehive and the ant hill are cities of a sort, but they are cities that are built by the unavoidable necessity of instinct. The cities of human beings, on the other hand, can be built only by the free and historic oblations of individual persons. The family is not instinctive so much as it is priestly. There is a great deal about brothers and sisters that will make them look alike, think alike, and laugh alike. But there is nothing about them that will make them a *city* except the exercise of their own priesthood. That is why no one can tell in advance how long it will take for given members of a family to turn the necessities of common origin into the virtues of priestly oblation. The most gracious ones may do it by ten or twelve; the surly and the bitter may not make a start even by seventy. It is so easy to give — and to take — umbrage at the crucial work of separation. The operation is designed, of course, to make a free union possible; but error, ignorance, pride, and prejudice lie perpetually at the door. There are often gaps — sometimes unclosable gaps — in the history of a family. Sons and father, brothers and sisters misread the purpose of their drawing away from one another. The letting go that was to be a prelude to taking up again becomes an outright rejection. The break *for* history becomes a break *in* history, and the *we* that might have formed degenerates, not back into *thou* and *thou* — that is an irretrievable condition — but into opposing *hims* or *hers*. The second-person singular must rise to the first plural or sink below itself to the third: *she* is only the cat's mother.

The weaving of the web of a close family, therefore, while it is one of nature's noblest works, is also one of her most difficult. That, I think, is why we generally find that it is our relatives at one remove who, in fact, become our first true consanguine oblations. It is the children of our parents' brothers and sisters with whom we commonly fall into something very like love. "Kissing cousins" is not simply an allusion to dirty games in the attic; it is a hint of the priestliness of Adam and Eve. A boy takes years to get far enough away from his sister even to see what she really looks like, let alone enter into a priestly mutuality with her. But the same boy may very well accomplish just that in the course of ten minutes with his cousin Mary at the age of twelve. That he will no doubt go on to try to accomplish a good deal more than that — or, better said, less than that, other than that — is beside the point. That is not what makes the oblation, but what unmakes it. He has seen *somebody* with his own eyes; the proclamation of *us* as an offered city, as opposed to *us* as an unavoidable crowd, has gone thundering through the fibers of his being.

But perhaps the chiefest and easiest of the early oblations of children is the lifting up not of their cousins but of their cousins' parents. It is in the offering of uncles and of aunts that we first use our priestly powers. Long before we can see our parents, we look with gladness upon their sisters and brothers. There is no greater historical gift than a brace, a set — a baker's dozen, if at all possible — of uncles. (Dutch uncles will do as well as blood uncles; indeed, the inequities of nature make them almost indispensable. No boy's or girl's priesthood should be imperiled just because their grandparents failed to have enough children.)

I distrust mightily the modern world's love of sorting people into all kinds of aptitude and ability groups at early ages, but if I were called upon to do it, I would be interested in only one division; the separation of the unpriestly from the priestly. And I stand ready with a one-question test that will do the job infallibly. *Ten-year-old children who would not rather live with their Uncle Henry or their Aunt Martha are children to be watched with the gravest suspicion:* their priesthood should have been operative long since. They will not be able to choose their own father or mother for years, but if they cannot offer their uncles now, we may well have unhistoric monsters on our hands. Such children should not, of course, be banished. They need help, therapy, treatment. Accordingly, they should be provided, perhaps at the government's expense, with a deluxe set of uncles for oblation. A 210-pound water skier, for a start, and a 140-pound model-locomotive builder to go with him. And, if available, a poetry reader, a crane operator, an amateur violinist, and a judge of good whiskey. And, above all, an uncle who can tell jokes that will grow hairier as the children grow taller. Their cure would not be long in coming. The therapy is well-nigh infallible.

Beyond the confines of the family, however, the possibilities for early and instant oblation multiply and abound. One of the saddest features of our present mode of life is the continuing disappearance of the town, the village, the neighborhood. There are neighbors who are even more easily offered than uncles! But if the young are not exposed to them, if there are no stoops and porches to display them, no open basement windows through which to address them, no back fences across which to reach out to them — if there are only barren apartment corridors and porchless development houses — the world has ceased to be the seminary it might have been.

Nonetheless, the priesthood of Adam fights back. Even in the desert of the modern world, children still walk with open, wondering eyes. They offer whatever neighbors they can find, and the offerings they make are often their best as well as their first. The oblations they make later will be more conscious and, therefore, more self-conscious. Pride grows along with priesthood; the ability to wreck increases with the power to build. But, adult or child, they — and we — offer.

God binds us into histories we did not choose that we may go forth from them into cities of our own shaping. The actual offerings we make in the confines of family and neighborhood are seldom as important as the habit of oblation that we form in the first years of our priesthood. Give children only reality and open eyes — give them a father to struggle with and a mother to misunderstand, give them cousins to kiss and aunts to make them pies, give them uncles to offer and large neighbors for oblation — and you will, by every one of those exchanges, move the world another inch away from chaos. It takes more than that to build the City; but without that, it cannot be formed at all.

10. *The Black Mass*

Hilaire Belloc says somewhere that nothing is so hard as
ending a book. He advances a number of reasons, chief
among them the home truth that there is always something more to be said. I would like, without dissenting from his
original motion, to offer an amended and more precise version: there
is nothing so hard as making it *possible* to end a book. The trick of
turning a really neat back splice is not accomplished at the end of
the rope; you must begin a certain distance in, tie a proper crown
knot, and work carefully from there. The neatness and elegance of
the finished splice depend on preparation.

But more than that, they depend on the proper handling of
the reversals of direction in the rope itself. There are very few subjects
of any importance that can be ended by proceeding straight ahead.
One of the neglected categories in literary criticism is what I would
call the Grand Adversative — the *But* Paramount — of a book. It
is the point at which the author, having built his case by paying
attention to matters of his own choosing, begins to feel the pressure
of other matters he has so far kept at bay. He has achieved consistency
by selection, but — there it is, you see: *But* — there are all kinds
of inconsistencies waiting for him among the things as yet un-
selected.

If he does not deal with them — if he omits entirely the Grand
Adversative — his book will not end at all, but simply unravel like
an unspliced rope. If, on the other hand, he tries to tie up his loose

ends with assurances from other and alien subjects, his book will end, all right, but it will lack the naturalness and integrity it might have had. A rope can indeed be whipped over with string — the problem of mere unraveling can be solved from the outside — but it cannot then be said that the rope itself has a good end. The string has come in as a *deus ex machina* to save the day. Accordingly, if a book is to have both an end and an *honest end,* the author will have to do precisely what a good seaman does: he must use only his proper subject, tie the crown as best he can, and splice backwards. He must take up the But Paramount with both hands and work it right into the heart of the matter.

▼   ▼   ▼

Concede the validity of the concept of the priesthood of Adam and Eve. Concede further the effectiveness of all the allusive arguments for it based on marsh reeds and marriage beds, on kissing cousins and offered uncles. Concede even, *per impossibile,* that this entire book so far has achieved triumphantly all that it set out to do. Concede all that, and you will still have every right to be skeptical about the whole business. I have showed you some marvelous passages of history. *But.*

But: your history does not look much like them. But: the world's history does not look much like them. And, for a final, honest But: my own history, my family's history, and my parish's history do not look much like them. There is just enough correspondence with them to make the argument temptingly plausible. But on any given day there is more than enough bad history, wrong history, unhistory to send it sprawling every time. My relations with my children, my parents, and my uncles are anything but gorgeous and grand. We all hold innumerable mortgages on each other, and we have frequently threatened foreclosure. Oblation has run only a poor second to use. And my relations with my parish and with the many others who have had the questionable fortune to get within shouting distance of me are not much better. If we are making history here, we are making it in exceedingly small quantities. Adam may be the agent of meaning, but he takes a lot of days off. Most of the time it's hard to believe that anyone is minding the store.

And the same is true of the rest of the world, as you know perfectly well. Most marriages are poor oblations at best: shoddy offerings by lazy priests. And a good many of them are worse than that: demonic oblations, perversions of priesthood, *black Masses*. And if you add only the contents of one issue of a daily newspaper — if you look only at one previous day's record of what humankind has done about history in politics or in architecture, in love, law, or religion — you have come to a perfectly adequate statement of the But Paramount in the subject of the priestliness of humankind.

Be sure, however, that you state it correctly. It is not the simple adversative involved in this sentence: All right, grant that Adam is the priest of the world; *but* why, then, doesn't the world look better than it does? That is only a *But* Paravail, an enlargement of the semicolon. It raises no problem that priestliness cannot explain. The question it asks can be answered, simply and honestly, by saying that the world is a mess because we have been false and wicked priests. Indeed, I have already said as much long since. The But Paramount, on the other hand, is a deeper and more majestic consideration — one that appears not in the first sketches of the argument but only in the large and nearly finished drawing. It is the adversative contained in this passage: Grant everything you have said about priesthood and history. Grant also the perversion of priesthood as the explanation of bad history. But if priesthood is the reason for both history and *un*-history, must you not despair for good of ever achieving meaning at all?

That But, you see, is no mere elaboration of a semicolon; it is a word with power, a dark and sovereign lord. Though it speaks in a question, it utters a challenge. For it sees clearly that if it is Adam the priest who makes history, and Adam the priest who wrecks history, then history is a subject that may as well be dropped. It looks the author straight in the eye and says: You have produced a tender and amusing account of meaning, *but you can't make it stick!* You have shown us Adam the priest continually bent upon shaping; you have displayed our love of offerings *in order that . . .* of oblations *for . . .* of priestly acts *so that. . . .* But to all of it, the real story of our priesthood simply says: So what? So nothing! Sew buttons on your old man's coat! If we build only to break, if the architects of meaning spend most of their time in the wrecking business, why bother with them at all? *Carpe diem,* or take the gaspipe, but don't waste your time trying to make sense out of nonsense. The wound is incurable; make the patient comfortable and quit.

There, at last, is the real problem of history: not that we neglect it, but that even when we work at it we pervert it. Take a marriage that, after five years or ten, goes bad. Talk to the people involved during the final hours of the shipwreck. There was once, of course, a common history in that marriage: the two of them came together in mutual oblation and jointly shaped a new meaning of their lives. But in those last hours you will be able to find no trace of it. They will have drawn apart into separate histories. As far as they are concerned, the versions they are now presenting are, and always have been, true. But anyone who heard them years before knows better. The long recitals of grievances, the bills of particulars that go into the legal depositions, are precisely *new history.* The old chronicles, the old facts, are indeed still involved; but they have become the elements of a new and sinister offering.

"On the night of April 7th, 1960, I left the house after an argument with my wife. Upon returning, I found she had locked all the doors and windows. When I tried to gain entrance, she called the police, reporting that a prowler was outside her house. Since my wallet and papers were inside the house, the investigating officer refused for at least ten minutes to believe that I was her husband. This was only one of many such humiliations."

Do you want to know what is sinister about that? At the bottom of the affidavit is a signature and a date: John Smith, 10 June 1965. Notice: April 7th, 1960; June 10th, 1965. Five years. Five years of marriage after the dire event. But, according to them, only five years of waiting until they discovered what it meant, until they found how it could be offered, until they finally made history of it. But that is impossible. The very persistence of the marriage from 1960 to 1965 is proof that there was at least another, and possibly a better, offering of that event, a different and happier oblation. The event was, no doubt, irksome enough at the time, but days or weeks later they probably laughed about it and told it to their friends as a joke at their own expense. That is what is sinister about the new oblation in 1965: it is an unsaying of meaning, a *black Mass,* a reversal of reality, a priestly destruction of history.

When you have seen enough such offerings, you acquire two things: a new appreciation of the power of humankind to give shape and meaning to events, and a deep dread of the meanings people actually bring forth. You come to a despair over the ability of the white Mass to withstand the perverting power of the black — to an increased awe of priesthood and to a profound distrust of priests. You begin to see how easily unmeaning triumphs over meaning. After all, if a marriage survives for ten years — if it survives even for ten months — the amount of solid, right offering involved must be great indeed. Day after day, week after week, mutual oblations are made in sincerity and truth. And day after day, week after week, to some degree at least, even wrong oblations are offered up in forgiveness and love. But once the black Mass begins in earnest, the white one ceases as if it had never been. All the same elements are now present: the same priests, the same altar, the same events. Now, however, they are offered backwards and upside down — not for the creation of shape but for its obliteration. What took years to build is torn down in a month. The whole tissue of mutually offered events in a common life is rent from top to bottom; what survive are two typewritten depositions of five and nine pages respectively.

And if you want to see it writ large instead of small, go from the history of marriage to the history of nations. How much of the priestliness of Adam has gone into the building of civilization? How many oblations, how many white Masses did it take to build the cities of physics, of music, of poetry? The answer is vast beyond calculation: millions — billions of priests have built and built well. But how much will it take to say the black Mass over it all? Very little. How many matches did it take to burn the library at Alexandria? How many buttons will have to be pushed for the blast that will unsay all the oblations of Western civilization?

There, then, is the Grand Adversative in all its power. If fourteen pages of turgid prose can destroy fourteen years of real life, one affair wreck a marriage, one betrayal finish a friendship; if one morning's plot can fell a kingdom or one weekend of sedition, privy conspiracy, and rebellion put an ancient city in its grave, what chance does meaning really have? The problem of evil is not that there is so much of it that we can't see the good, but that there is so little of it — and yet it still wins.

In the assassination of a Lincoln, a Kennedy, how much was really wrong? Not the gun. The hammer fell with its rightful, authoritative snap, the chamber was its own powerfully rigid self, the powder burned in faithfulness to its nature, and the barrel held the bullet in its course. Was it perhaps the eye of the assassin? No. Light entered the intricacies of its lens, was inverted, fell upon the retina, and was translated infallibly by the brain. Everything was gloriously right: the assassin's aim and the reflex of his finger, the resistance of the wounded flesh and the effectiveness of the bullet itself. A vast concert of things true to themselves, and only one thing really wrong: a priest saying Mass backwards. But that one thing is enough: the flower of a generation slumps in the seat, an era ends, and the tissue of meaning breaks beyond repair.

Cease ye from man, whose breath is in his nostrils: for wherein is he to be accounted of? It is his very priesthood that destroys the world. *This is my first and my last saying, that it had been better not to have given the earth unto Adam: or else, when it was given him, to have restrained him from sinning. O thou Adam, what hast thou done? for though it was thou that sinned, thou art not fallen alone, but we all that come of thee. For what profit is it unto us, if there be promised us an immortal time, whereas we have done the works that bring death? And that we should be shewed a paradise, whose fruit endureth forever, wherein is security and medicine, since we shall not enter into it? (For we have walked in unpleasant places.)*

After all our offerings and sweet savours, after all our tenderness and high good humor, we shall lie low in the grasses. We scatter the ashes of our history in the dust; the city of our solemnities sits broken and solitary. The last shape we impose upon the world is without form or comeliness; Adam's final word of meaning consists only of the unsaying of the Mass he should have offered.

▼   ▼   ▼

We come at last, therefore, to the question that has been waiting for us in the heart of history: What can be done with wrong history — with meaninglessness — to keep it from wrecking everything? The answer leads straight into paradox.

First of all, wrong history cannot be offered, must not be offered. It is perversion, reversal, denial; if it is touched at all, if it is admitted for one hour, it corrupts everything. The lie that is admitted into the tissue of a marriage destroys the tissue forthwith. The bigotry that is actually offered up by the priestly hands of a society — that is taken in *as* bigotry, and *as* right — gives that society an incurable wound.

But, secondly, wrong history cries out to be offered, must be offered. Adam builds the web by taking all things into priestly hands and lifting them into the exchanges of the City. If even one evil, if even a single piece of wrong history fails to be offered, the City will go down in defeat. If the power of darkness cannot somehow be taken into the tissue of the web, it will destroy the web as it always has.

Thus the paradox: Evil *must not* be offered, for it corrupts the priest; yet evil *must* be offered, or else the priest will have no power over it. Let me follow it a little further. We have words for all the possible oblations of wrong history. For the mere rejection of it, we have *blame* and *condemnation;* for the mere acceptance of it, we have *condonation* and *winking at iniquity;* and, for the paradoxical act that accepts and rejects it at once, we have *forgiveness.*

Once again, take a marriage. Into that marriage admit an affair, and into the affair admit eventual disclosure. Behold, you are ready to write a treatise on the oblation of evil. Assume the husband is the — let us avoid words that raise questions — the perpetrator of the affair, the *agent* of it. His wife then becomes the spectator of it, the one against whom, before whom, *to* whom it is done — let us call her the *patient* of the affair.

For the *agent,* the priestly possibilities of the situation are four: he will first attempt to keep the affair from becoming a priestly problem by leading two lives, by offering at two altars. For as long as nobody important finds out, and for as long as he has the stamina and the interest to put up with the wear and tear, he will be able to avoid facing the fact that he is only one priest and the shaper of only one history. Needless to say, the days of such double offerings are the golden days of an affair, the times of plural benefices and of fat livings in the country. They are the happy times before the reformers move in and spoil everything.

We have, however, already admitted the thing that ends them. The agent's wife finds out, and the fat is in the fire. So far he has avoided the terrible demands of his priesthood: he has used it not to make history but to play at histories. But now he finds that even his play has been a making. The double life, the double history, turns out to be a painful and unmanageable fact. Enter here, therefore, the truly relevant possibilities for his priesthood: blame, condonation, or forgiveness.

Blame. If he simply rejects the history of his affair — if he, in a paroxysm of remorse, blames himself, torments himself, condemns himself — he will hardly escape what he has made. Short of suicide, no man's remorse is proof against passion and involvement. Shame is not a viable ascetical notion; blame is a sleazy theological concept. He will, for a while, stay clear of his mistress; but by and by he will, like Jeshurun, wax fat again and kick, and the last state of that man will be worse than the first.

Condonation. On the other hand, if he simply accepts what he has done — if he *condones* the affair, glories in it, justifies it — he is no better off. He is, and remains, a being of one history who is trying to function in two. He will learn soon enough that the others in his history — his wife, his mistress — are beings of one history themselves. He may condone the arrangement, but when all is said and done, they probably will not. He will be attempting an offering that the other sharers in his priesthood — his concelebrants — will not put up with. Late or soon, he will find himself with one altar only — and badly shaken in the bargain.

[139]

Let me set aside for a moment the *forgiveness* which the agent must extend to himself, and turn to blame or condonation as they are found in the *patient* — in his wife.

Should she attempt merely to reject, to blame her husband, she destroys the very offering in whose name she issues the rejection. To be sure, she cannot, any more than he, *accept* the affair; but if she simply blames, she rejects her husband along with it. He may have been a fool to divide his history, to inaugurate two concelebrations, but, fool or not, he has done it, and in dead earnest. The more profound her rejection, the more scathing her blame toward him, the more effectively she destroys the only real Mass she herself has to say.

But if she condones, she does no better, for then she becomes another foolish priest, another ineffectual architect of two meanings, two histories, where only one is possible. Blame may be destructive, but at least it recognizes the realities of the situation. Condonation is monstrous. The "understanding" foursome who have swapped wives and husbands are engaged in a collegial black Mass for the unsaying of all their meanings. The "intelligent" couple who wink at each other's iniquity and arrange a whitewashed marriage, or a cool and passionless divorce, wreck history in the name of happiness. And, without going into it, the society that makes it increasingly possible for such impossibilities to be achieved is a society that is sick at the heart. It is trying to preserve the city without preserving the priestliness that alone can build it.

Forgiveness. It is *forgiveness,* then, in both agent and patient that is the only viable priestly exercise. Forgiveness in the *agent* as the acceptance of priestly responsibility for the impossible history he has made. Forgiveness *toward himself* that, without blame and without condonation, accepts the affair, but accepts it *as wrong.* Forgiveness as the only real option in the whole tissue of his life. But forgiveness — mark it well — as an act of almost unimaginable difficulty: forgiveness as a passion, a crucifixion — as an imminent destruction of himself by the admission into his being of the awful contradictions he has wrought.

And forgiveness in the *patient* as the same thing: the acceptance of the affair, but the acceptance of it as wrong. A sufferance more gracious than any condonation, and a reproof more austere than any blame. A more awful forgiveness, no doubt, for no agent sees his monstrousness as it is in the eyes of his victims. And a deeper passion, a more deadly cross, a more certain destruction, for no agent feels the full force of what he has done to his patient. But without the acceptance of suffering there can be no forgiveness. History is made, or unmade, by the *acts* of Adam the priest; but history can be saved only by his *passion.* Unless evil is taken *out,* the City cannot be built; but unless it can be taken *up,* it cannot be taken out at all. Somehow, therefore, we must rise above both blame and condonation — they only leave wrong history free to roam at large — and we must enter into the high mystery by which that history is not destroyed but offered, hidden, *sequestered,* in the heart of the passion of the priest.

▼   ▼   ▼

I do not intend to belabor the point much beyond that. The last reversal of the Grand Adversative is already in sight. It is simply this: But who can afford to be that kind of priest? For the lighter and lesser perversions of history, we may all do well enough. The sins of ignorance, the catastrophes that, almost accidentally, grew greater than anyone meant them to be, the evils that, even by the victims, were never felt in all their dark power — these we can manage. Inattention spares us the full assessment of the cost. But with the recognition of *deliberate* evil by the agent, and with the bearing of the *full weight* of it by the patient — there, the oblation begins to be expensive.

It is not enough to say it demands charity. That is hardly a candid answer. Anyone who finally sees what is involved will realize that such charity is not only rare; it is deadly. Evil is no mere diagram; it is the power of darkness, and it can do things — vast and ugly things — to anyone who, even to forgive it, gets close to it. To offer up evil in a passion of forgiveness is, for all practical purposes, to let evil have its way and, in all likelihood, to be destroyed by it. The passion is followed by a crucifixion, and the crucifixion by death and the tomb.

And pacifism is not the answer, either. It is still another instance of an error that is only an inch away from the truth. As a diagram of the passion, as an insistence that the only way to get evil *out* is to take it *in,* it is right. But as it is commonly presented — that is, as a recipe for the effective conquest of evil as a formula to end wars — it is impossible. The only logical result of pacifism is the death of the pacifist. Evil is much too ambitious to be impressed by the idea that easy targets should not be hit.

If, therefore, there is ever to be a Passion that will turn the trick, if there is to be an Agent with hands clean enough not to be defiled by the poison of his own guilt, if there is to be a Patient with a heart great enough to face the monstrousness of evil and still be willing to take it in — if there is to be a Pacifist who can survive his own charity — something will have to be done to the priesthood of Adam. It will need not only *repair* to restore it to its natural operation, but also *enlargement* to raise it to a new and mysterious working by which it can be defeated and still win. What then?

Two things. First of all, human nature must not be discarded. We are the priests of the world; to build the City without us, to make history run its course apart from our ministrations, would be victory at the price of junking the world we know. The new priest, therefore, must be us — must be human. But secondly, for the renovation, human nature alone is not enough. Somehow, the second Adam will have to be able not only to survive but to triumph gloriously over the disaster of his charity. And for that — I shall, as I promised, say it out at last — you need God. Not a *deus ex machina* who comes in to save the day by irrelevant marvels, but a *Deus Incarnatus* who can be human enough to die in his priesthood, but God enough to rise from the dead.

I said I would not belabor the point. I shall not. By the grace of God we have such a redeemer: Jesus Christ, the Incarnate Word, the Second Adam, the Great High Priest. He was despised and rejected. He walked among us, and the world said a black Mass over him. But in his Death and Passion, in his Resurrection and Ascension, he takes all our words and reads them right again. Ever since, with or without conviction, we have made that offering the determining point of history: the cross is where the triumph of meaning becomes possible. Without the victory of evil that it permitted, so much history would have been lost that salvation would be meaningless. But without the sequestering of evil that it achieved — without the taking of meaninglessness into the heart of the only Priest who could afford it — the City would forever go unbuilt.

He has tied, you see, a back splice to end all back splices. In the very nick of time — at the end of history's rope — the tongues of flame in-fold into the crowned knot of fire, and the fire and the rose are one.

11. *Epilogue*

LECTOR: Well?

AUCTOR: Well, what?

LECTOR: That sounded like an end to me. Do I assume correctly that that is all you have to say?

AUCTOR: Yes and no. Belloc was right. An author can go on more or less indefinitely; but it is best if his book does not.

LECTOR: What do you feel you have omitted?

AUCTOR: Aha! You will not catch me as easily as that. I have made whatever argument I can manage for my case. The rope is spliced back. If it does not reach you, I am sorry; you must cast about for a longer piece.

LECTOR: You have nothing to add, then?

AUCTOR: I did not say that. If you like, I can end as I began: *next to,* but not *on,* the subject.

LECTOR: But is that consistent with your principles?

AUCTOR: Consistency is the hobgoblin of small . . .

LECTOR: Never mind. Just end.

AUCTOR: I must ask you then to join me in a recurrent — not fantasy, but — distracted occupation of mine.

LECTOR: I am in your hands.

AUCTOR: Today is Friday. In the Latin, that is *feria sexta,* the sixth day of the week. On the sixth day, according to the first chapter of Genesis, God made the living creatures of the earth: cattle, creeping things, and beasts. A little later in the same day he also made the Adam in his image and after his likeness: male and female — for dominion, for fruitfulness, for multiplication, and for the replenishment of the earth.

LECTOR: Now, really, does anyone in this day and age seriously believe . . .

AUCTOR: I have no idea. I am not addressing myself to the point. Let me finish.

A good while after that, on the Friday of the Preparation of the Sabbath of the Passover, God *remade* the Adam by a passion, a death, and a resurrection in the human nature he had taken to himself. As a result, for most of the Fridays since, Christians have undertaken to fast in honor of the day.

LECTOR: May I ask where all this leads?

AUCTOR: There is no need. I am almost there.

Finally, it is a practice among certain Christians to make the day more notable still by the recitation of the English Litany. It is, no doubt, a custom honored more . . .

LECTOR: Spare me that. I gather I am about to be invited to pray.

AUCTOR: Yes and no again. I began by taking you on a walk. I end likewise. The Litany is a devotion designed to be used *in procession,* a prayerful circumambulation, if you will, of the City. The church walks through the world, and in her passing she lifts all things into her oblation: marsh reed and shabby village, offered uncle and broken marriage. No triumph of priesthood is too high for her attention; no failure, no distraction irrelevant to the Passion by which she returns history to God. Even if you do not pray, come these last few steps, just for the walk.

▼　　▼　　▼

O God the Father, Creator of heaven and earth;
Have mercy upon us.

O God the Son, Redeemer of the world;
Have mercy upon us.
O God the Holy Ghost, Sanctifier of the faithful;
Have mercy upon us.
O holy, blessed, and glorious Trinity, one God;
Have mercy upon us.

The day before yesterday, I drove through a suburban development. I saw there:
three women gossiping at the end of a driveway;
five preschool children playing with toy dumptrucks;
a man, obviously a husband, repositioning a lawn sprinkler in accordance with his wife's shouted directions;
a man, obviously a salesman, leaving his parked car and knocking on the door of a house;
another man, not obviously either a husband or a salesman, walking in a front door without knocking;
three women still gossiping, but more animatedly than before.

Why, O Lord, do we do it? What was it that we had in mind? Why are we so bent on toys and lawns, on marriages and assignations? Pity us, Lord; this is all the City we have. We mean well, O God; we mean to *mean*. We have done nothing here that was not the fruit of our priesthood. Why do we not build better? Why do our children hate us, why must our neighbors talk, why are our husbands so closed?

Remember not, Lord, our offences, nor the offences of our forefathers; neither take thou vengeance of our sins; spare us, good Lord, spare thy people, whom thou hast redeemed with thy most precious blood, and be not angry with us forever.
Spare us, good Lord.

Wednesday night, first jointly, then in separate interviews, a married couple told me:
that they had both retained lawyers;
that they both had their faults, but that it made no sense trying again if the other party wouldn't try too;

that his wife was sick;
that her husband was sick;
that he hit her;
that he never really hit her;
that his mother ran his life;
that her mother ran her life;
that the church was unreasonable to expect people to go on
forgiving.

O Lord, what did we do wrong? All we wanted was to build;
why do we live now in ruins? Spare us the misery of our priesthood.
From all evil and mischief; from sin; from the crafts and assaults
of the devil; from thy wrath; and from everlasting damnation,
Good Lord, deliver us.

On Thursday morning, I went, as usual, for my walk, and
bought, as usual, my daily copy of *The New York Times:*

Humphrey Thinks Wagner Will Run
Senate Bars Ending Aid to U.N. Debtors

O Word Incarnate, we are in love with meaning; we are
obsessed with 44-point caps and with 30-point upper and lower
case. We impose shape endlessly; but history escapes us still.
O Wisdom, who reachest from one end to the other, and
mightily and sweetly orderest all things: Come and build the
City for us in thy Passion.

From all sedition, privy conspiracy, and rebellion; from all false
doctrine, heresy, and schism; from hardness of heart, and contempt
of thy word and commandment,
Good Lord, deliver us.

On Thursday afternoon, I said prayers for a man in the last
extremity of life. A sad trickle of saliva lay in the corner of his
mouth. Uphold him, O God, in the communion of the Catholic

Church, and in the confidence of a reasonable, religious, and holy hope; and uphold us all, O Lord, in the face of a meaningless end to seventy-three years of meaning.

I walked home and smelled liver and onions on a side street. A man would be a fool not to come home to such a wife. Drive despair from us, O most Merciful.

By thine Agony and Bloody Sweat; by thy Cross and Passion; by thy precious Death and Burial; by thy glorious Resurrection and Ascension; and by the Coming of the Holy Ghost,
Good Lord, deliver us.

This morning, I rehearsed with my sons: three pieces from the *Musica Brittanica.* The Lupo *Pavan* went best: the ornamentation began to come out right. But one of them yawned while he was playing, and the other breathed in the wrong place. I became angry and abusive.

Tonight I play a concerto for recorder and chamber orchestra. It is all over now but the postmortems. "Don't think about getting through it; think only of playing musically. The Siciliano must lilt; the downbeats must lift, not fall. The entrance after the second *tutti* in the *allegro assai* must be proclaimed with brilliant articulation."

Accept in mercy, O Lord, whatever it is that we so weakly have in mind. Spare, O God, in the universal shipwreck of the world, our love of shape and meaning, and grant that we have not trained these hands only to unstring them in death. In spite of fears, make us bold in our priesthood. Lift for us, O Lord. Lift our places and our times, lift creek and harbor, Tom and marsh reed, lift even broadloom and vinyl; receive into thy Passion all that we build, and in thy ruin make us whole again.

In all time of our tribulation; in all time of our prosperity; in the hour of death and in the day of judgment,
Good Lord, deliver us.

▼   ▼   ▼

I leave you there. The walk is as wide as the City; the Litany is as large as life itself, and no distraction is alien to it. Caught up in the Passion, we plead freely for the laborers in the vineyard and for the unity of nations, for the restoration of the erring and for the comfort of the weakhearted; and for women in childbirth, for prisoners and captives, for fatherless children and widows — for all people everywhere who, in the priesthood of Adam, have said their Masses and laid away their vestments, who have offered as they could afford, but who found history too expensive for them; who, if they are to build the City at all, will build it only in the Passion of a better Priest than Adam.

For, by the disaster of his charity, God plays out at last the Game that began with the dawn of history. In the Garden of Eden — in the paradise of pleasure where God laid out his court and first served the hint of meaning to humankind — Adam strove with God over the tree of the knowledge of good and evil. But God does not accept thrown-down racquets. He refuses, at any cost, to take seriously our declination of the game; if Adam will not have God's rules, God will play by Adam's. In another and darker garden he accepts the tree of our choosing, and with nails through his hands and feet he volleys back meaning for unmeaning. As the darkness descends, at the last foul drive of a desperate day, he turns to the thief on the right and brings off the dazzling backhand return that fetches history home in triumph: Today shalt thou be with me in *Paradise.*

God has *Gardens* to give away! He has cities to spare! He has history he hasn't even used! The last of all the mercies is that God is *lighter* than we are, that in the heart of the Passion lies the divine Mirth, and that even in the cities of our exile he still calls to Adam only to catch the glory, to offer the world, and to return the service that shapes the City of God.

12. Preface

If you object that this is an odd place for a preface, my only answer is that this has been an odd book, and that there is no point in trying to switch off the oddity this late in the day. Prefaces are a strange genre, anyway. An author may pretend that he is simply addressing a foreword to his readers, but in fact he is in the sly business of taking out insurance against reviews that miss the point.

Any policy he buys, however, is of dubious value. For one thing, if a book doesn't make its own point, no preface in the world can save it. For another, if a critic has a tin ear, whistling the same tune in another key won't help. And for a last, the author's claim on the reader's attention extends only to what he has written, not to what he thinks about it all. Authors are almost the last people in the world who should be allowed to comment on their own books.

That being the case, it would, no doubt, be wisest to suppress the preface altogether. I am torn, however: the cool waters of wisdom only partly quench the thirst for insurance. Accordingly, I give you a preface, but I print it at the end. Here at least, if you read it, you read it when I wrote it — after the book, and after you have come to your own conclusions. And if perhaps you are wise enough not to read it at all, we part company while we are still such friends as we have become.

▼   ▼   ▼

Admittedly, this book has been more allusive than direct. Permit me a brief apologia for the style. The offhandedness is deliberate. I have a conviction that, in the present shipwreck of philosophy — particularly in the absence of any working concept of the analogical nature of all discourse about God — it is safer not even to attempt to speak directly. The best of the classical theologians, of course, had a firm grip on the doctrine of analogy and sprinkled their works liberally with *caveats* and cries of *nescimus*. Every theologian worth his salt walked with one foot on his affirmations and the other firmly planted on the *via negativa*. Unfortunately, however, a good many of their heirs, assigns, and devisees fell into the trap of thinking that the categories of traditional dogmatics had somehow succeeded in getting straight at what God and his action were really like. The result was that the all-important sense of *Mystery* promptly left by the back door and, with it, the possibility of germane theology.

After that, the only solution anyone could think of was to leave the front door open in the hope that germaneness would wander in off the street. Theology, however, cannot be saved by inviting other disciplines in to do its work. We have had sociological theologians and psychological theologians; we have had mathematical theologians and evolutionary theologians; and lately we have been treated to the theologians of linguistic analysis and historical skepticism. None of them has done much to rescue the party from boredom: the gala theological blowout of the age to come turns out to be just one more slow leak.

Germaneness cannot be restored from the outside. The bright new theologians of systematic doubt are no improvement over the bad old theologians of straight-line certainty. The whole lot of them are guilty of trying to deal directly with what can only be handled analogically; the difference between them is simply that in the new breed the failure of analogy has led them to stop talking about God altogether, while the old boys continue to act as if they know more than they do. But silence is no solution. We go on talking about God anyway, whether the theologians do or not; we even, on occasion, talk *to* him. Given that fact, the only responsible thing for theology to do is to try to save its own party by its own methods: that is, it must either formally refurbish the doctrine of analogy, or else it must find a way of speaking that will, informally, do the same thing. In choosing the allusive rather than the direct approach, I have, I hope, opted for the latter.

I have avoided straight exposition because I think that in a world that has lost the sense of Mystery it can only mislead. We do not need to have either God or creation *explained* to us; we are already sick to death of explanations. We have forgotten, you see, not what reality *means,* but how it smells and what it tastes like. The work of theology in our day is not so much interpretation as contemplation: God and the world need to be held up for *oohs* and *aahs* before they can safely be analyzed. Theology begins with admiration, not problems. If we walk through the world doing psychedelic puzzles rather than looking at reality, if we insist on tasting the wine of being with our nose full of interpretive cigarette smoke, the cure is not to hand us better puzzle books or more lectures on wine. We must be invited to *look* at what is in front of us and to get rid of those nasty cigarettes. And that perhaps is the place where this apologia can come to rest as far as the style of the book is concerned: I have written you a little tirade against smoking while you taste how gracious the Lord is.

Having justified my indirection, however, I want to go a little further and try to locate myself in the present theological landscape. Some of the things that I have dealt with allusively can be treated at least a little more directly, and I propose to have a go at three of them. They are the alienation of human beings from reality, the nature of God's action in the world, and the place of the Passion of Christ in history. Accordingly, I give you three short essays and, for the present at least, thereafter hold my peace.

Alienation

We have been treated lately to a number of solemn harpings on the subject of our estrangement from the world we inhabit. Books and articles conjure up visions of poor old Adam stumbling lost and lone through the automated and computerized age to come. If we are to believe the accounts, humanity is on the verge of technological unemployment. We may feel lonely now, but just wait until the electronic brains do *all* the work.

The menace is generally billed as brand new, but it has a familiar ring to it. It seems to me to be only the latest phase of one of the oldest diseases of modern people: their deep-rooted unwillingness to allow being to be itself, their penchant for over-interpreting the obvious, their refusal to drink their reality neat. Almost from the first moment of their philosophical maturity they are trained to think of the world in terms of a glibly popularized science. "That table over there," the high-school sophomore is told, "is actually not a table at all. It is really a cloud of electrons." For fourteen years Sally has thought otherwise, but she has been in the dark. Now she is invited — more, she is *told,* on pain of intellectual disgrace — to face the light of the new day.

Obedient girl that she is, Sally obliges. As she thinks the matter through, she comes to see that her tomato sandwich cannot possibly be a tomato sandwich, and that her breakfast egg is not really an egg. What matters most about everything, she learns, is not what she knows it to be, but some mysterious and abstract stuff that she is told it is made of. Consequently she acquires, at least by implication, a guilty conscience if she decides to spend much time acquiring a taste for such accidental superficialities as *things* and *substances.* If she cares seriously about how her eggs are cooked, she had better not mention it in intellectual circles.

What Sally finds out eventually, of course, is that she has been slipped a very tiresome kind of mickey. She is the recipient of a *Weltanschauung* that is a crashing bore. It takes all the fascinatingly solid differences between things and writes them off as only apparent — as merely accidental determinations of an endless and monotonous raw material: the true substance of the world is the tasteless subatomic tapioca out of which it is made. And *that* is all she is to be served — not simply for dessert but for breakfast, lunch, and dinner, world without end.

The really fearful thing about such a view is that it stands the world on its head. Real *things* — substantial beings — are written off as of secondary importance: the distinction between sharp razors and dull razors is dismissed as so fine that it hardly matters. The difference between a properly cooked and an overcooked soufflé is practically nil. It is the infranuclear oatmeal that really counts. And yet everyone in his right mind knows better than that. A dull razor is no razor at all, and is to be cursed roundly. And a dry soufflé . . . well, that is more than sufficient cause for weeping. If you rob us of our right to such rages and tears, you court disaster.

For insofar as we believe what we have been taught, we will become bored, estranged, and . . . alienated. The world around us will seem far too accidental for real care. It will be worthy only of manipulation — or worse. And we ourselves will sit solitarily important in a world which, as we meet it, doesn't *matter*. To be sure, because of the legacy of Christian civilization, we will probably go on believing that somehow human beings, with their rights and duties, their privileges and obligations — with their individual status as *persons* — do matter. But on that basis a human being is only the last raisin in an ocean of rice pudding. It makes for a lonely life.

The alienation of modern people stems not from the incidental advances of their technology but from a philosophy that has turned them into metaphysical freaks: they are the last inexplicably substantial beings in an otherwise relative world. No *thing* keeps them real company. Far from being a materialistic age, we are a devilishly spiritual one. Having forsaken the true concrete individuality of *things* — having made care about differences philosophically disreputable — we are left only with diagrams of reality to keep us going.

At this writing, I learn that my eggs no longer need to be done at all — either to a turn or to a crisp. My supermarket will sell me an envelope of powder that, when dissolved in milk, will provide an instant breakfast. No matter that I once thrilled to a nicely boiled egg in a thin china cup. It is time now for me to face the facts of life. Eggs don't matter, and my sensibilities don't rate. All the foolish substantialities of the past must give way to the new truth: what counts is the juxtaposing of my nutribility and the envelope's nutritiveness. And what a confrontation *that* is: abstract cheek laid against immaterial jowl, and the devil take the whole shooting match.

No wonder we're bored. However important the substrate of the world may be to scientific analysis, it will not do as a substitute for philosophy. The physical question of what beings are made out of can never be allowed to preempt our proper metaphysical concern with what being *is*. Our alienation, our boredom, our estrangement can be cured only by the recovery of a philosophical sanity that will allow us to meet *things* face to face. An egg is an egg, and must be saluted as such. And china is china, and all things are themselves: mushrooms and artichokes, wine and cheese, earth and stars and sky and ocean. It is *things* that matter, and our cure waits for the restoration of our ability to care about them.

It will be an uphill fight, though. Pleasant as the idea sounds, the world is anything but ready for a revival of Christian materialism. It is more than ready for a revival of *religion,* of course; but religion and Christianity are by no means the same thing. The proclamation of the Gospel is the announcement of an embarrassingly concrete and material piece of work by God in history. The salvation it offers operates by the assumption of humanity into the Person of God the Son and by the incorporation of the rest of the race into the sacred humanity so assumed. It is a bit too crass and earthy to rate as a gorgeous piece of spiritual philosophy.

Accordingly, the world's inveterate lust for lovely spiritualities will cause it to look almost anywhere before it seriously considers Christianity and all it implies. The winds of the times have begun to blow out of the East politically and psychologically; if I may venture a little prophecy, I think that they will also shortly blow us a revival of religion. It may well be that the next major intellectual fad will be Oriental spirituality. There are, in fact, signs that it has already begun: the psychedelic cults, with their little trips into the inner spaces of the mind, are the outriders of a movement that will systematically prefer the exploration of "consciousness" to the savoring of *being.* When it arrives in force, religion Eastern-style will be the order of the day, and the Judeo-Christian tradition will have a hard time finding houseroom anywhere except in the basement of unspiritual superstitions.

There will, of course, be attempts to offer spiritualized and therefore fashionable versions of Christianity. (The God is Dead movement is, in many respects, a reaction to just that sort of thing. Unfortunately, however, it falls prey to the very errors it opposes. To replace intemperate reliance on the sacred with excessive faith in the secular is to achieve nothing. It simply forces the secular to do the work previously done by the sacred and, by just so much, to lose its true secularity. Christian materialism sees the two orders as complementary, interpenetrating, and inseparable; but it never tries to make one of them do the work of the other.) But the greatest damage from the windstorm of the East will not be sustained by Christianity — that can, in time, take care of itself; the real wreckage will be the collapse of any workable notion of history.

If you adopt a philosophical outlook that makes *things* unimportant, you automatically make history meaningless. It is the cats and the alligators, the rivers and the hills, the kings, the bankers, and the girls in the back room that make the world the way it is. If you seriously eliminate them from consideration, the only thing left is to import an assortment of gods, fates, and ghosts to run the show in their absence. You may manage to make it sound a little like the Gospel, but it will be the furthest thing in the world from it. Christians believe, of course, that God himself is the ultimate Lord of history, but the Gospel of the Incarnation insists that he does not rule at the price of turning things and people into ciphers. And that brings me to the second little essay.

The Action of God in the World

The recent debates over the Death of God have managed to propose all the right questions about God and history in almost all the wrong ways. The press, of course, has given the impression that the real point of the discussion was whether God existed or not, and no doubt at least a few of the principals in the debate have been guilty of saying as much. At least some of them, however, have seen that the real relevance of their comments lies elsewhere.

Outside the realm of straight dogmatic theology (where the reality of God has always been a *datum* and not a problem), questions about the existence of God must be dealt with in terms of the only subject that has an honest claim on them: metaphysics. Accordingly, the problem of the existence or non-existence of God can hardly be advertised as the hottest issue of the twentieth century, brought to light only recently by new and daring thinkers. Rather, it is a piece of unfinished metaphysical business dating from the eighteenth century in its present form, and from the fourteenth century if you trace it to its roots. It is not the doctrine of God that is the main problem of contemporary theology; it is the doctrine of Man, the doctrine of the Secular, the doctrine of History.

There, you see, is the sad part of the promotion given to the recent debate. Nearly every man Jack of the new theologians has had a lot to say about Secularity, about Culture, about Human Nature, about History. But far too many of them have been shunted off, either by the press or by their own inadequate metaphysic, into a discussion of Deity. Their common sense and good judgment — their feeling for the heart of the matter — landed them squarely in the right neighborhood; but their less-than-adequate friends talked them into working the wrong side of the street.

Even when they managed to stay on the right side, however, their insistence on a divorce between the sacred and the secular made it difficult for them to arrive at a respectable doctrine of secularity. Modern people's problem, you see, is no more about the nature of the secular, pure and simple, than it is about the nature of God, pure and simple. It is, when all is said and done, about the nature of their interaction. Our confusion is over a world which *simply* does not seem to need God, and over a God who *simply* does not seem to be at work in the world. With our penchant for simplicities, you see, we have managed so to limit both the sacred and the secular that we have set them at odds with each other. I suggest that the only way to get them back together is to get that word *simply* out of the discussion, and to restore to its rightful place the biblical dimension of *Mystery*. The world will never be clear to us until we stop insisting that it be plain.

To begin with, the world has never *simply* needed God. He is too skillful a creator to have left evidence of his direct action lying all over the lot — and he is too serious about creating a world that will stand on its own feet and blow its own nose. Good theologians have always held that God's *immediate* work in creation (that is, the work in which, if you could examine it, you would find God's own hand on the throttle) has always been *mysterious*. God intimately and immediately bestows the act of being upon each existing thing, but that bestowal occurs at the roots of reality. The only evidences of his creativity that you and I can manage to investigate lie higher and are in the realm of his mediate action. Everything that is empirically ascertainable about the world lies in the realm of secondary causes — in the province of gloriously independent *things* which, thank you very much, *simply* act for themselves, but which God, by the *Mystery* of his creative act, causes to be. The secular, you see, can be just as secular as it pleases and never suffer a moment's divorce from the sacred. God constantly holds the world in being, and he constantly pronounces it very good. It is only when the world tries to take its simplicities without a good stiff shot of Mystery that it becomes the bore it so frequently is.

That leads to the second point. In this marvelously produced world of secondary causes, God has never (or at least, barring miracle, almost never) acted *simply*. From time to time, he has filled a water pot with wine or provided fish sandwiches for a crowd, but most of the time his action has been more mysterious than that. His relationship to my cleaning of my fingernails, or to your writing of a letter to the editor, or to any of our alliances in love, marriage, or politics has been complex. He has caused us without causing *them;* he has been Pure Act without infringing on creation's action; and he has been the sovereign Lord of History who, having bestowed upon each thing its little plot of being, has been content to put up with some fearful and wonderful farming. The courteous Creator of the worlds, if he rules at all, does not seem to rule by simplicities or to guide history along straight lines. His creatures stand *extra nihil* and *extra causas* only by his largesse; but by that same largesse he allows them to act as if they owed nothing to anybody.

His work in the world, therefore, and the world's need of him have always been mysterious, inscrutable, anything but self-evident. The presence of the sacred in the secular has been a bit difficult to keep a finger on, and people have accordingly been entirely too ready to abandon the embracing of the Mystery in favor of simple sacredness or simple secularism. We have been treated to all kinds of theories about the world, and I have dealt with a number of them in the third chapter. Through it all, however, both the Sacred and the Secular have gone on being their own marvelously and mysteriously interpenetrating selves. No doubt we should have caught that hint long ago if we had been listening to Scripture or even to such a lowly discipline as dogmatic theology. The classical descriptions of God's work in creation, for example, are anything but simplicities. To say that he creates *ex nihilo* is hardly to limit him to a straight-line approach to the world. And to refer to him as Necessary Being, or as the *movens non motum,* is to invoke not plain reasons but logical absurdity as the root of explanation. The note of Mystery, of paradox, is the hallmark of classical theology.

And if Mystery is the rule in the work of creation, how much more so in redemption? What is the call of Abraham but the announcement of God's action by mysteries rather than by simplicities? He will bless the world in the seed of a man who has no seed, and whose seed he will later command to be destroyed. What is the history of Israel but the story of the peregrinations of the body of the Mystery? It is no straight-line success story. Israel's *simple* triumph appears to have occupied a period of about an hour and twenty minutes in the whole history of the world. For the rest, all the way up to its flowering in the Cross, the Resurrection, and the Church, it is a rhapsody of unsuccess, an epic presentation of the theme of God's triumph through failure, of his reasoning through paradoxes, of his action through passion — in a word, of *Mystery* as his chosen vehicle.

There, then, is the hint of the true relationship between the sacred and the secular. It has never been a case of simple action or of simple need. To be sure, the world of secondary causes moves in simplicities, small and great. The cat jumps at the mouse, and the iron leaps to the magnet, and people build houses, and nations create institutions — all on intelligible lines. But those very lines are drawn on the utterly mysterious slate of an unnecessary world held in being by Necessity Himself. Again, women tell lies, and men water stock, and marriages are broken, and six million Jews die in ovens — all in nice, straight, intelligible lines. But those lines, too, are drawn on the slate of the secular held in being by the sacred. And in their case (which is the case of the world as it is now) it is precisely the Passion of Christ through which the sacred mysteriously rules history. And that brings me to the last essay.

History and the Passion

In chapters ten and eleven, I spent some time on the point that without the Passion of Christ, and without an unceasing intention to draw all that we are and have into that Passion, no history can be saved. I held the point off until the end of the book, and even then hit it only one more or less direct blow. It was part of the allusive approach. Nevertheless, though the blow was lightly struck, the point about the Passion is, in fact, the point of the book, and I want to enlarge a little upon it here.

That the world does not accept Christ Crucified comes as no surprise. The cross is not pretty. Worse yet, it is paradoxical, scandalous, vulgar, and, all in all, far beneath the dignity of anyone the world is willing to recognize as God. It is, as Saint Paul said a long time ago, a stumbling block to the Jews and a lot of foolishness to the Greeks. What does come as a surprise, though, is the fact that the church seems to find it as hard to swallow as the world. The one group of people who should be expected to find it the wisdom and power of God in history are the very ones who, more often than not, try to unload it at the earliest possible moment. We preach almost anything before we preach Christ Crucified. The upshot of it is that the world finds both our diagnoses and our prescriptions irrelevant.

We have talked so often about soundness and sanity that we have given ourselves and our age the impression that the goal of Christianity is the miraculous achievement of health and goodness here and now — that history is to be repaired simply, and from the outside. Worse yet, we have tacitly suggested that Christianity will be manifested best and chiefly by the healthy and the good, which usually ends up meaning (God help us) by us. The church has more or less openly hoped that it could be a kind of free ulcer-clinic, AA chapter, and general faith-healing dispensary — the very present help that could keep people out of the clutches of the head shrinkers and medicine men.

This was, perhaps, inevitable. After all, we do believe in a God who restores all things — we do confess the triumph of goodness. We say to the sick world, Come here and be cured: be healed of your ills, be made whole of your maladjustments, be lifted up in triumph over your vices. God wills your health, your balance, your goodness; come, take Grace, and rise.

It is all true. But we have acted as if it were the whole truth or, better said, as if we could safely state it that way to a fallen race and have them get it right. As a matter of fact, however, something more must always be added. Tell people only that much, illustrate it with Jesus' miracles of healing, root it in the general beneficence of God, and they will inevitably draw themselves a Mary Baker Eddyish picture of Christianity that will not square either with the Gospel or with life.

Take Christ's miraculous acts of healing. How universal were they? How far should they be allowed to form the basis for our everyday expectations? How many of all the sick did he cure? How many demoniacs did he heal? Not many by any estimate — far too few to touch the aggregate misery even of his own day. His cures themselves were always more like signs than solutions. Lazarus went to a second grave: he was raised from the dead, but not from dying.

His real problem was met elsewhere than in the miracle. And the rest of the Gospel picture is the same. Those whom Christ cured by his miracles remained fundamentally what they were — creatures still trapped in the agony of a fallen world. Either he must have a deeper remedy, or he was guilty of merely symptomatic treatment, of giving anodynes to the incurable. Unless he has succeeded on another level, his program of healing here and now is not only a failure, but a cruel one.

The same point can be proved by the pastoral ministry, if we are honest enough to take a good look at it. How often are the disturbed really calmed? How many marriages headed for the rocks actually manage to avoid them? How many destructive loves do we ever succeed in taming? Not many. We kid ourselves into thinking we are successful healers by the expedient of writing off the vast army of incurables. But for all that they are not cured. By and large, the unhealed simply leave our studies and our pews and take their sickness somewhere else. The loudest and clearest offer they heard from us was the outside chance of a miracle here and now, and when that failed us, we failed them. How must our Gospel of simple healing have sounded? What must it be like to hear only a medicinal or a psychiatric Christ? Must they not gather that we have a message only for a select clientele — that we are all right for the resilient and for the well-endowed by luck and nature, but that we will not do for the common run of humanity who know that they are trapped in their agony and are not about to bounce back? Mustn't our message to them sound like the harsh and uncomplimentary word of Christian science to the incurable: Sorry, Charlie, but the trouble is yourself; you need to work up some more faith before you can play in our league. Monstrous!

Of course, the whole trouble is themselves. They knew that; that is why they came. But that we should make it sound as if their problem is after all a matter of a human more or less — that we should hint ever so subtly that with us the trouble has ceased to be ourselves, that the passion is over, and that, in us who have the firstfruits of the Spirit, the creature no longer groans and travails — this is what confounds them. God forgive us. To them, it must be as if the Gospel had never been preached, as if Christianity were only a miraculous form of moral rearmament. We seem to have had nothing to say to the defeated unless they could somehow win, no message for the defenseless unless they could manage to put up their dukes. The trouble is indeed themselves. That is the meaning of original sin. But the answer to original sin is not miraculous deliverance from its consequences. In the end, the only real deliverance is on another level. It lies not in the curing of our symptoms but in the drawing of our diseases into the Mystery of the Passion. What Christianity promises is not the removal of evil from this world but the taking of this twisted world into the Mystery of Christ's suffering, death, and resurrection.

The root of the problem is our inveterate tendency to relapse into believing that the fallen human race can still manage a straight-line solution to its difficulties. Somewhere in Bonhoeffer there is a passage in which he insists that we cannot pursue any good directly in this world, that it will be achieved, if at all, only paradoxically — through the Passion. That is right. Not that there is anything intrinsically wrong with the straight-line approach; it remains our natural mode of operation. But it just won't work in a fallen world. It was what we were made for in Eden, and it is what we are promised in heaven. Adam was meant to be able to say: There is my wife — I choose to love her; there is my God — I choose to serve him. And he was meant to bring it off. He was to have proceeded to the deliberate fulfillment of his nature as successfully as the cat proceeds to the mouse.

But, with the Fall, our faculties weaken and grow confused. We love; but our love is confounded by self-interest and does unlovely things. We serve; but our service dishonors. To be sure, the straight-line approach is still open to us. We can still get our spaghetti from plate to mouth, recover our strength by a nap, be loving to the child we delight in. But it is no longer the triumphant process it was designed to be. Our love does as much harm as good, our health is not indefinitely recoverable, and even the spaghetti obeys us only as long as we stay clear of senility, paralysis, and death. There is nothing we can do now that we are not imminently in danger of being unable to do at all; there is nothing we can do well that we may not, under slightly different circumstances, do very badly indeed.

Now when Christ came to save this Adam, can it possibly be that he took so little notice of our real condition as to hand us a gospel of self-improvement and miraculous spiritual healing? Can he really have said "Sorry, Charlie" to the whole groaning and travailing world? Is it even thinkable that he is going to write off our catastrophe and hand us a metaphysically inconsequential picnic in its place? Of course not. He will indeed provide the picnic (no honest Christian can get around the lavish, even slightly vulgar, beneficence of God — heaven may be analogical pie in an analogical sky, but pie in the sky it remains). There can be no quarrel with the happy ending of the divine comedy. But there is every reason to quarrel with our failure to grasp that he saves us *in* and *through* catastrophe, not out of it in any straight-line sense. The deliverance of Christ is in his Passion. It is in the Passion that the Incarnate Word of God exercises his Lordship over the broken and dishonored fragments of history, and it is our failure to take that to heart that makes our Gospel sound irrelevant to modern ears.

Humanity is a mess, and the world at its most perceptive knows it. We may be a nice mess, a warmhearted, well-intentioned shambles, but we remain intractable. Why, then, are we so reluctant to come out and say flatly that it is precisely the mess that is Christ's real *métier?* We have put crucifixes on our altars for centuries, but we have too seldom proclaimed the point. It is precisely the impossible, the horrendous, the hopeless, the useless that is the occasion of his work. He is here to draw our debacle into his and to bring his Passion into ours. He will not save failures with the proviso that at some stage of the game they must quit being failures and snap to. He will, himself the great failure, save them *in* failure, *by* failure. He will never tell Charlie that the years amid thorns and thistles are a waste, suitable only for regret and speedy replacement. He does not, in short, tell Adam that his life so far is irrelevant. His yoke is easier than that, and his burden lighter. We have only to come as we are. It is to our condition that Christ has stooped; we have only to endure to the end to be saved. And what does the enduring involve? Only an offering of our passion to Christ, only an invitation of Christ's Passion into ours. No doubt we will fail in that, as we fail in all else; no doubt we will do it by fits and starts, as we do everything; but provided we do it at all — provided (dare we say it? . . . Mercy Himself constrains us) provided we do it even once, provided only perhaps that someone else does it *for* us — the God who creates in failure comes with power. After that, who is to judge by appearances?

Admittedly, it must be *done.* The Mystery by which the Passion rules history does not operate without us. It is part of the crassness of the Incarnation: Adam — humankind — remains the agent of history: God reigns over the world, but he reigns through the *human* Body of Christ. Christianity preaches no mystique of suffering, no spiritual equation of miseries, but the drawing of the sons and daughters of Adam into the sacred humanity of Christ through the acts of their own history. True enough, the rewards of the laborers in the vineyard bore no relation to the size of their efforts — that is the Mystery of the free grace of the Passion. But only those who *worked* were rewarded — and that is the mystery of human agency. It takes both sides of the paradox to do history justice. Yet when all is said and done, what the world most needs from the church is not so much instruction about the nature of the Mystery as a glimpse of the Mystery itself operative in us. It already knows its own passion and the vastness of the shipwreck of history; it waits for us to show it the power of Christ's Passion and to lift our human agony into his.

Adam and Jesus, you see — history's agent and history's Lord — have been in the same room all along. What a pity we have so often failed to introduce them.

The Third Peacock

The Problem of God and Evil

To those whom I have taught —
for teaching me most of what I know

Introduction

When *The Third Peacock* was originally published, it began not with a systematic delineation of the "problem of evil" but rather (as you will see in Chapter 1) with a fantasy about the delight of God in the act of creation. My feeling was, and still is, that most attempts at theodicy — at proving that God is good even though the world is full of badness — start off wrong. First, they paint a picture of a very good God indeed: all-wise, all-knowing, all-powerful, all-loving — in fact, the supreme exemplar of just about any virtue you can fasten an *omni-* onto. Next, they produce a grim montage of all the horrors in the world: war, disease, pestilence, cruelty, betrayal, deceit, plus any other evils, natural or moral, they care to include. Then, desperately but gamely, they set about the thankless job of trying to reconcile the beauty of the first picture with the ugliness of the second.

There are two drawbacks to that approach. First, it contains a built-in temptation to get rid of the discrepancy by fudging one of the pictures until it matches the other. Either God has to be toned down into a kind of incompetent who can't be expected to do anything about the mess the world is in, or the mess has to be prettied up until it can be explained away as a blessing in disguise. In neither case, though, is the problem reckoned with, let alone solved; it is simply attenuated into a non-problem.

The second drawback is more fundamental: this "reconciling" approach flies in the face of biblical facts. Attenuating the problem of evil is, from a scriptural point of view, exactly what God refuses to do. From Genesis to Revelation, he seems instead bent on aggravating it. Unlike the generations of theologians who have been at pains to prove that his public image is not as bad as it seems — who can give you dozens of reasons why the unsavory world he runs is really not his fault — God goes bravely through the entire history of salvation caring not a fig, apparently, for what anyone thinks of him. He is by turns loving and arrogant, bloody and merciful. He promises and does not deliver, he delivers but does not help, he helps in ways that are no help at all — and when he is asked for explanations, he responds only with riddles.

He calls Abraham, for example, and then tells him to kill the only son through whom the call can be fulfilled. He selects Moses and then tries to murder him in an inn. He chooses the people of Israel and then allows them to be flattened, century after century, by every steamrolling superpower in the ancient world. He conquers sin in Jesus' death and then lets sinners go on mucking up the world exactly as before. He overcomes death in Jesus' resurrection and then leaves everybody just as mortal as ever.

But enough. The point is this: if God seems to be in no hurry to make the problem of evil go away, maybe we shouldn't be, either. Maybe our compulsion to wash God's hands for him is a service he doesn't appreciate. Maybe — all theodicies and nearly all theologians to the contrary — *evil is where we meet God.* Maybe he isn't bothered by showing up dirty for his dates with creation. Maybe — just maybe — if we ever solved the problem, we'd have talked ourselves out of a lover.

You may object, of course, to such a line of speculation. Indeed, if you're in your right mind, you'd better object to it: it sets standards for the conduct of God's love affair with the world that are lower even than our standards for lunch with an enemy. But you should also understand that your objection has been voiced before — and by experts — to no particular effect on the divine style of loving. The Bible itself is filled with complaints of ill treatment. From Moses, to Elijah, to the psalmist, to Job, to the prophets, to Jesus himself, there goes up from its pages, apropos of one bit of divine perfidy or another, a persistent chorus of "How could you *do* this to me?" And yet God neither apologizes nor explains, and he certainly makes no effort to solve the problem of evil for them. He just goes on arranging rendezvous after disreputable rendezvous, no matter how little anyone thinks of his choice of trysting places.

For your comfort, I do realize how unsatisfactory all this must seem: your thirst for theodicy is being deliberately left unquenched, your itch for understanding not given the benefit of the smallest theological scratch. But just suppose with me for a moment. Suppose that both the thirst and the itch were really for something quite other than intellectual solutions. Suppose that your restlessness for answers was actually — as it was with Job, with Augustine — only the tip of the iceberg, only the upper tenth of a heart's unquietness that could be satisfied by nothing less than the *presence* of this admittedly exasperating God. Ah, then perhaps you see: what a loss it would be to settle for the small beer of theodicy or the short reach of the theological hand. What a shame to palliate the symptoms and leave the deep dis-ease uncured.

This book, therefore, takes a radically different approach to the problem of evil. Instead of asking (on the basis of largely unscriptural theologies), "Why isn't God as good as our intellectual conclusions tell us he should be?" it addresses itself to more manageable if more uncomfortable questions — namely, "What, in fact, has he actually revealed himself to be like?" and, most important of all, "What do we (not he, please note) propose to do about it?" It strives, in other words, for realism above all else. It takes seriously not some abstract notion of deity but the kind of deity the God of the Judeo-Christian Scriptures seems to fancy himself as being — however inconvenient that may turn out to be from a theological point of view. And it suggests in the end that we will be better off accepting the bad manners of a real lover than constructing for ourselves the convenience of a cosmic Lord Fauntleroy Doll.

But lest you think this is either a novel theological approach or, worse yet, an abandonment of theology altogether, let me give you a longish example from Scripture to prove that such realism has always lain at the heart of genuine theological method.

In the composition of the four Old Testament books of the Kings (commonly referred to in English as 1 Samuel, 2 Samuel, 1 Kings, and 2 Kings), a formidable theological mind was at work. The author's object was not simply to present the history of the Chosen People from Samuel, through Saul, through David, through Solomon, through the division of the kingdom, right up to the beginning of the Babylonian Captivity; it was to develop a theological understanding of the relationship between the will of God and all those diverse events and personages. Very early on, therefore, the author of the books of Kings developed a master idea: he decided that the reason the history of God's people went so badly was that their kings regularly and flagrantly transgressed the Law of God.

This theory of historical disaster as God's punishment for leaders' sins went swimmingly for a while. Eli the priest, for example, had disobedient sons; therefore the Philistines defeated the people of Israel. Next, God sent Samuel the prophet to straighten things out, but the people insisted that what they really needed was a king. Neither God nor Samuel thought much of that idea, but eventually they both relented and allowed Saul to become king. Then, however, when Saul disobeyed by failing to destroy the Amalekites utterly, God told Samuel to replace Saul with David. David did fairly well and so passed the kingdom along to Solomon; but Solomon had strange wives who worshiped strange gods and thus, when Solomon died, the kingdom fell apart.

The theory did even better when it came to explaining the terrible history of the divided monarchy: king after king, in the northern as well as the southern kingdom, failed to obey the Law of God. The high places of the pagan cults were not torn down, the laws forbidding intermarriage were not observed, and, in general, every king did what he ought not to have done and left undone what he ought to have done, and there was no health in the whole sorry lot of them.

As the theory became more and more attractive, however, so did a corollary implicit in it. Little by little, the theological mastermind behind the books of Kings found himself entertaining ever more enthusiastically the proposition that, if only a king would come along who would really really — *really* really — keep the Law . . . well then, everyone would see that both the theory and the corollary were totally accurate descriptions of the way God did business in history. Because *then,* with *that* king, all the disasters would come to a grinding halt and everything would come up roses.

It was at this point that the God of bad manners (especially when it comes to dealing with theologians) decided to throw one of the great sucker pitches of all time. Very near the end of our beloved writer's monumental work (in fact, in the twenty-second chapter of 2 Kings) God serves up to him Josiah, king of Judah — and he drops a sinking curve right across the plate: *Josiah keeps the Law.* Our theologico-historical genius finally has a ball he can hit: Josiah reinstitutes the Deuteronomic Code; Josiah shuts down all the Canaanite high places; Josiah purifies the Temple at Jerusalem and makes it the only center of worship; Josiah keeps the Passover as it had not been kept since the days of the Judges nor during all the days of the kings of Israel or of the kings of Judah. In short, our author receives from God the very king his theories have been itching for over the course of three and four-fifths volumes. And finally, in verse 25 of chapter 23, he takes the swing of his career at it: "Before him there was no king like him, who turned to the Lord with all his heart, with all his soul, and with all his might . . . nor did any like him arise after him."

And then, guess what? *Josiah dies. In battle. Slain by Pharaoh Neco of Egypt. Who then takes over Jerusalem, but shortly loses the whole shooting match to Nebuchadnezzar, king of Babylon. Who then leads the Chosen People off into the Great Captivity.* "So much," God says, "for *that* theology. Go back to the drawing board and try again."

To give credit where credit is due, the author of the books of Kings almost did just that. Immediately after his paean to Josiah as the answer to a theologian's prayer, he begins verse 26 of chapter 23 with a word that should probably be given a special name to mark its place in the history of theology. Perhaps we could call it the Great Adversative, or the Grand Nevertheless, or the Ultimate However, or the Quintessential But Still. In any case, and by any translation, there it sits: tossing his entire theory into the fire of historical fact, he writes (King James Version), "*Notwithstanding*, the Lord turned not from the fierceness of his great wrath" — and with the words turning to ashes in his mouth, he records the details of Josiah's demise.

To be sure, he found himself unable to sustain that kind of theological fact-facing for very long: in the two remaining chapters of his work, he goes back to implying that his theory of divine intervention to punish the disobedient and reward the obedient is still as good as new. But for one gloriously honest moment there, he really did see its falsehood, and he paid to the truth the ultimate tribute of that *nevertheless* by which he threw away a lifetime's theologizing.

But even if the author couldn't sustain the honesty, the God who inspired Scripture could, and did. In the writings of Jeremiah during the Captivity and in those of Deutero-Isaiah after it, there are hints that God's relationship to the course of history may be more profound and more paradoxical than the theory of punishment and reward ever imagined. A notion begins ever so slowly to surface: The suffering of Israel may be not simply retribution but the very sign of the Mystery of God's own action — of his own involvement — in history. Israel's role as the Servant of the Lord may well be fulfilled more in its failures and defeats than in its successes. And, to carry that notion all the way to what Christians believe is its fulfillment in Jesus, the theological road is open at last to the vision that it is in the midst of our disasters, rather than by deliverance out of them, that God fulfills the promise of his love. In other words, the way is open to the Good News that God in Christ doesn't wait for the world to save itself. Instead of standing at some antiseptic distance from our agonies and our failures, he comes to meet us in the very thick of them: in Jesus, he dies in our death, he becomes sin for our sins, and in the mystery of his resurrection — *without faking a single bit of history* — he invites us to believe that he has made all things new.

I apologize for so long an illustration; but now, perhaps, you see. Christian theologians who address themselves to the problem of evil should treat it as a mystery to be entered, not as a puzzle to be solved. That, accordingly, is just what this book tries to do. At times whimsically, at times earnestly — never solemnly but always seriously — it invites the reader all the way down into the heart of the problem, into the divine complicity in the nightmare at the bottom of the world. If that isn't the way most theologians have dealt with it, it nevertheless remains the way Scripture, considered from start to finish, deals with it. The supreme act by which God makes history come out right — the still, reconciling point of the whole turning world — is the very nightmare of the cross itself. This book simply tries to remove the theological blinders that keep us from seeing — in both our own case and God's — the way things really are.

I am delighted that Eerdmans has seen fit to reissue *The Third Peacock* in this new volume. While the body of the work remains substantially unchanged, I have taken the opportunity to make what I hope are improvements in the text. I'm happy that the book is once again in print, and I wish all its readers Godspeed.

1. Let Me Tell You Why

Let me tell you why God made the world.

One afternoon, before anything was made, God the Father, God the Son, and God the Holy Spirit sat around in the unity of their Godhead discussing one of the Father's fixations. From all eternity, it seems, he had had this *thing* about being. He would keep thinking up all kinds of unnecessary things — new ways of being and new kinds of beings to be. And as they talked, God the Son suddenly said, "Really, this is absolutely great stuff. Why don't I go out and mix us up a batch?" And God the Holy Spirit said, "Terrific! I'll help you." So they all pitched in, and after supper that night, the Son and the Holy Spirit put on this tremendous show of being for the Father. It was full of water and light and frogs; pine cones kept dropping all over the place, and crazy fish swam around in the wineglasses. There were mushrooms and mastodons, grapes and geese, tornadoes and tigers — and men and women everywhere to taste them, to juggle them, to join them, and to love them. And God the Father looked at the whole wild party and said, "Wonderful! Just what I had in mind! *Tov! Tov! Tov!*" And all God the Son and God the Holy Spirit could think of to say was the same thing: *"Tov! Tov! Tov!"* So they shouted together *"Tov meod!"* and they laughed for ages and ages, saying things like how great it was for beings to be, and how clever of the Father to think of the idea, and how kind of the Son to go to all that trouble putting it together, and how considerate of the Spirit to spend so much time directing and choreographing. And for ever and ever they told old jokes, and the Father and the Son drank their wine *in unitate Spiritus Sancti,* and they all threw ripe olives and pickled mushrooms at each other *per omnia saecula saeculorum. Amen.*

It is, I grant you, a crass analogy; but crass analogies are the safest. Everybody knows that God is not three old men throwing olives at each other. Not everyone, I'm afraid, is equally clear that God is not a cosmic force or a principle of being or any other dish of celestial blancmange we might choose to call him. Accordingly, I give you the central truth that creation is the result of a trinitarian bash, and leave the details of the analogy to sort themselves out as best they can.

One slight elucidation, however. It's very easy, when talking about creation, to conceive of God's part in it as simply getting the ball rolling — as if he were a kind of divine billiard cue, after whose action inexorable laws took over and excused him from further involvement with the balls. But that won't work. This world is *fundamentally* unnecessary. Nothing *has to* be. It needs a creator not only for its beginning but for every moment of its being. Accordingly, the trinitarian bash doesn't really come *before* creation; what actually happens is that all of creation, from start to finish, occurs within the bash: the raucousness of the divine party is simultaneous with the being of everything that ever was or will be. If you like paradoxes, it means that God is the eternal contemporary of all the events and beings in time.

Which is where the refinement in the analogy comes in. What happens is not that the Trinity manufactures the first duck and then the ducks take over the duck business as a kind of cottage industry. It is that every duck, down at the roots of its being, at the level where what is needed is not the ability to fertilize duck eggs but the moxie to stand outside of nothing — to *be* when there is no necessity of being — every duck, at that level, is a response to the creative act of God. In terms of the analogy, it means that God the Father *thinks up* duck #47307 for the month of May, A.D. 1723, that God the Spirit rushes over to the edge of the formless void and, with unutterable groanings, *broods* duck #47307, and that over his brooding God the Son, the eternal Word, triumphantly *shouts,* "Duck #47307!" And presto! you have a duck. Not one, you will note, tossed off in response to some mindless decree that there may as well be ducks as alligators, but one neatly fielded up in a game of delight by the eternal archetypes of Tinker, Evers, and Chance. The world isn't God's surplus inventory of artifacts; it is a whole barrelful of the apples of his eye, constantly juggled, relished, and exchanged by the persons of the Trinity. No wonder we love circuses, games, and magic. They prove we are in the image of God.

Still, though, after you've said that the delight of God is the deepest root of the being of everything, you have to watch that you don't wander off into another error. It's fine to see beta particles, electrons, and DNA molecules, guppies, geese, girls, and galaxies as responses to immediate divine enjoyment. Just remember that what's sauce for the goose is also sauce for the cancer cell, the liver fluke, the killer whale, and the loan shark — that if God is holding all things in being right now, he's got some explaining to do if he hopes to maintain his reputation as the original Good Guy. Or, more accurately (since God steadfastly refuses to show up and explain anything, except by announcing mysteries and paradoxes), *we've* got a lot of explaining to do if we are to go on thinking of him in terms of his reputation.

In short, any talk about creation brings you very quickly to what is called the problem of evil. It should be noted, however, that the problem arises only in certain circumstances. If you can manage to believe in two Gods, for example — one good and one bad — there is no problem. Evil, in such a system, is as much a part of the show as good.

The same thing would be true if you believed that the world was made by God not out of nothing but out of some primeval matter, some *Urstoff* or original glop that God didn't make and that he was simply stuck with. Then you could blame evil on the sleaziness of the raw materials he had to work with and get God off the hook by saying he's doing the best he can.

The problem of evil, in short, exists only for those who believe in God, who believe he made all things out of nothing, and who are stuck with a theology of delight which says that all beings, bar none, exist because he thinks they're just dandy. In other words, it is an invention — in the proper sense: a *discovery* — of the Judeo-Christian tradition with its God who, right at the beginning of the Bible, keeps muttering "Good, Good, Good" at the end of each day's work.

Judeo-Christian theologians, however, have not always done too well by their discovery. More often than not they have set up the problem of evil in a way that made their attempts at theodicy — at justifying the ways of God to man — seem ridiculous and even cruel. Some of them, for example, solved the problem by saying that God allowed evil in order to teach people useful lessons and make them better persons. You know: he gave us pain so we'd learn to keep our hands out of the fire, disappointments in order to teach us persever-ance, unkindness from others to help us grow in charity, and so on. The trouble with that, of course, is the *and so on:* torture, to teach us what? cancer, to improve us how? earthquakes, to advance civi-lization in what way? the whole bleeding, screaming, dying, lying, cheating, rotting carcass of a once-beautiful world to uplift us when?

It simply won't wash. For a few great souls, poverty may be a blessing; for most of us, it is what it is: a curse. Now and then a terminal disease ennobles; most of the time, it's miles from being even the best of a bad job. To set up God as an instructor who uses such methods is to make him the warden of the worst-run peniten-tiary of all. The atheist who would rather have no God makes far more sense than the pietist who will take that kind of injustice lying down. The atheist at least sounds like Job; the pietist sounds like hell.

Let's begin, then, by saying that there is ultimately no way of getting God off the hook for evil. By and by I'll make use of a distinction between evil and badness, reserving *evil* for deliberate perversions of being by creatures with free choice, and using *badness* to refer to all the other collisions, contretemps, and disasters in the world. Even that distinction, however, helps only slightly. It enables you to blame *voluntary* evil — sin, if you will — on persons other than God; it does not, of course, exculpate God from the responsibility for making free beings in the first place. Sure, my brother-in-law is the one who got drunk and punched me in the nose; but then, why is God so all-fired insistent on preserving my brother-in-law's freedom to gum up everybody's life? Sin is possible only because God puts up with sinners.

The quick retort that I object only to other people's freedom — that I find my own precious and will defend it against all comers — is true enough. It is not, however, an answer to the question of why any of us should be free in the first place. It says only, perhaps, that I am enough of an opportunist to agree with God in my own case — that I like the divine-image business when I profit from it; it sheds no light on the mystery of why he should keep such a shop when he knows it is, at least half the time, a losing proposition.

The last gasp on this line of defense is to say that the fact that he keeps backing such a bad show proves how highly he regards freedom. True enough. And on a good day, when the sun is glistening on the snow, when your bowels are not in revolt, and when your brother-in-law has phoned to say he can't make your dinner party, it sounds pretty good. But in the stormy season, in the thick of our own and others' sins, it's only one inconvenient mystery used to cover another.

God is still firmly on the hook. (That he is actually on the hook, of course, is God's own final answer to the whole matter. According to the Gospel, he himself hangs on the cross with the rest of his free creation. If you believe that, it is great comfort; it is not, however, one whit less a mystery.) There is, therefore, even in the fullness of Christian revelation, no untying the knot of freedom. Even in the relatively simple case of moral evil, where you can find somebody besides God to blame for what's wrong at the party, it remains true that things go wrong only because of his stubborn insistence on keeping the party going no matter what. Theodicy is for people with strong stomachs.

Literally. If the case for moral evil is difficult, the case for natural evil — for what I choose to call *badness* — is positively distasteful. There is, of course, no question but that bunny rabbits are lovely. But to allow one's theology of creation to rest content with paeans to all that is cuddly and warm is to ignore precisely half of creation. The rabbit is indeed good, and, in his own mute way, he aggressively affirms his own goodness. The coyote is good too. But when the coyote, in the process of affirming her own goodness, contemplates the delectability of the rabbit, it turns out to be a little hard on the rabbit.

The world of delight that the Trinity holds in being is a rough place. Everything eats everything else, not only to the annoyance of those who get eaten, but to their agony, death, and destruction. The rabbit himself does in the lettuce, the lettuce impoverishes the soil, the big fish eat the little fish, the little fish eat the shrimp, the shrimp eat the plankton, the rivers eat the mountains, and the sun eats the rivers. And the human race is no exception. Modern children probably think it is: for them, turkeys are not killed and bled; they are mined from freezer cases in supermarkets. In fact, however, humanity has, even at its best, more than a lion's share of the world's blood on its hands. What to say, then, about the goodness of a God who makes a world so full of badness?

Wrong solutions come to mind at once. Paying attention only to what is lovely has already been mentioned: it simply ignores the problem. A more serious error is involved in trying to fob off all the killing and eating on sin — to tie natural badness to moral evil and to say that, if it hadn't been for sin, all the animals would have been vegetarians. That, however, is a bit much. It involves, as someone once observed, the saber-toothed tigers waking up the morning after their creation and wondering why the God who designed them to eat grass gave them so damned inconvenient a set of choppers. Such a gambit never solves the problem of theodicy. It simply arranges to have somebody else's ox gored.

Furthermore, even a vegetarian creation is no answer. It is only our human chauvinism that is satisfied when literal bloodshed is ruled out. The lettuces still, in their own way, take a dim view of having to cease being lettuces; as they can, they fight it. One of the deepest mistakes in theology is to start our discussions of the major activities of creation too high. We act as if only we were free, only we had knowledge, only we were capable of feeling. That's not only false; it's mischievous. It makes us a lonely exception to the tissue of creation rather than a part of its hierarchy.

Finally, it is not at all apparent in such a solution just how sin managed to bring about the general debacle of a bloody creation. It was bloody and destructive long before the only available sinners — human beings — showed up. To argue that our work was to be the reformer of that destructiveness and that, by sin, we welshed on the job is, of course, possible. It is, however, a bit apocalyptic. It is not easy to see how we, even in our present competency, are able to do much about weaning mackerel away from their fondness for silvers. And to postulate such wonders as our work from the beginning is to revert to the worst kind of prelapsarian aggrandizement of human nature — to return to those strange theologies by which Adam and Eve before the Fall were made entirely of stainless steel and Teflon, and knew Greek, Chinese, and the periodic table of the elements by heart.

To repeat, it just won't wash. However much we may be able to make a case for the lion's lying down with the lamb in the eschatological fullness of things, it remains true that no wise lamb thinks much of the idea right now. No, the atheist, once again, is right, and the pietist is barking up a tree that never existed. Nature *is* red in tooth and claw. The badness of creation is inseparable from the goodness of creation. It can indeed be argued that moral evil, sin, perversion — the willful twisting of goodness toward nothing — is not necessary to the shape of the world; but there is no way of getting simple badness out of the act. What's good for one thing is bad for another. The human race was no doubt meant to be a kind of referee in the game, to lift it into something higher, wider, and handsomer. But that we ever had even an outside chance of abolishing here and now the game of lion eat lamb, crow eat carcass, bugs eat crow is simply beyond reason.

Whether a solution to the riddle is possible, of course, remains to be seen. Only one thing is clear: there will never be a solution until we stop faking the facts. The world is a very rough place. If it exists because God likes it, the only possible conclusion is that God is inordinately fond of rough places. From earthquakes to earthworms, it is all his doing. One or the other of them gets us in the end; here begins, therefore, the consideration.

2. Let's Take Stock

Let's take stock of what we've come up with so far: Evil is assignable to freedom; freedom has to be blamed on God. Now if we're facing facts, that means that God has dangerously odd tastes: he is inordinately fond of risk and roughhouse. Any omnipotent being who makes as much room as he does for back talk and misbehavior strikes us as slightly addled. Why, when you're orchestrating the music of the spheres, run the awful risk of letting some fool with a foghorn into the violin section? Why set up the delicate balance of nature and then let a butcher with heavy thumbs mind the store? It just seems — well, *irresponsible.* If we were God, we would be more serious and respectable: no freedom, no risks; just a smooth, obedient show presided over by an omnipotent bank president with a big gold watch.

At least so it seems, until you think about it. Then everything turns around and you're back on God's side before you know it. Try writing a fairy tale on the safe-and-sane view of the universe.

The princess is under a curse. She is asleep and cannot be awakened except by an apple from the tree in the middle of the garden at the Western End of the World. What does the king do? Well, on the theory that a well-run, no-risk operation makes the best of all possible worlds, he gets out his maps, briefs his generals, and sends a couple of well-supplied divisions to the garden to fetch the apple. It is only a matter of getting an odd prescription from an inconveniently located drugstore that doesn't deliver. He uses his

[183]

power and does the job. The apple is brought to the palace and applied to the princess. She wakes up, eats breakfast, lunch, and dinner forever after, and dies in bed at the age of eighty-two.

Everyone knows, of course, that that's not the way the story goes. To begin with, the garden isn't on any of the maps. Only one man in the kingdom, the hundred-year-old Grand Vizier, knows where it is. When he is summoned, however, he asks to be excused. It seems that he's scheduled to die later that evening and therefore cannot make the trip. He happens to have a map, but there's a complication. The map has been drawn with magical ink and will be visible only to the right man for the job. The king, of course, inquires how this man is to be found. Very simply, says the Vizier. He will be recognized by his ability to whistle in double stops and imitate a pair of Baltimore orioles accompanying each other at an interval of a minor third.

Needless to say, the king calls in his nobles, all of whom are excellent musicians. They whistle, sing, and chant at the paper, but nothing appears. They serenade it with airs to the lute and with pavans played by consorts of recorders, sackbuts, shawms, and rebecs, but still no luck. At last the king, in desperation, tells them to knock off for lunch and come back at two. He goes up on the parapet for a stroll and, lo and behold, what does he hear but somebody walking down the road whistling double stops like a pair of Baltimore orioles!

It is, of course, the Miller's Third Son, local school dropout and political agitator. The king, however, is not one to balk at ideologies when he needs help. He hauls the boy in, gives him the map, and packs him off with a bag of Milky Ways and a six-pack of root beer. That night the boy reads the map. It seems pretty straightforward, except for a warning at the bottom in block capitals: AFTER EN-TERING THE GARDEN, GO STRAIGHT TO THE TREE, PICK THE APPLE, AND GET OUT. DO NOT, UNDER ANY CIR-CUMSTANCES, ENGAGE IN CONVERSATION WITH THE THIRD PEACOCK ON THE LEFT.

Any child worth his root beer can write the rest of the story for you. The boy goes into the garden and gets as far as the third peacock on the left, who asks him whether he wouldn't like a stein of the local root beer. Before he knows it, he has had three and falls fast asleep. When he wakes up, he's in a pitch-black cave; a light flickers, a voice calls — and from there on all hell breaks loose. The boy follows an invisible guide who's wearing a cocked hat and descends into the bowels of the earth; he rows down rivers of fire in an aluminum dinghy, is imprisoned by the Crown Prince of the Salamanders, is finally rescued by a confused eagle who deposits him at the *Eastern* End of the World, works his way back to the Western End in the dead of winter, gets the apple, brings it home, touches it to the princess's lips, rouses her, reveals himself as the long-lost son of the Eagle King, and marries the princess. Then, and only then, do they live happily ever after.

Do you see? It is precisely improbability and risk that make the story. There isn't a child on earth who doesn't know the crucial moment — whose heart, no matter how well it knows the story, doesn't miss a beat every time the boy gets to the third peacock on the left. There is no one still in possession of humanity who doesn't recognize that moment as the sacrament of all the unnecessary risks ever taken by God or man — of the freedom that we cannot live with, and will not live without. True enough, it explains nothing; but it does mark Mystery as our oldest, truest home.

Fascinatingly, if you turn from fairy tales to sport or games of chance, you get the same result. What is bridge or poker but the unnecessary pitting of our ability to control against the radically uncontrollable? What is football or baseball but the ritualization of risk? What lies at the root of our fascination with gambling, probability, and odds except a deep response of approval to the whole changing and chancy world? And what is love if it is not the indulgence of the ultimate risk of giving one's self to another over whom we have no control? (That's why it does no good to explain freedom by saying that God introduced it to make love possible. The statement happens to be true, but it doesn't illuminate much. The question still remains: Why *love?* Why *risk* at all?) The only comfort is that if God is crazy, he is at least no crazier than we are. His deepest and our best are very close.

The safe universe may be a nice place to visit; but when we're in the market for a home, we don't go to the overstuffed bank presidents with their model worlds. We head straight for the same old disreputable crowd our family has always done business with: the yarn spinners, the drunk poets, and the sports who caroused all night in mother's kitchen, and whose singing filled the stairways where we slept.

▼ ▼ ▼

Admittedly, that is a fey and slightly quixotic justification for freedom. But since it is all you are about to get from me, I propose to move on. Our problem with regard to freedom is not simply that we foolishly object to the risks involved; it is that, even when we accept them, we go right on acting as if the risk extended only to human beings. In our pride, we limit the discussion of freedom to humanity and then have the nerve to wonder why we feel lonely as the only free creatures in a deterministic universe.

The corrective to all of that takes us back to the act of creation and to the question of the precise relationship between God the Creator and all the comings and goings of the universe itself. I've already said that God is not simply the initiator or beginning cause of creation; he is the present, intimate, and immediate cause of the being of everything that is. When we say that God is the First Cause, we don't mean the first of all the causes in time. We are not trying to chase him down by going from me, to my father, to my grandfather, and so on, till we stumble upon God making Adam out of dust, or apes, or whatever. We are not going *back* in history but *down* in the present; and we are saying that when you get all through explaining that my fingernail exists because of my body, and my body because of its physicochemical structure, and its structure because of the particles in the atom — that when you have chased down all the intermediate causes that make being *behave* the way it does, you are still going to have to hunt for an ultimate cause that makes being *be* in the first place. You need a first cause to keep all the secondary causes from collapsing back into nothing; and, since they obviously don't collapse, the First Cause must be right in there pitching all the time.

That may or may not appeal to you. Obviously, it is a version of one of Saint Thomas's arguments. I don't put it in here, however, to prove the existence of God — only to make sure that you know what I mean when I say First Cause. If the rest bothers you, let it pass; what's already been said is enough to pinpoint the problem.

Look at it. You have God holding everything in being *right now.* You also have the assorted creatures he holds in being eating banana splits, making love, rabbits, or plankton, as the case may be, and generally doing what they please and/or can get away with. What is the connection between the act of God that makes them be and their own acts as individual beings?

The answer must be twofold. To be utterly correct, you have to say that the connection is real but mysterious; more about that later. For all practical purposes here, however, it will do quite nicely to say that, by and large, there is no connection. Unless you are an occasionalist — that is, one who thinks that God is the only actor in the universe and that the whole history of the world is just a puppet show put on by him — then you must grant that it is the rabbits who make rabbits — and for entirely rabbitlike and non-divine reasons.

Consider the stones on the seashore, how they lie. Why is this oval white pebble where it is? Is it here because God himself, in his proper and divine capacity, reached down an almighty hand and nudged it into place? No. God knows where it is, of course, because he is the cause of its being and, in the exchanges of the Trinity, holds it in continual regard. For the same reason, he also knows what it does. But he is not, for all that, the cause of its doing its own thing. The pebble lies in its place because of its own stony style — and because the last wave of the last high tide flipped it two feet east of where it is now, and the right hind leg of my neighbor's dog flipped it two feet west. It is not there because God, either in person or by means of some preprogrammed evolutionary software, has determined that it must be there.

The pebble, in short, lies where it does *freely.* Not, of course, in the sense that it has a mind and will and chooses as we choose, but in the sense that it got there because of the random rattling about of assorted objects with various degrees of freedom. The waves are free to be waves, to be wet and to push. The pebbles are free to sink and to collide and to break. The dog is free to scratch fleas and chase birds. This whole mixed consort then comes together and makes whatever kind of dance it can manage. God may be the cause of its being, but he is, for the most part, only the *spectator* of its actions. He confers upon it the several *styles* of its freedom; it is creation itself, however, that struts its own stuff.

In other words, any realistic view of freedom has to start way below human nature. It has, in fact, to start with the smallest particle of actually existing reality. No matter how restricted anything is — no matter how deaf, dumb, and determined it may in fact be — it is at least free to be itself and is therefore, by the creative act of God, free of direct divine control over its behavior.

Needless to say, such a position doesn't sound particularly religious. As a matter of fact, it isn't. Religion is one of the larger roadblocks that God has had to put up with in the process of getting his messages through to the world. The usual religious view is that God has his finger in every pie and, as the infinite meddler, never lets anything act for itself. People bolster such ideas by an appeal to Scripture, pointing out things like the parting of the Red Sea, or Elijah starting fires with wet wood on Mount Carmel. That won't do, however. To be sure, I am not about to make a case that God *can't* do miracles — that he can't from time to time stick in his thumb and manufacture a plum if he feels like it. Nor am I going to maintain that he can't answer the prayers of those of his free creatures he has bizarrely said he would take advice from. All I want to insist on here is that most of the time he doesn't meddle, that his ordinary policy is Hands Off.

Obviously, it is just that policy which produces the roughness of creation. On November 1, 1755, in the midst of one of the most theologically optimistic centuries in all of history, the great Lisbon earthquake occurred. At that time, most believers had come to hold a theory of the relationship between God and creation which assured them that God took personal care of every contingency and was especially diligent about arranging for the safety and welfare of the elect. Likewise, most unbelievers had nursed themselves to the conclusion that the world was about as perfect a piece of machinery as was possible and would go on functioning smoothly forever.

In either case, the Lisbon earthquake came as a shock; the intellectual tremor was as great as the geological one. How, everyone asked, in a world so well run by God or nature, could such a disaster occur? Why, the theologians wondered, didn't God take care of his elect? What had gone wrong?

The answer, of course, was that nothing had gone wrong — with the universe. What had happened was that the theological theories had been formulated without paying enough attention to the facts of creation. What happened in Lisbon was indeed assignable to God, but not for the reasons people then advanced. Some said it proved there was no God; others hunted for evidence of wickedness sufficient to warrant so fearful a punishment. The trouble with all such attempts to understand was that they went beyond the evidence. First of all, in spite of a few episodes in Scripture where God slapped down sinners, he nowhere promised that he would be a universal moral policeman. Too many scoundrels died in their beds and too many saints went out in agony ever to permit such a notion to be advanced realistically. In fact, when God actually showed up in Jesus, he resolutely refused to judge anyone. Far from being on the side of the police, he ended up being done in by the very forces of righteousness who were supposed to be his official representatives.

Secondly, if God's role in the world was that of a perpetual Mr. Fixit, it had not, to say the least, been particularly self-evident. Once again, consider the facts. When he showed up in Jesus, he did a few miracles. He calmed a storm or two, healed a handful of the sick, and fed two crowds by multiplying short rations. If we are being realistic, however, we cannot hold that these things were the announcement of a *program* for the management of creation. They were, of course, signs to identify him as the manager — and they were evidence of the compassionate direction that he intended his management to take. But as a program, they were a flop. Too many uncalmed storms remain, too many unhealed sick, too many hungry and halt. Indeed, when he did his consummate piece of managing, it turned out to be the ultimate act of non-interference: with nails through his hands and feet, he simply died. Whatever else that was, it was the hands-off policy in spades.

No, the Lisbon earthquake was not God's fault for any of the reasons assigned to it by unrealistic theologies. It was God's fault simply because he made the earth the kind of thing it is. If he had made it out of one solid homogeneous block, then it would not have developed a surface condition liable to cracks and shifts. But since he actually made it out of molten slush — and set it to cool not in an annealing oven but in frigid space — it was bound to develop a somewhat unstable crust before its center cooled and hardened. Again, if he had not made trees and grass, ducks and geese, sheep and oxen, men and women free to wander about the earth in accordance with the several styles of their freedom, he could no doubt have arranged to have the site of the city of Lisbon unoccupied by anything liable to be injured by earth tremors. Obviously, however, he had no such restrictions in mind. Everything was left, barring miracle, to fend for itself with what freedom it had. It was indeed horrible for so many to die such a dreadful death; it was not at all horrible for the crust of a partly cooled casting to shift a bit under the circumstances.

Once again, we are back to the necessity of facing facts. The world, insofar as we can see, is not stage-managed by God. Neither is it a place in which a few free beings like us fight a lonely battle against vast armies of totally determined creatures like lions, sharks, and mountains. It is rather a place in which all things are free within the limits of the style of their own natures — and in which all things are also determined by the way the natures of other things impinge upon them.

It is precisely the free goodness of the Crown Prince of the Salamanders, as he himself conceives it, that makes so much trouble for the Miller's Third Son in the bowels of the earth. It is the marvelous aptitude of aluminum to conduct heat that makes the rowing trip down the river such a trial to the admirable sensitivity of the human backside. There is no badness except by virtue of the goodnesses that compete with each other in the several styles of their freedom. We have not yet, therefore, solved the problem; we have only descended to a deeper level of consideration. The question *now* is: In a situation so radically and deliberately out of God's control, how does he bring it all around in the end? If he has power — and uses it as he claims — why does it look as if he has none?

3. *The Heart of the Problem*

T he heart of the problem beats strongest in the confrontation between Jesus and the Devil in the wilderness. The account as we have it is condensed and stylized, but the realities are still clear. After Jesus has fasted for forty days and has meditated, presumably, on his coming redemptive work, the Devil makes three suggestions about the best way to get the job done. Christian piety usually hands the Devil the short end of the stick, but it's worth the time it takes to turn the tables and give him his due.

In the first place, the story doesn't cast the Devil simply in the role of the bad guy. On the old Christian theory that the Devil is a real being — a fallen angel, in fact — he couldn't possibly be *all* bad. Insofar as he exists, his *being* is one more response to the creative delight of the Trinity. Being as such is good. There is no *ontological* evil. (*Whether* the Devil actually exists, of course, is a question of fact, the principal evidence for which lies in Scripture. About that, you will have to suit yourself. About the *possibility* of his being, however, you have no choice: he is neither more nor less likely than a duck. A priori objections to his existence are simply narrow-minded.)

Furthermore, the story does not require that we consider all of his *behavior* bad. Perhaps even his motives were good. After all, his suggestions to Jesus are by no means either unkind or unreasonable. What is wrong with suggesting to a hungry man at the end of a long retreat that he make himself a stone sandwich if he has the power to render it digestible? It is perfectly obvious that Jesus ate again sometime, either on the forty-first day or shortly thereafter. He did not acquire his reputation as a glutton and a winebibber by fasting for the next three years.

Likewise, it was not necessarily mischievous of the Devil to urge Jesus to jump off the Temple and make a spectacular landing. As the Grand Inquisitor pointed out, people need to see some proof of power if they are to believe. They wander through life like donkeys; a good whack with a miraculous two-by-four might be the very thing to get their attention. Even the suggestion that, in return for Jesus' loyalty, the Devil would hand over to him all the kingdoms of the world is not, on the Devil's principles, such a bad idea. It's simply a rather sensible with-my-know-how-and-your-clout-we'd-really-do-some-good kind of offer. After all, God, who was supposed to be running things, wasn't doing a very obvious job of it. Since, in his own view, the Devil was still the Prince of this world — allowed by the divine courtesy to keep his dominion even after his fall — perhaps he could be excused for hoping for a little more cooperation from the Son of God than he ever got from the Father.

In any case, the clincher for the argument that the Devil's ideas weren't all bad comes from Jesus himself. At other times, in other places, and for his own reasons, Jesus does all of the things the Devil suggests. Instead of making lunch out of rocks, he feeds the five thousand miraculously — basically the same trick, but on a grander scale. Instead of jumping off the Temple and not dying, he dies and refuses to stay dead — by any standards, an even better trick. And finally, instead of getting himself bogged down in a two-man presidency with an opposite number he doesn't really understand, he aces out the Devil on the cross and ends up risen, ascended, and glorified at the right hand of the Father as King of Kings and Lord of Lords — which is the best trick of all, taken with the last trump.

No, the differences between Jesus and the Devil do not lie in what the Devil suggested but in the methods he proposed — or, more precisely, in the philosophy of power on which his methods were based. The temptation in the wilderness is a conversation between two people who simply cannot hear each other — a master-piece of non-communication. If you are really God, the Devil says, do something. Jesus answers, I am really God; therefore I do nothing. The Devil makes what, to him and to us, seem like sensible sug-gestions. Jesus responds by parroting Scripture verses back at him. The Devil wants power to be used to do good; Jesus insists that power corrupts and defeats the very good it tries to achieve.

It's an exasperating story. Yet, when you look at history, Jesus seems to have the better of the argument. Most, if not all, of the mischief in the world is done in the name of righteousness. The human race adheres devoutly to the belief that one more application of power will bring in the kingdom. One more invasion, one more war, one more escalation, one more jealous fit, one more towering rage — in short, one more twist of whatever arm you have got hold of — will make goodness triumph and peace reign. But it never works. Never with persons, since they are free and can, as persons, only be wooed, not controlled. And never even with things, because they are free, too, in their own way — and they turn and rend us when we least expect. For a long time — since the Fall, in fact — we have been in love with the demonic style of power. For a some-what shorter time, we have enjoyed, or suffered from, the possession of vast resources of power. Where has it gotten us? To the brink of a choice between nuclear annihilation or drowning in our own in-destructible technological garbage.

However we may be tempted, therefore, to fault the divine style of power — however much we may cry out like Job against a God who does not keep hedges around the goodness he delights in — however angry we may be at the agony his forbearance permits, one thing at least is clear. The demonic style of power, the plausible use of force to do good, makes at least as much misery as the divine, if not more. The Devil in the wilderness offers Jesus a shortcut. Jesus calls it a dead end and turns a deaf ear. The great, even well-meaning challenge to the hands-off policy comes and goes, and God still insists on playing the Invisible Man, on running the world without running it at all. The question is put loud and clear: Why in God's Name won't you show up? And the response comes back as supremely unsatisfying as ever: to show up would be to come in your name, not mine. No show, therefore. And, of course, no answer.

▼   ▼   ▼

Try another tack.

The difficulty with the policy of non-interference arises not only in redemption — in God's purported action to straighten out a bent creation; it arises just as acutely in what he does to hold creation in being in the first place. He never tips his hand there, either.

In spite of the way it is bandied about popularly and even scientifically, the notion of creation is not, and cannot be, a category of physical science. By any ordinary definition, God is not a physical being. Therefore, if all the investigative devices at your disposal rely on the detection of physical phenomena, none of those devices is going to register the presence of God. It doesn't matter whether you are going *back* in time to discover the act by which he initiated the whole process, or *down* in the present to find the hand that makes it be right now; you are never going to find anything except the results of that act, the works of that hand. He may be operating full blast, or out to lunch, or retired, or nonexistent; but physical investigation isn't going to provide you with a single clue as to which is really the case. *Meta*physical investigation, of course, is another matter. A philosophical inference that there is a Creator is perfectly possible; so is a theological assertion to that effect. Both of those disciplines have room for the concept of creation. But in physical science it is only an infrared herring, an invisible quarterback offsides and out of bounds.

While we are at it, this is the place to add a word about the general subject of other hunting expeditions that try to turn up spiritualities in a material world. From time to time, people try to prove the existence of things like the soul, or the mind, or even such ordinary pieces of business as cause and effect by an appeal to physical science. None of it ever succeeds — and none of it can. There is nothing that happens *in this world* — up to and including the action of God himself in this world — that doesn't happen on some physical basis. There is no love without hands, arms, and hearts to give it expression. There are no thoughts unless there are brain cells to make the thinking process possible. There are not even any miracles without physical starting and stopping points. Jesus goes to the wedding feast. Plain water in jugs is succeeded by first-rate wine. Even if he had done the trick with a magic wand, however, there still would have been nothing but wand, jugs, water, and wine that was susceptible of material investigation.

That means, if you think it through, that there is nothing here that can't be faked on a physical basis. Since there is no mystical experience without some accompanying physical activity in the brain, it's perfectly possible, if you have the techniques and equipment to produce the proper brain waves, to obtain an effect indistinguishable from true mysticism. We have known that, of course, for a long time: ether makes philosophers of us all, and so does the newer and more potent panoply of hallucinogens and mind-expanding drugs. But as we become cleverer, we had best be prepared for a vast increase in the power to fake. Since everything a human being does is done physically, our race of geniuses will someday succeed in producing something that can do everything a human being does. What we will not succeed at, however, is finding a physical basis for deciding whether we have made a human being or only a gorgeous troll. For that we will still need a philosopher or a drunk poet — someone, at any rate, who knows the difference between having a blood pump and having a heart.

The technicians, of course, will try to argue us down. In the kind of world we live in, the *reductionist* argument is always possible: love is only endocrine secretions; thought is nothing but electrical disturbances in brain tissue; miracle is simply a physical incongruity for which we have not yet found a physical explanation. But, by the same token, the reductionist argument is always specious. Anybody who holds that there is more to reality than physical phenomena can rebut it in an instant. Question: How do I know that the whole idea of God isn't just a bunch of electrical impulses in some cells in my head? Answer: How do you know that electrical impulses in brain cells are not God's chosen device for communicating to me the reality of a spiritual nature not otherwise accessible to me? Score? Zero, zero. Time to drop the reductionist argument and get on with the real job.

Apparently there is just no way of getting God to tip his hand. His power as such — even in so direct a use as miracle — remains invisible. The thing to do, therefore, is to stop looking for barefaced manifestations of it. Accordingly, I propose simply to assume his power and then to try and see its relationship to the radical freedom of the things God holds in being. Such a procedure may gall you; you have, perhaps, a congenital aversion to arguments that assume what they set out to prove. In fairness, however, please note that I am not trying to prove anything — only to reach a possible understanding of certain classic assumptions. What I am doing is indeed circular, but it is not argument; this is sightseeing, not proof. If the Devil had spent a little less time throwing dares at the Mystery and a little more time just walking around it, he might have discovered what this book is looking for and saved us all a lot of trouble.

What we need, then, is a good instance of an apparent conflict between the fact that things are free and the assertion that God is, at least in some sense, stage-managing history. I suggest, as that instance, the evolution of the human race — an event that, by all accounts, has been one of the chief battlefields of the conflict. Its circumambulation takes a little time, but it may do some good.

Take first the points of agreement. There is no question, on anybody's theory, but that human beings showed up *at some time* in history. The accepted modern wisdom puts that time very late indeed in the total picture; but even the biblical story has us show up at the end of God's six-day working week. In other words, everyone is agreed that something *happened,* either to the dirt or to the monkeys, to bring about the phenomenon called human nature. Nobody says that we were present from the beginning, or that our appearance needs no explanation.

Second, on the basis of a renewed seriousness about the freedom of the world, the more discerning representatives of both the theistic and the non-theistic sides tend to rule out any determinism about the

advent of human beings. For a long time, of course, secular evolutionists talked as if they had a completely deterministic proposition on
their hands — as if, in the constitution of matter itself, there was a
fully programmed evolutionary scenario. Worse yet, they sometimes
even implied that, if only you had enough time and could duplicate
the right conditions, you would get the same world all over again.
Mercifully, that kind of talk has pretty much ceased. While everyone
admits that mutations of fruit flies under laboratory conditions prove
the possibility of all sorts of evolutionary leaps, most people concede
that such experiments have nothing to say about where, when, and
how such jumps might take place in a world full of earthquakes, floods,
and snowstorms. To be sure, when the first little slimy whatsis
slithered up on the beach, it must have had evolutionary capacities *de
luxe.* But perhaps it survived its first day only because the sun, which
might have fried it to a crisp, was behind the clouds on that particular
Tuesday two hundred million years ago.

Theistic thought has improved similarly. The standard
nineteenth-century godly response to the menace of evolution was
to say that if evolution was indeed the reason why things turned out
the way they did, then it achieved that result only because God had
previously *involuted* all the developments. Instead of a secular computer program, they posited a religious one; but with no better
result. An electrochemically oriented divine puppet master is still a
puppet master; any world run that way doesn't smell even vaguely
like the one around us. We have come, therefore, to a more realistic
view. Evolution "causes" nothing; it is merely a description of a
sequence of results. You might as well say that *history* caused the
failure of Napoleon's Russian campaign. It's things that cause things,
at whatever opportunities and in whatever styles they can manage.
Evolution or History or the Divine Plan or whatever — all of them
are, at bottom, *descriptive* and not determinative categories. We have,
in short, finally come to the point of being able to see the world —
even the world run by God — as a fairly loose show. The fear of the
Lord's tightness has been the beginning of at least a little secular
wisdom.

At any rate, so much for the agreements. What, against that

background, can be said about God's relation to the appearance of humankind in the world? On the physical side we must, of course, hold out for the freedom of things. On the theological side, however, it seems that we are stuck with a paradox. There doesn't seem to be any way around the necessity of saying that God actually thought up, and arranged for, human evolution. The *mechanics* of the biblical "Let us make humankind in our image, according to our likeness" can be sat loose to; the *theology* of the phrase is inescapable: humankind is one of God's own bright ideas. He has got exactly the species he wanted; but how in the world did he do it?

Possibility Number One: God is adaptable, if nothing else. As the Supreme Realist, he takes what he gets. He puts all the stones of creation into an infinite tomato can, shakes them up, dumps them out, and says, "Just what I had in mind." He is, in short, a spectator and nothing but a spectator.

Such a view does very nicely by the freedom of things. It will not, however, leave you with anything even halfway like the God who supposedly instigated the Bible. To begin with, miracle is impossible if God is only an infinite Watchbird. Furthermore, if he is simply the passive acceptor of all that is, you would expect him to express no opinions or preferences about anything. Needless to say, that is a limitation that the God of the Judeo-Christian tradition does not seem to have heard about. Try selling Pharaoh the doctrine of Divine Utter Complacence.

What really makes such a view impossible, though, is the theology of delight with which both the Bible and this book began. God actually has *likes;* and nobody, not even God, can have likes without having dislikes. If Adam is the apple of his eye, then anybody (including Adam) who beats up on Adam is bound to end up on the divine s. list. If that's not true, then things are really in rotten shape. If God is merely passive, evolving along with his creation and nodding meaningless approval at everything, that's the worst news of all. We might just manage to put up with an eternal Puppeteer or an omnipotent Tyrant or even an infinite Predestinarian Monster; but to live forever under the sappy smile of an everlasting *klutz* who doesn't give a damn about anything is simply too much.

Possibility Number Two, therefore: God runs the world by incorporating into the being of everything a *nisus* or tendency toward himself. Human beings, accordingly, show up when they do because God always wanted human beings, and therefore built into the natures of prehuman things a drive or thrust toward humanity. Evaluation? Close, but no cigar.

First, it is a bit short on the freedom of things. A built-in tendency looks suspiciously like the old preprogrammed computer, even if it's posited as part of the very nature of things. It sounds too much like a distinction without a difference — like a verbal and not a real solution of the problem.

Second, while a nisus sounds better than a built-in drive or thrust, it is hard to see how any of them are compatible with the hands-off policy that God seems to honor. A pushy God is a pushy God; it doesn't change things simply to hold that his pushiness exerts itself at the roots of being rather than farther up the tree.

Third, at least in the case of the human style of free will, the innate-thrust theory simply contradicts the facts. We are quite capable of making this lovely pinball machine of a world read TILT. There is no subtle nisus that we can't, by the push of a button or the slow alteration of our genes, play full and final hob with. If God is to be handed a workable device for running creation, it would be a good idea to make it more foolproof than this one. Nisus is nice, but rebellion is more robust. Out with it, then. On to Possibility Number Three . . .

4. *Which Requires a Chapter by Itself*

. . . which requires a chapter by itself to do it justice.

Having thrown out the idea of a nisus because it involved God's doing too much, we are still under the necessity of finding some concept that will not leave him doing too little. There's no use getting rid of a busybody of a God only to find yourself with a substitute who spends eternity drawing unemployment checks.

Accordingly, let me shift the focus of the word *doing.* Most analogies to the creative act of God are unfortunate. Our heads are filled with pictures of responsible little watchmakers and painstakingly careful craftsmen whose products, once brought into being, no longer have any connection with their maker. God's relationship to the world should not be expounded like that. It deserves an analogy that is . . . well, more intimate. What he does to the world, he does *subtly;* his effect on creation is like what a stunning woman does to a man.

In the ordinary sense of the word, she doesn't "do" anything. She needs neither hooks nor ropes nor bumps nor grinds to draw him to her. He doesn't cry out to her, "Don't just stand there; do something." It is her simple standing there that does him in for good. She doesn't touch his freedom, and she doesn't muck about with the constitution of his being by installing some trick nisus that makes Harry love Martha. (Sex, of course, is a nisus, but I'm talking about romance, not sex. If you can't see the difference, you're on the wrong analogical bus.) All she has to do is be — and Harry's clock is wound. All in green his love goes riding, and, to the bizarre accompaniment of fleet does, red roebucks, swift sweet deer, and four lean hounds, his heart falls dead in the silver dawn.

So God with creation. He makes it, yes. I suppose we shall have to leave him a small shop in the basement of his being where he keeps busy at the day labor of first causing and prime moving. But after that, he doesn't *make* the world; he *makes out* with it. He just stands there, flaunting what he's got and romancing creation around his little finger without moving a muscle.

If, out of mere curiosity, you have to ask how he does that trick, I have to admit I have no answer. But then I've never met a man or a woman who drew others by love and knew how *they* did it, either. The lover is always just as surprised as the beloved. But if you ask in all seriousness how God does it — as if that were a question that needed an answer — then you and I are not only on different buses; we are in different worlds. My answer to you in that case is, "Who cares *how* he turns the world on, as long as he does it — as long as he gets his way by attractiveness, not pushiness." The job of theologians is not to unscrew the inscrutable. Their highest hope is not that their analogical discourse will unveil absolute truth, only that it will make as little trouble as possible. Their criteria are more aesthetic than metaphysical. (I admit that, if pressed to a metaphysical conclusion, I would claim that this particular analogy lies pretty close to the truth. It rests, it seems to me, on a real *analogy in being* between us and God: we turn each other on because we are made in the image of a God who is always on the make. I recognize, of course, that that begs the question; I can't prove my claim. It does have a lovely smell, though. It may be just another circular argument; but the kitchen it prowls around reminds me of the best dinner I ever had.)

Therefore, I'm not averse to playing with the analogy in connection with the first appearance of human beings — or of anything else, for that matter. What is so *attractive* about God that it enables him to draw the world into being? Well, on the basis of the doctrine of the Trinity — in which the Father eternally *thinks up* the world, the Spirit eternally *broods over* the idea, and the Son eternally *calls* the world out of nothing into being — maybe it is simply that creation falls, lovely head over round heels, for all that divine fuss over it. Martha moves toward Harry first of all because of the romantic intimation by which she perceives the marvel of his being, leaping upon the mountains, skipping upon the hills, showing himself through the lattice. But she falls hardest at the discovery that he always thinks, broods, and says her name: You are beautiful, O my Love, as Tirzah, comely as Jerusalem, terrible as an army with banners. Rise up, my Love, my fair one, and come.

More than that, under his love she *becomes herself:* she blossoms into a fullness of being. *How* she thus evolves is not at all clear; *that* it happens is as plain as day. We talk about her clothes, her hair, her skin being more *becoming* than they were. We recognize in her a process not of ceasing to be what she was and becoming some alien thing, but of being called into the fullness of her own being. We see not a foreign perfection forced upon her from the outside, nor yet some inevitable development deterministically built into her bones; we see a creature in pursuit of her own goodness as pronounced by her lover. He calls her forth, her eyes like doves' eyes, her breasts like twin roes among the lilies, and the smell of her garments like the smell of Lebanon — all the things she always could be but never was until they were spoken by him whose name is like ointment poured forth — and she says, Draw me, we will run after you. The king has brought me into his chambers; we will remember your love more than wine.

Admittedly, it is a long fetch from that to a workable application of the analogy to the way God moves the world. Just how the creatures who now lie in the Upper Devonian layer remembered a love more than wine is not obvious; perhaps it will always remain a mystery, sequestered in the mind of Teilhard's "omega point." All we will ever discover, even with great luck, are the mechanisms by which they moved. We will be able to say that the beloved rose up by placing most of her weight on her right leg and using her left arm to steady herself — and that, once up, she ran at a speed of eight miles per hour for a distance of three hundred feet. But the mystery to which she responded remains a mystery still; the ultimate explanation of her whole action is itself inexplicable. Once again, admittedly, no proof. But, once again, the scent of something great.

Do you see? What we really feel the need of when we talk about evolution is precisely the one thing physical science cannot supply: a final reason for it. Its day-to-day devices we may master; but the ultimate desire by which it works escapes us. Oh, I know. Using a word like *desire* for the force that moves the evolutionary process rubs you the wrong way. Nevertheless, I still think it's on the right track. First of all, because it is the only category that can let you have both a free world and a successful God without welshing on either. As I said, I am a theologian — that is, someone concerned to describe creation and God in words and images that do the least damage to all the facts. Desire, or something like it, is the only idea that does the job.

Just to take the curse off it, though, I should point out that it is neither my idea, nor is it new. It is an old notion that has, unfortunately, been out of fashion since the seventeenth century. As Owen Barfield pointed out, modern physical science has not been an unmixed blessing. Its earthiness, its particularism — its refusal to ask or answer sweeping teleological questions — enabled us finally to pay attention to things in themselves. But it cost us a view of the universe in which things responded to God by love.

When medieval woman went out on a starry night and looked up at the heavens, she saw, in one sense, just what you and I see in modern times: innumerable dots of light on a black background. But when she came to explain to herself *what it was* that she saw — that is, when she tried to *understand* what she was looking at — she came up with something very different from our understanding. To us, the heavenly bodies are discrete hunks of matter spinning through space in obedience to assorted laws such as inertia and gravitational attraction. To her, however, the stars and planets moved not in empty space but in a vast envelope that she called "mind" or "wisdom"; and they moved not in obedience to mute physical laws but by *desire* for the highest good. In other words, to her the planets were part and parcel of a world in which all things interacted and moved in hierarchy. The stars in the sky and the blood in her veins were both participants in a vast, harmonious, and, most important of all, loving universe.

It was just that view of the world which the tidal wave of modern science shattered. Needless to say, it was, in some ways, a view whose hold needed breaking. As long as you thought of blood, for example, as moved by desire within the hierarchy, there was not too much likelihood of your discovering the actual mechanism by which blood circulated within the body. Likewise, as long as you saw the planets moving around the earth in an envelope of wisdom, you were not inclined to raise the question of their actual orbits around the sun.

And yet. For all the benefits the scientific view brought us, it involved a devastating loss. The medieval universe was a friendly, rational, desiring — and desirable — place. The human beings who inhabited that universe felt at home and even important. They were there because of care. The modern universe is not so warm and toasty. It is huge, impersonal, and mute. There is no music of the spheres — only silent, mindless laws. We are not at home in such a universe; we are just insignificant pieces of stuff lost in a crowd of vastly bigger but equally insignificant pieces. After four hundred years we cower like skid-row bums on the doorstep of an indifferent creation. We long for a square meal and a kind word, but we're afraid to believe it when we hear it. Mention a universe run by desire for the Highest Good and, for all our loneliness, we can hardly bring ourselves to trust it.

But if we still believe in the real God as he revealed himself — and in the real world as science has displayed it — what else is there? If we're still committed to not going back on either proposition, why not give the old, participative, desiring universe a face-lift and put it to work once again? Why not try once more, for all our sophistication, to see the world as the beloved thing whose heart wakes even while it sleeps in the dawn of prehistory? Why not try to hear it rise up at the voice of its Beloved — at the calling of God the Son, who, with the Spirit and for the Father, woos it into being and life? Why not look once again for the Word who *fortiter suaviterque*, mightily and sweetly, orders all things — for creation's Love riding forth all in green and, upon the Virgin's fiat, coming down to be Jesu, Joy of Man's Desiring? It's not a case of substituting a mystery for a plausibility, only a matter of letting a lovely mystery take over from a mindless one. If there is even an outside possibility that there really are feet beautiful upon the mountains, what a shame it would be not to run after them!

5. *Time Out*

Time out at this point, however, for a bite of lunch.

The story of the Miller's Third Son was more apt than it first seemed. I've been leading you, along a path of analogies and concessions, into the doctrine of creation; the journey, however, begins to look more like a slowly winding descent into the bowels of Mystery itself. Not only are we getting farther and farther from the daylight of mere intelligibility; we are getting closer all the time to the smell of something dreadful down below in the dark. Somewhere along the line, the third peacock on the left had his way with us. While we still have a little light, therefore, and a halfway decent footing on the concept of a world run by desire, I suggest we sit down on this ledge and ease ourselves.

In the best stories, the standard bill of fare is, I believe, cold venison pie, a good red wine, a couple of apples, and some nuts; in any case, that, plus a little conversation, is what I have for you. Of course, if you are one of those sincere types whose conscience makes you eat sandwiches at your desk and work straight through the lunch hour, you had best skip to the next chapter. This theological lolling about in the middle of a quest will make you even more impatient with me than you already are. If, however, you are any kindred spirit at all, have a slice of venison pie and as many pulls on the jug as you like. Theology may be a necessary evil; but there is no excuse for earnestness at noontime.

Venison pie? It's one of the great alfresco delicacies. I have, ever since I put away childish things, made a firm rule: I will eat well-prepared indoor food outdoors, and suitably delicious outdoor food indoors; I will not, however, put myself in the double jeopardy of eating outdoor food outdoors. If I'm to suffer ants, spiders, dirt on my hands, and stones under my backside, I must have a touch of civilization to take the curse off it. I'm not so degenerate as to *insist* on the wicker basket and the red-and-white checkered cloth — just degenerate enough to be unalterably convinced that everything tastes better if you have them.

At any rate, venison pie is the archetypal pie that everything else is as easy as. You take a pie plate large enough to accommodate the remainder of your venison stew (which you have made with a good red-wine marinade plus some onions and mushrooms — but without potatoes, dumplings, carrots, parsnips, or rutabagas). Next you line the plate with plain pastry, put in the stew, add a top crust, crimp the edge, cut a *round* hole in the center, and bake till the pastry is nicely browned. You then cool it in the tin, wrap it in foil, and throw it in your knapsack. With a Cabernet, if you can afford it — or a four-liter jug of red plonk, if you can carry it — there is no sickness that destroyeth in the noonday against which you will not have at least a fighting chance. *In vino veritas. Prosit!*

It occurs to me, however, that this may be the first time you have ever had a drink with a dogmatic theologian. If that's the case, let me disabuse you of the prejudices you're more than likely to have. You see, while there have been some of our number who have been "dogmatic" in the pejorative sense of the word, the best of us are the most modest and tolerant people on earth. Contrary to common opinion, dogmaticians are not people who make up their minds first and then tailor the facts to suit their conclusions. They are theologians who accept — on the, to them, likely basis of faith — a number of facts, and who then proceed to tailor their theories accordingly. They are, in a word, the compulsive housekeepers of the church's intellectual apartment, the maids who modestly sweep up the room after everyone else has done his thing.

Permit me a slightly professional illustration. If you ask liturgical theologians (those gallingly authoritative types who tell you the proper way to worship) what is necessary for a valid celebration of the Lord's Supper, they will inform you that you need, among other things, an invocation of the Holy Spirit, or *epiclesis*. They arrive at that conclusion by observing that all the really dandy Christian liturgies have one. Dogmatic theologians, on the other hand, will tell you that all you need is Christ's words of institution, or something that refers to them. They arrive at their conclusion not by judging what makes the best liturgy but by canvassing all the liturgies that have been considered valid and striking the lowest common denominator. They are concerned not with achieving the ideal but with leaving as few invalid Masses as possible lying about in history. They are, in short, not idealogues but broad-minded citizens of the particular world they have chosen to inhabit.

And what is true in liturgy is true everywhere else. What dogmaticians say about the Trinity they say not because *hybris* has led them to think that they know what God is like, but because they are simply trying to keep track of a clutter of assertions about oneness and threeness. Their claim is not that they *understand* but that they *deliver* — not that you will finally be able to comprehend the contents of the package, only that there will be nothing missing when you get it.

In other words, it's paradox, not intelligibility, that is the hallmark of dogmatic theology. Observe: God is not man, and man is not God; nevertheless, Jesus is both God and man. Those, you will admit, are the assertions of someone who is concerned with more than neatly systematic theories — of a type of mind dedicated to providing you not with answers but with the raw materials that will enable you to ask the right questions. The best dogmaticians do not argue for the faith; they simply display it and let it fend for itself.

Which leads me to an important distinction. For a long time, apologetics — the art of presenting plausible arguments in favor of the faith — has been considered the absolute queen of theological disciplines. All nonbelievers, and most believers, have lived in the secret fear, or hope, that some hotshot apologist would one day produce the argument that would laugh the enemies of the Lord straight out of court. When you think about it, though, that isn't likely to happen. If the action of God is as mysterious as it seems, it probably isn't going to be susceptible of simple explanations. Waiting around for the light of intelligibility to go on is the guaranteed way to stay in the dark.

Accordingly, it has always seemed to me that the best apologetic of all is dogmatic theology itself: not an attempt at the explanation of things divine but a hunt for those analogies that will display the beast of the faith in all its oddness. That is why I said that the chief tests employed by dogmatic theologians are always aesthetic, not narrowly rational. They try to come to an appreciation of the given, not to an explanation of it; to a knowledge not of what it means but of how it feels. You can work a lifetime trying to make the Trinity intelligible and get nowhere; you can spend five minutes on it and begin to see its colors light up the world. If I had one piece of advice to bequeath to Christian theologians, it would be: Stick to the dogmatic last. We are, when all is said and done, only preachers of a word we have received. When we stand up on Easter morning and say, "Christ is risen!" we are not arguing for the abstract possibility of resurrection; we are simply announcing what was announced to us. We arrive in our several pulpits not as the bearers of proof but as the latest runners in a long relay race; not as savants with arguments to take away the doubts of the faithful but as breathless messengers who have only recently spoken to Peter himself: *The Lord is risen indeed* (gasp, gasp) *and has appeared* (pant, pant, pant) *to Simon!*

Have a little more wine and pass the jug.

The point is that once you master the true method of dogmatic theology, you become the most tolerant of all dispensers of doctrine. Admiration sets you free. Your only real work is to display paradox; after that you can take or leave anything. People rush up to you, for example, and ask for the Christian position on birth control; you find yourself liberated from the necessity of believing that there is a Christian position. Your arsenal of truths consists chiefly of the revealed doctrines of the faith (roughly, the Apostles' and Nicene Creeds — the assertions of which are all quite brief and fairly factual); after that, all other pronouncements are simply the opinions of assorted Christians. They may run from the *obiter dicta* of Harry in the fifth pew to the encyclicals of John Paul II, but none of them has quite the same stature as the statement that on the third day he rose again. You have, at long last, gotten out of the question-answering business and back into the Gospel-proclaiming business where you belong.

And what a relief that is! Most of the mischief in Christian theology is caused not by answers but by questions. When I was in seminary back in the bad old days, I came across a Roman tract about the Communion fast. It had been reprinted from one of those question-and-answer columns featured by pious magazines. It was signed "Disturbed." I don't remember the answerer's name, but it was undoubtedly something like Paschal O'Flaherty, O.F.M. Cap. "Disturbed" apparently had been lying awake nights wondering about possible sins against the pre-Communion fast as it was then practiced. His question was: May I still receive Communion if, prior to the Mass, I have a nosebleed and swallow some of the blood? Father O'Flaherty responded with a distinction: If the blood proceeds *out* of the nose and into the mouth, the fast is broken, and you should not receive; if it proceeds through the back of the nose and down the throat, the fast is not broken, and you may receive as usual.

It is almost my favorite illustration of bad theological method. As soon as you tell it to people, they break up. How ridiculous, they say! But think about it. What's wrong with the answer? It makes good sense. Since it is precisely *eating* that breaks the Communion fast — and since all ingestion is not necessarily eating — the answer makes a perfectly sensible distinction between supralabial and infraglottal ingestion. What is wrong is not the answer but the question. Father O'Flaherty's answer is not foolish; his folly lies in giving any answer at all. A good dogmatic theologian would have said something like "Oh, come now!" and changed the subject.

More pie?

I heard once of a bright young thing who walked out on an inquirers' class and never came back. It seems that an earnest type in the group had asked the priest whether there were any babies in heaven. The reverend gentleman replied, "No, everyone in heaven is thirty-three years old."

Again, a case not of a bad answer but of a dreadful question. If by "thirty-three" you mean what the ancients meant by it — namely, the symbolic age of maturity, the age of Christ in his fullness, the minimum signification of the Latin word *saeculum* — it makes excellent sense: God makes all things perfect in heaven; there will be no half-baked human beings there. If, however, you cannot count on that rather antiquated sophistication in your hearers, you had best recognize the question as a hopelessly high-flying canard and shoot at something more profitable. The only right dogmatic answer to it in this day and age is "I don't know, and neither does anybody else. Let's just say that if God can be trusted to bring heaven off at all, he can be trusted to do it nicely for all concerned."

What dogmatic theologians need above all, you see, is horse sense. Once they admit how little they really know, they can cut the ground out from under almost all their critics. For example, one of the commonest charges against theology is that human language about God is anthropomorphic and therefore, as far as God *in himself* is concerned, meaningless. The idea is that when I say God is loving or good or just or powerful, I'm simply extrapolating human qualities — that my God is nothing more than a hoked-up version of a human being.

The proper dogmatic answer to that is to concede the point. Of course I don't know what God is like *as God:* "No man hath seen God at any time," and all that sort of thing: "My ways are not your ways," saith the Lord. But if there is in fact an *analogy in being* between God and us, then human concepts may very well turn out to be analogous to the divine reality. The objector can, of course, reply, "Poppycock! Prove there is such an analogy in being." But the answer to that is "The human race has almost universally assumed it without proof. Darers go first. Prove there isn't one."

When I say that God *knows,* I am obviously using an analogy: I don't understand what the divine knowing is really like; I'm simply grappling for it with the only concept I have. But the same thing is true when I try to describe knowledge that's on a lower level than mine. When I say my dog *knows* something, I may, in my arrogance, presume that I'm expert about all the details of her knowing. But I'm really just as much in the dark about my dog as I am about God. She knows; yes, indeed. There is an analogy in being between her and me, and it works nicely. I spend time — and profitably — training her to know what I mean when I say "Fetch my slippers"; I do not, unless I'm an idiot, spend any time trying to train the ottoman to do likewise. But even when I have trained my dog to know, do I know *how* she knows? Am I in the least aware of what it is really like for her to *recognize* and *understand* on her own level? I would be an even bigger idiot if I thought I was.

Horse sense. Or dog sense. *All* human language about non-human things is anthropomorphic for the simple reason that the only talking animal we have so far discovered is dear old muddle-headed *anthropos*. If our language about God turns out to be invalid, it will be so not because it was human but because there was no God to talk about. If there actually is a God, however (and that, obviously, is another question), what we say about him is like what we say about everything else: it's a poking about in the dark by means of analogies. It may be tricky, but it's not necessarily false.

Have an apple.

There are lots of instances of the same thing. People object, for example, to the story of the ascension of Christ into heaven. They trot out all kinds of impressive stuff about how the ancients believed in a three-story universe in which heaven was really straight up. They point out that since we no longer believe in that kind of world — since we know that what's *up* here is really *down* in China — we have to demythologize the story and get back to some kernel of truth inside the disposable husk of first-century cosmography.

It sounds good, but it isn't even baloney, let alone venison pie. In the first place, no orthodox Catholic or biblical theology requires you to get Jesus farther than the first cloud. After that, you can do what you like. If you think heaven is just another ten thousand feet above his head, go ahead and think it. If you want to be sophisticated and say heaven has no spatio-temporal referent, go ahead and say that. It's an open ball game.

Secondly, the argument tries to have it both ways; it can be run through with its own sword. The objectors are quite willing to give the authors of the ascension story — Saint Luke, for instance — credit for *thinking up* a cleverly mythologized account of the basically indescribable mystery of Christ's exaltation. Why aren't they equally willing to give Christ credit for *acting it out?* I'll tell you why. Because they have a prejudice against miracles based not on modern cosmography but on nineteenth-century monistic materialism. The horse-sense answer to the whole problem is that if he's God, he can jolly well do what he wants. If he's not God, of course, we're stuck; but, once again, that's another question — and it has nothing to do with the particular brand of celestial mechanics you happen to buy.

You could multiply illustrations all afternoon. Just one more for good measure. People object to the idea that the Bible is the Word of God just because it is full of oddities, contradictions, and dunderheadedness. Admittedly, there have been theologians who tried to maintain that God literally wrote it all himself — or dictated it to infallible secretaries — and that all the riddles of Scripture were put in just to keep our faith on its toes. Well, if you like that theory, you're welcome to it; I happen to think it's rather unflattering to God. What seems more reasonable to me is to assume that God did indeed decide to come up with a bookful of words that would be his Word, but that when he cast about for some word-producing agents, he found that all he had arranged for in his infinite wisdom were human authors. Accordingly, he did whatever he did to inspire the several writers of Scripture and settled for what he got — or, better said, perhaps, he got what he wanted, plus a lot of other sometimes vivid writing that he took as part of the bargain: inflated census figures, rhapsodic reporting of sleazy royal carryings-on, and a fair amount of just plain wrong geography.

My theory about the divine inspiration of 1 Corinthians, for instance, is that God sized up Saint Paul on a particular evening and felt that this was the night to get him to tear off the definitive statement about the paradox of the divine power. Saint Paul, obedient to the inspiration of the Spirit, promptly responded with chapter one in all its glory: the foolishness of God that was wiser than men, the weakness of God that was stronger than men, and the absolute centrality of the Passion of Christ to the divine management of history. In the process, however, he also produced a rather feebleminded list of people he thought he remembered baptizing — and followed it up with three chapters full of sexual hang-ups and a couple of pages of absolute waffling on the subject of speaking in tongues. First Corinthians has sixteen chapters not, I think, because Saint Paul neatly rounded off his argument at that number but because God, taking pity on subsequent generations of commentators, inspired him at that point to go to bed.

Be that as it may, however, my own inspiration is to pack up the remains of lunch and get back on the road. It has not, perhaps, been a total loss: wine is always more pleasantly carried in the stomach than on the back, there is a slice of pie left for later, and you have had the benefit, if it is that, of hearing me explain some of the theological assumptions I have so far foisted on you. In any case, there are still nuts to eat while we walk.

Onward and downward . . .

6. Into the Divine Complicity

. . . into the divine complicity in the nightmare at the bottom of the world.

We had a brush with it right at the beginning of the book: the fact that there is no possibility, in this kind of world, of getting badness out of the act of creation. If both chicken hawks and chickens proceed from the delight of the Trinity, then God is the author of badness as well as goodness. But we woke ourselves up before the worst part of the dream by blaming it all on freedom. We said that freedom is marvelously heady stuff even if it is a pain in the neck.

It wasn't a bad way of shaking off the terror by night the first time around, but it won't work now. Once you've got to the point of seeing the world as run by desire for the overwhelming attractiveness of God — and once you have more than just a pain in the neck to cope with — you want an answer that recognizes the outrageousness of it all, not just an intellectual fast shuffle with a fairy-tale deck. If God draws the world by desire — if the creative Word is really *romancing* into being not only chicken hawks but cancer cells, brain tumors, and all the pestilences that walk in the darkness — then he is guilty of something more than a merely laissez-faire attitude toward freedom, of simply tolerating what goes wrong and shrugging it off with an "Oh, things will be things." He is guilty of irresponsible and indiscriminate flattery. He romances the chicken hawk and the chicken at the same time; he sings the praises not only of the beloved child but of the tumor that slowly

[216]

destroys her sanity. In other words, God is a two-timer; half of his creation is always sitting up nights and crying its eyes out.

Follow that down. As with all two-timers, it's not so hard on the lover as it is on the beloved. God doesn't suffer the consequences. First of all, since he knows everything *eternally* — since both the oldest star and the newest, shortest-lived beta particle have been in his mind as long as he has had a mind — he never has to worry about losing any of the goodnesses he calls into being. Poor little old creatures may not enjoy their participation in the creative bash for very long, but as far as God is concerned the party goes on forever.

Secondly, since he keeps his own participation in his creatures on a strictly spiritual and highfalutin level (God, classically, is neither part of nor connected to creation), no thinnest skin ever comes off the divine nose, no matter how many barroom brawls and knife fights creation gets into. He does indeed behold the gore along with the goodness, but it's creation, not God, that feels the crunch. Maybe it even bothers him. But it's still hard to feel very sorry for *him*.

(That, by the way, is what's really wrong with oriental-style religions of indifference — the kind that carry on about God writing straight with crooked lines and using good and bad as if they were just different-colored threads. It's all very well if you're God, or if you're one of those altogether admirable types who can spend a lifetime meditating your way into some nirvana that approximates the divine indifference. But if you're just a common garden slob who cries all night because they have taken away your beloved and you know not where they have laid him, then frankly it looks like a sellout to a con job: the great eternal cat lecturing the mice on the beauties of being eaten, and the mice lining up in the streets to fill the hall. Once again, the only thing that feels right is to cry out against it all like Job: We're your creatures, dammit; we've got *some* rights, haven't we?)

In short, while it's just barely possible, by fabricating an ersatz divinity, to tolerate the divine complicity in badness *metaphysically*, it remains unacceptable *aesthetically*. You may philosophize your way into thinking that goodness is worth the risk; but in a world where half of creation is always on the rack, the only thing you can *feel* is that no risk could ever be worth this badness.

Once again, therefore, no answer; and once again, down a little farther.

Our resentment has complex roots. It goes beyond the easily explained distaste that the chicken has for the chicken hawk's advances. Nothing enjoys being killed. After the kill, however, the chicken's own goodness, so recently enjoyed, ceases to be much of a problem for chickendom. True enough, a few chicks may, for a while, retain some sensitive memory of their mother's wings, but even that passes. The situation is tolerable. God has his eternal knowledge of the chicken in all its goodness, and the chickens don't have long enough memories to give them anything but a short-term problem with pain.

It's memory, you see, that puts the sting in our knowledge of badness. God is lucky: he never loses a thing. The chickens are equally lucky: they lose everything. But we are just enough of a mixture of God and chicken to be able to hang on to the worst of both worlds. We haven't got God's divinely intellectual eternal referent of the beloved child before the brain tumor, but we do have a clear memory of a beautiful eight-year-old — a poignant knowledge of what the child's true goodness was really like. Coupled with that, however, we have the actual presence of a deranged child. If we were more divine — or less — it wouldn't be so bad; as it is, it's horrible. It's precisely the remembered goodness that becomes a burr under the saddle of our mind. We run wild intellectually. We lose sight of any possible balance between goodness and badness and call all things meaningless. Things once sweet in our mouth grow bitter in our belly. That we once conversed lovingly with this now alien mind is carrion comfort. The only sane thing we can think of is to curse the day in which we were born and the night in which we were conceived. Why was not sorrow hid from our eyes? Why did the knees receive us? or why the breasts, that we should suck? Only the grave makes sense, where the wicked cease from troubling and the weary are at rest. It is death that we long for, that we dig for more than for hid treasures. Our sighing comes before we eat; our roarings are poured out like the waters. We were not in safety, neither had we rest, neither were we quiet; yet trouble came: the arrows of the Almighty, the poison that drinks up the spirit, the terrors of God. In the end, though, we do grow quiet. Our once-glad eye surveys the divine banquet of creation and gives the final withering word: *It has no more taste than the white of an egg.*

No answer, again. But this time we have finally hit bottom.

▼   ▼   ▼

What shall we say now about the divine complicity?

I've already warned you that I'm not an apologist but a dogmatician — that I'm committed not to explaining anything but to hefting it long enough to see what it feels like. For me, therefore, the question is not whether all this can be justified. I suppose it can't be. What I want to get at is the more modest question of whether God has in fact (that is, in his revelation) addressed himself to the problem at all. We may indeed feel like throwing him out of court; nevertheless, if only for the sake of being fairer to him than he is to us, one more look at his announced plan for the management of this losing proposition won't hurt. If it fails to butter his parsnips, so much the worse for him; at least it isn't going to break any more of our bones than already lie scattered before the pit.

The first thing to say is that there's no question but that he has actually promised to make a good show of creation. Quite apart from the subtleties and the paradoxes of the New Testament — which, for all their underhandedness, still end up with the King of Kings riding in on a white charger to make creation his bride without spot or wrinkle — there is the Old Testament, with God himself actually showing up in history every now and then to part a Red Sea or cater a quail dinner.

But what an embarrassment it all turns out to be! Time and again, he fosters the hope of help by the promise of help: "Ask, and you shall receive; knock, and it shall be opened to you." "The Lord whom you seek shall suddenly come." But he doesn't come dependably enough to keep the hope going. All the advertisements of his help sit squarely against a constant landscape of situations in which no help ever comes — and for which there probably is no help, anyway: of battles that the Philistines are bound to win, of impossibilities that even God is not about to convert, and of inexorabilities like death that not even the resurrection of Christ makes a dent in.

If he does help, therefore — if we are to try to believe him in spite of the evidence — how on earth does he do it? Do we have any analogy that might shed light on a divine succor that, as far as anyone can see, makes not one material whit of difference to the creatures he promises to rescue?

Go back a little to the concept of a *desiring* universe, created by the attractiveness of God as God, falling upward like a ton of infatuated bricks for the sheer flattery of the Word. The beauty of that comparison was that it was personal, not mechanical. It saved the freedom of creatures because it allowed us to see God not as *doing* something — not as meddling, pushing, and shoving — but as *being someone fetching.* It gave us not a divine watchmaker but a divine lover. Try it again here.

In the Christian scheme of things, the ultimate act by which God runs and rescues creation is the Incarnation. Sent by the Father and conceived by the Spirit, the eternal Word is born of the Virgin Mary and, in the mystery of that indwelling, lives, dies, rises, and reigns. Unfortunately, however, we tend to look on the mystery mechanically. We view it as a fairly straight piece of repair work that became necessary because of sin. Synopsis: the world gets out of whack; perverse and foolish, oft it strays until there is none good, no, not one. Enter therefore God with incarnational tool kit. He fixes up a new Adam in Jesus and then proposes, through the mystery of Baptism, to pick up all the fallen members of the old Adam and graft them into Christ. Real twister of an ending: as a result of sin, humanity ends up higher by redemption than it would have by creation alone.

However venerable that interpretation is, though, it is not the only one. As long ago as the Middle Ages, the Scotist school of Franciscan theologians suggested another. They raised the question of whether the Incarnation would have occurred apart from sin; and they answered yes. In other words, they saw the action of God in Christ not as an incidental patching of the fabric of creation but as part of its very texture. For our purposes — in this context of a world run by desire for God — that opens up the possibility that the Word in Jesus was not so much *doing* bits of busy work to jimmy things into line as he was *being* his own fetching self right there in the midst of creation.

And there you have the bridge from a mechanical to a personal analogy to the divine help. When we say that a friend "helped" us, two meanings are possible. In the case where our need was for a Band-Aid, a gallon of gas, or a push on a cold morning, we have in mind mechanical help, help for times when help was at least possible. But when nothing can be helped, when the dead are irretrievably dead and the beloved lost for good, what do we mean by telling Martha how much help she was to us in our need? She *did* nothing: she rescued no one from the pit, she brought no one back from the ends of the earth. Still, we are glad of her; we protest that without her we would never have made it. Yet we know perfectly well we could have gotten through it just by breathing in and out. That means, therefore, that what we thank her for is precisely *personal* help. It was her presence, not the things she did, that made the difference.

So with God, perhaps. Might not Incarnation be his response not to the incidental irregularity of sin but to the unhelpable presence of badness in creation? Perhaps in a world where, for admittedly inscrutable reasons, *victimization* is the reverse of the coin of being, his help consists in his continuous presence in all victims. At any rate, when he finally does show up in Jesus, that is how it seems to work. His much-heralded coming to put all things to rights ends badly. When the invisible hand that holds the stars finally does its triumphant restoring thing, it does nothing at all but hang there and bleed. That may well be help; but it's not the Band-Aid that creation expected on the basis of mechanical analogies. The only way it makes any sense is when it's seen as personal: when we are helpless, there he is. He doesn't start your stalled car for you; he comes and dies with you in the snowbank. You can object that he should have made a world in which cars don't stall; but you can't complain he doesn't stick by his customers.

Nevertheless, being broad-minded, Jesus is blithely paradoxical — or inconsistent, if you like. He reserves the right to start your car for you at such times and places as you and he can work out in conference. Have mercy on me, son of David, says the woman of Canaan; and after a little verbal fencing and a few good ripostes, her daughter is made whole from that very hour. It's exasperating. Tidy minds would find Jesus easier to take if he never helped at all. If he's going to make a principle out of victimization, why does he shilly-shally around with occasional answers to prayer?

Once again, it's the mechanical analogy that makes the mischief. Answers to prayers for help are a problem only when you look on God as a divine vending machine programmed to dispense Cokes, Camels, lost keys, and freedom from gall-bladder trouble to anyone who has the right coins. With the personal analogy, things are better. The Word is like Martha: Given the circumstances — given the kind of free world he has chosen to make — he will do the best he can by you. It isn't that he has a principle about not starting cars — or about starting them. What he has a principle about is *you*. Like Martha, he loves you; his chief concern is *to be himself for you*.

And since he is God, that is no small item. His presence in the victims of the world — his presence in the cases where even *his* best is none too good — is still the presence of the Word who romances all things into being. Stuck out there in the snowdrift, you may feel that he should be doing something more than just trying to make out at a time like this, but he obviously doesn't see it that way. He knows the home truth that grief and love-making are only inches apart. In his own dying, while he hangs helpless on the cross, he still, as the eternal Word, flatters nails into being nails, wood into being wood, and flesh into being flesh. Love is as strong as death; there may be waters God does not overcome, but there are no waters that can drown the loving of the Word.

One important refinement, however. People sometimes get the impression that the Incarnation showed up for the first time rather late in the history of the world — that it was not only a patch job, but a patch job after awful and irretrievable damage had been done. Once again, though, it's not as simple as that. There are all kinds of hints that the Incarnate Word is not a late intruder, but rather that he is somehow coterminous and contemporaneous with the whole history of creation.

First of all, there is the fact that for God, at least, the Incarnation cannot possibly have been an afterthought. He has no afterthoughts. He didn't one day decide to create and then the next day decide to become incarnate. In his customary eternal style, he always thought of both. Secondly, even the Creed, for all its brevity, suggests that Christ, by "descending into hell," was in some way dealing with those who weren't lucky enough to be born A.D. — that his redemption was somehow available to all of creation right from the start. Finally, there is the witness of the passages that deal with what is usually called the "cosmic" rather than the simply time-bound Christ: Christ the Rock that followed the Israelites in the wilderness; Christ the Lamb slain from the foundation of the world; even Christ the one foreordained *before* the foundation of the world.

His incarnate presence, then, is the presence of the Mystery of the Word in all victimization. But, because this is a temporal world — and because in a temporal world no mystery is ever visible except under a sign — God sacramentalizes the Incarnation. He presents it under a supreme and effective sign in Jesus. The only way to keep track of an invisible man is to put a hat on his head — or in this case, a crown of thorns. Jesus is neither other than nor a reversal of what the Word does at all times throughout the fabric of creation. He is the Mystery of the Word himself in the flesh. His cross, therefore, is no accident; it is the sacrament of the shared victimization by which he has always drawn all things to himself.

To be sure, in the end he allows himself one success. He rises from the dead. For one morning — and for forty confused days — he takes his hand off the mystery of his working and says, "There! I meant every word I said. The party will come off. Lion and lamb, wolf and kid, will all lie down together. Victimizer and victim will eat at my supper. They shall not hurt or destroy in all my holy mountains. I will wipe away all tears from their eyes." And then, as the apostles stand dumbfounded on the hilltop, he disappears. He claps his hand back over the Mystery and says, "But not yet. I have the keys of hell and death, but till the end, I am as good as dead for you. You will meet me in the Passion — in the heart of badness where I have always been. Together, we will make up what remains of my sufferings; in the agony of all victims we will draw the world into the City of God."

From there on, Mystery reigns absolutely. It is, I grant you, such an incredible piece of business that no one can be faulted for not believing it. There is no proof, only odd signs that are even more obscure than Jesus himself: a little water, a little bread, a little wine. But if you decide to believe it, what must be done is clear enough: you tend the signs and adore the Mystery as best you can; you join your victimization to his; and you say, Jesus, I love you, I love you, till you finally run out of breath.

And then . . .

If it should all happen to be true . . .

7. *The Hat on the Invisible Man*

. . . the hat on the invisible man will have been the very thing that brought us home at last. Or, to update what we used to say back in the days when we were more barefaced about it all: JESUS (as the sacrament of the Word) SAVES; Outside the Church (because it is the sacrament of Jesus) There Is No Salvation; and even, Ten Thousand Cheers for the Pope! (duly collegialized, of course).

I'm aware that you may have a violent reaction to the turn I've just executed. Some nerve! you say. He quotes Job, knocks God, drags us down to the bottom of the pit — and then has the gall to slip in a plug for organized religion! A fine guide he turned out to be!

By way of a soft answer to your wrath, let me point out that I'm not your guide — or anybody else's, for that matter. I'm simply one of the travelers trapped with you in the bowels of creation. We are all, like the Miller's Third Son, equally in need of a guide. My contribution to our mutual journey has simply been to direct your attention to a peculiar cocked hat bobbing along just ahead of us in the darkness and to suggest that if there is indeed an invisible man under it, he might turn out to be useful — especially if he knows how to get us out of the spot we're in.

For a slightly firmer answer, I have a choice of two different lines of argument. On the one hand, I can deny the charge. "Organized religion" is a misnomer. The church — anybody's version of it — may look fearsomely organized from the outside, but once you're in it, you have to be deaf, dumb, and blind to avoid the conclusion that it's the most disorganized venture ever launched. Its public image may be that of a mighty lion on the prowl; what it really is, in this day and age at least, is a clowder of uncoordinated pussycats falling all over each other.

On the other hand, I can let your accusation stand and make a useful distinction: the church is obviously not totally disorganized. At various times in history it has been clever enough to get itself into the teaching business, the building business, the real-estate business, the law-enforcement business, the government business, and the witch-hunting business. Its real business, however, was never any of those things. If I'm on the right track, the principal function of the church is to be the sign of the Mystery of the Word — which is precisely what we mean when we call the church the *mystical* Body of Christ. The principal function of its members, therefore, is the tending of those particular bits of felt and ribbon by which the church can be recognized as the hat it is supposed to be — specifically, and to be brief about it, the Scriptures and the sacraments.

Obviously, it is not the easiest thing in the world to be content with such a vocation. The church could, with perfect propriety, be what it once was: a bunch of landless nobodies who met in caves. Its bishops, priests, and deacons (whom I take to be essential ribbons on the hat) could be tax collectors, tentmakers, and fishermen, and still be the signs of the Mystery they were intended to be. Nobody was under any theological necessity to put them on salary or to build them nifty buildings to do their mystical signifying in. Human nature being what it is, however, it was quickly noted that if there was no need for such gussying up, neither was there any theological objection to it. A priest in sneakers saying Mass in a basement is not *more* of a sign of the Mystery than a priest in a gold chasuble consecrating the wine in a diamond-encrusted chalice. Accordingly, once it was realized that gold, diamonds, and property might go begging, and that pension plans, fringe benefits, and annual increments were not necessarily sinful, the church jumped gleefully into the assorted business opportunities that offered themselves. (It jumped into some sordid ones too, but that's neither here nor there. We're above *that* kind of argument.)

In spite of all such goings-on, however, the subject of organized religion has got to come up at this point. If the working of God in both creation and Incarnation is a mystery — that is, if it is always radically invisible — then there is no sense in our getting snootily spiritual about its obvious need for some down-to-earth manifestations. Either God left us to our own guesswork about the spiritualities he was up to, or he didn't. If he didn't, then he had to give us at least a few materialities to provide us with an intellectual handhold. No doubt his originally sparse signs have been multiplied and embroidered; but there doesn't seem to be any way of cooking up a decent version of the Gospel that dispenses with them altogether. If God is doing anything more than just sitting up in heaven and handing out free advice — if he really is *doing* something down here that he intends to let us in on — then, by the necessities of our nature and his, he is forced into sacramentalizing it.

In other words, there can never be a completely spiritual version of the Christian religion. Not that it hasn't been attempted. There have always been itchy souls in the church who are allergic to materiality. For example, you find Christians who argue that if the deepest reality of the Eucharist is the presence of Jesus himself, then the signs of bread and wine are mere symbols that can be switched around at our pleasure. Beer and pretzels, or crackers and milk, will do just as well.

Their fallacy stems from forgetting that the sacraments are precisely hats on an invisible man. To be sure, if the Word had decided to wear a beer-and-pretzel hat instead of a bread-and-wine hat, he would have been perfectly within his rights: it's his head and his hat. But once he has announced that the bread-and-wine hat is his choice for the late afternoon of the world, we had best keep a careful eye on *that*. It is, after all, the only one under which we *know* he has promised to make himself available.

Needless to say, he's also available and active everywhere else: you can look up the invisible man on the golf course any time you like. That's not the point. The problem on the golf course is that it's hard to be sure you've got hold of the right invisible man — or, indeed, of anything more than one of your own bright ideas. It's not a question of presence; it's a question of how to know when you've grasped it. If I'm right, for example, the Mystery that the Eucharist signifies is present throughout creation; the Incarnate Word does not become *more present* at the Mass than he is elsewhere. What happens at the consecration is that his presence is sacramentalized for us under a device of his own choosing. We have his assurance for the device of bread and wine; the best you can say about beer and pretzels is maybe — which you could just as well say about ducks, dogs, or dandelions.

Once again, the mischief is caused by mechanical analogies. Most of the bad trips in eucharistic theology have been caused by attempting to explain how, in the consecration, God "confects" something new. If we resort to a personal analogy, however, things are less gross. On that basis we assert not that God *does* something he never did before on land or sea, but rather that he *bees* (forgive the barbarism; English has always needed a more aggressive word than *is*) — that he *bees* what he has always been, but under a special sign.

The sacraments, accordingly, are not mere representations; they are the very realities the church has always claimed they were: the Holy Communion is Jesus himself, really and effectively; Baptism is the power of God grafting us into Christ; the ordained priesthood is none other than the priesthood of the Word himself. The sacraments, however, do not have an exclusivity in these things. The priesthood the priest bears is not something the layperson lacks: if Baptism gives us the fullness of Christ, there is nothing left for ordination to *add*. Rather, the sacramental priesthood is an effective sign, a notable outcropping, of what the whole church has. It is every Christian's invisible priesthood packaged and labeled for easy use. Likewise, at the Eucharist, Jesus does not show up in a room from which he was absent. The eucharistic "change," it seems to me, is neither a quantitative nor even, properly, an ontological matter. It's qualitative — a clear but subtle shift in God's style that makes it possible, under the form of an occasional meal, for his creatures effectively to take the Word's constant mystery of victimization and victory into their ordinary exchanges.

It is when you come to Baptism, however, that this line of reasoning bears the best fruit. The church has always had a problem explaining its relationship to the world. By far the commonest view is the Noah's Ark theory: The human race is out there bobbing around in the drink. Nobody can touch bottom; they all just tread water till they drown. Up over the horizon sails the Ark of Salvation. Much bustle. Cries of "Man overboard!" and "Heave to!" Apostles, Martyrs, Popes, Confessors, Bishops, Virgins, and Widows lean over the sides with baptismal boat-hooks and haul the willing ones up over the gunwales. Assorted purblind types, however, refuse to come aboard. Sensible arguments are offered to them, but there are no takers. After a just interval, the Captain orders full speed ahead and, swamping the finally impenitent in his wake, heads the church for the ultimate snug harbor.

The trouble with that view, and with many another more refined, is that it forces you to limit the Incarnate Word's saving activity to the church. No doubt the church is the only place where you can be sure (by means of easily recognized sacramental hats) that you have a firm grip on what he's doing; but it doesn't seem right to imply that he isn't doing the same work everywhere else. I, if I be lifted up, says Jesus, will draw *all* unto me. *God* invented the ecumenical movement — and his version of it is not limited to Christians. The relationship between the baptized and the unbaptized is not a case of us versus them. The church is like the rest of the sacraments, an effective sign — a notable outcropping — of what all people already are by the Word's work of creation and Incarnation. The church is the mystical body because humanity is the mystical body. The only difference is that in church the Mystery wears a hat on its head. (Yes, Virginia, that is why a Christian lady always keeps her head covered in church: Saint Paul said a hat was power on her head because of the angels. You and I are the first people in history to have figured out what he meant.)

If you would like a little more serious documentation, consider the Christian teaching about the resurrection of the dead. If Christ dwelt and worked only in the baptized, you would expect that the unbaptized would be out of it completely. In fact, however, the promise that the dead will rise is surprisingly indiscriminate. At the Second Coming, *all* are given risen bodies; only *after* the General Resurrection are the lucky sheep separated from the uncooperative goats. Admittedly, you could argue that the entire business applies only to the baptized, but I don't think you can make it stick. It hardly seems consistent either with the divine justice or with the Word's drawing of all to himself to hand some baptized *schlemiel* a risen body after a lifetime spent as a nogoodnik and then to deny one to a real *mensch* just because he spent his days inside the Warsaw ghetto at the insistence of the baptized. (Don't overinterpret. I'm not saying that anyone is saved apart from Christ. I still buy outright Jesus' statement, "No one comes to the Father but by me." All I'm saying is that the work of Christ is wider than the sacramental manifestations by which it can be grasped. You may, in other words, be able to make it without Baptism; but you'll never make it without the Incarnate Word.)

Even that isn't as bizarre as it sounds. Right from the start, the church was confronted with the problem of saying something about good converts who unfortunately died before they were baptized. The problem was solved by the invention of the categories of Baptism of Desire (for those who died in their beds) and Baptism of Blood (for those who were helped into the larger life by Nero, Diocletian, and Company). It's only a short step from such an accommodation to the wider one I have suggested: Who's to say, since the loveliness of the Word draws all, that desire is possible only for those who have a conscious yen to become Episcopalians or Presbyterians? Who can limit the efficacy of his shared victimization when blood is being shed all over the world? Every year, on December 28, the church honors as saints all the little Jewish boys whom Herod killed while attempting to put the Incarnate Word out of business. Are we seriously prepared to rule out the possibility that, since the Word is still very much in business, there may be innumerable other innocents who might yet be holy on the same basis?

The upshot of all this is to refocus our attention on the church's true vocation. Perhaps it's time for it to retire from most of the plausible businesses it has been in for years and to start thinking about its real work as the sacrament of the Mystery of the Word. Perhaps it ought to stop justifying its pretension that it is the world's finest question-answering machine and the human race's chief of moral police, and accept the fact that things are a little more obscure and tricky than the Roman Curia, the Episcopalian Mini-Vatican, and the New York Conference of the United Methodist Church have so far seemed willing to admit.

In any case, one thing is certain: there's no point in trying to get all those cantankerous bureaucracies back together under the aegis of a greater bureaucracy still. The only useful thing for the church to do is join forces with God's already-operative ecumenical movement and learn again how to be a really clear sign of the Passion of the Word. For openers, this means rediscovering the Eucharist as the mirror of its true face; but that's only a start. After that, it probably means a whole new style of life — more care about *being* and less faith in *doing* — and a lot more humility in the process of opening its inevitably bureaucratic but so often unnecessarily flannel mouth.

▼   ▼   ▼

To all of this, two major objections can be raised. The first is that it's unethical — that it's dangerously indifferent to the prescriptive aspect of the Gospel — that it will lead the church to stop telling people where to head in and so encourage the world to aim straight for the rocks. To which the first response is: Don't kid yourself. Unless you've been asleep since the Middle Ages at least, you must have noticed that the world listens to the church with somewhat less than eager ears. It *likes* the rocks; find something better to tell it, or don't waste your breath.

The second response is more weighty. For the church to continue to act as if it were a kind of moral cop on the beat is to run the risk of perverting the Gospel. What I have suggested sounds immoral because God himself sounds immoral. Most of our journey in this book has been an attempt to get around the divine complicity in badness; but really, there never was much chance of success. And when Jesus finally appears as the ultimate sacrament of the Word, he doesn't help matters a bit. Parable after parable is deliberately designed to offend even the most elementary moral sense: full pay for workers who didn't earn it, and expensive parties for boys who blew their fathers' money on booze and broads.

Our trouble is that we've so long let ourselves be convinced that the Ten Commandments are the whole story that we're deaf to the outrageousness of the Gospel. The Ten Commandments are only what they are: ethical prescriptions — and negative ones at that. Even put positively, they have no more virtue than any other ethical propositions: they are true comments on the facts of life, valid expositions of the laws of human nature. The law of gravity is a useful observation too. It tells you that if you jump off the Brooklyn Bridge, you will pick up enough speed between the railing and the river to do yourself a probably fatal mischief. But it doesn't tell you whether jumping is a good idea or a bad one. That has to be determined another way: If you want to end it all, it's not a bad idea; if you want to get home to dinner, you think less well of it.

Likewise with ethical pronouncements. It's perfectly correct to say that truth-telling is good for human nature and that hating is bad for it. The comment is even slightly useful: if you care about keeping your human nature intact, you will avoid lying and try your best to love. But there are two important questions ethics cannot answer. The first is why you should want to keep yourself in tip-top human shape; and the second is what truths to tell and which people to love. The answer to the first depends on whether or not you think anybody is crazy about you. The answer to the second depends entirely on good taste.

Accordingly, we do both ourselves and the world a disservice when we imply that ethical strictures, if followed, will make people glad and wise. What they need to hear from us is that the Word loves the world enough to join it in its passion — and that he has exquisitely good taste. They have absolutely no need for a rescue team that stands on the beach and bores suicides with the news that they're drowning. They already knew that; what they really want to hear is some reason why they shouldn't go ahead and sink. Their life tastes like the white of an egg; only a church that knows what it means to be the body of the life-giving Word can possibly be salty enough to interest them.

Which brings us to a second major objection, based on the fear of quietism. To urge the church to concentrate on *being* the body of the Mystery — and to denigrate the usefulness of all the more or less plausible things it constantly *does* — is to run the risk of having it do nothing at all. Are we simply to return to the bad old days when, in the blissful assurance of salvation, we told the poor that their poverty was a blessing and justified the deaths of child laborers on the grounds that they were lucky not to have to spend any more time in this vale of tears?

No. The day-to-day actions of the mystical body may not be terribly useful — they may in fact be downright mischievous — but they are absolutely inevitable. The whole mixed bag of clever schemes, bright ideas, and gross stupidities is all we have. To be the body of the Mystery is to be the body of something you cannot take in hand as such. Accordingly, you take in hand what you can and then relax and trust the Mystery to work through you.

Ah, but! you say. That leaves us with nothing more than meaningless busy work.

No again. Precisely because the church is the body of the creating Word — of the Word who, in the fullness of his delight, romances all things into being — even its minor gestures, even its failures, must spring from a love for what he loves. It does not stay in the slums, work for the abolition of poverty, or lobby for civil-rights legislation just because there's nothing better to do. The church does it because the Word's body must affirm the goodnesses that the Word himself affirms — and if they are threatened, it must come to the defense of the victims in whom he suffers. The church's campaigns are not always successes; there are more helpless cases than not; and, saddest of all, its cures are frequently worse than the diseases it sets out to treat. But it cannot sit idly by. Come down ere my child die, says the world: if Jesus was moved to compassion by that cry, the church can do no less than second the motion.

It is not passivity that mirrors the Passion of the Word; it is the act of loving in the midst of the desperate helplessness of the world. Quietism is only a parody of victimization; resignation is a door into an empty house. The true Christ does not just stand and wait; he butts his head against the impossibilities until they crucify him; and then, having opened the door of the Passion, he invites the church into the deepest mystery of all.

8. The Rest of Our Journey

The rest of our journey, once we have passed through that door in the bottom of the world, is predictably unpredictable. The Miller's Third Son, following the cocked hat in the gloom, has no idea where he is going or what will happen next. Everyone who reads the story, however, knows that, whatever happens, he will make home safely. Mystery may never stop being mystery; but the happy ending comes on willy-nilly.

It can be argued that the whole business is just an elaborate game of wishing-will-make-it-so. There are answers to that. The first is the old anti-reductionist one-two punch: How do you know that this elaborate game of wishing-will-make-it-so is not the divine device for clueing us in on what, in fact, really is so?

The second is to trot out Pascal's "wager": No matter what happens, we're going to have to wander around down here in the dark of badness as long as we live; why not take a chance on the invisible guide? If he's for real, you win hands down; if not, you only lose what you had to lose anyway. It's a proposition no true gambler would refuse: the worst you can do is break even.

The third answer goes one step further: even if the invisible guide turns out to be the little man that wasn't there, he sounds nicer than the Crown Prince of the Salamanders. If the whispered love of the Word is a lie, it is at least more appealing than all the ghastly truths we have to put up with.

In the long run, though, who really cares about smart answers? On both sides of the fence, everyone whose head is threaded on straight knows there's no possibility of proving or disproving these things. What we think of them is always decided on the basis of taste. If you find something fetching about the idea of the Word making love to creation in the midst of its passion, you take to it; if not, you call a spade a spade and brand the whole thing a fraud, a fool's promise to do everything someday by doing nothing now.

But what you *do* about it all is another question. The world commonly assumes that the faithful are uniformly delighted, everywhere and always, by the faith. That's partly because they have never paid proper attention to the book of Job, and partly because the faithful are sometimes a bunch of fakers who refuse to admit their doubts. There are always days when honest Christians will feel that the promises of the Gospel are just so much incredible baloney. Even when they try to catch the last handhold — the *fact* of the resurrection of Jesus — it gives way, and they see it only as the delusion of a handful of peasants, inflated to cosmic proportions by a tentmaker with excess intellectual energy.

But what they *think* has nothing to do with what they *do*.

Ah, you say, intellectual dishonesty!

No. Or yes. It doesn't matter. You forget what kind of proposition we're dealing with. There's no harm in thinking I'm on the wrong bus when, in fact, I'm on the right one — as long as I don't talk myself into getting off the bus. We have been offered a guide who says he can bring us home; either he can or he can't. But what I think about him has nothing to do with *his* competence. I may believe in him with all my heart; if he's a fraud, it gets me nowhere. Or I may doubt him absolutely; if he really knows the way, I can still get home by following him.

You have failed to distinguish between *faith,* which is a decision to act as if you trusted somebody, and *confidence,* which is what you have if, at any given moment, you feel good about your decision. It's probably not possible to have confidence without faith; but it certainly is possible to act in faith when you haven't a shred of confidence left. Intellectual honesty is a legitimate hint for your own mental housekeeping; it has no effect whatsoever on things that already are what they are.

I suggest, therefore, that we stop this bickering and think about something more pleasant. We still have a long way to go. Have the last piece of venison pie while I tell you a classroom story.

When I teach dogmatic theology, I try to set up the faith on the same framework I've used in this book: the Trinity creating the world out of sheer fun; the Word romancing creation into being and becoming incarnate to bring it home; Jesus as the sacrament of the Word; and the church as the sacrament of Jesus. Having done that, I then ask the crucial question: How does the story actually end?

Invariably, I get all the correct but dull answers: The Word triumphs; creation is glorified; the peaceable kingdom comes in. And I say, Yes, yes; but how does the story *actually* end? The class looks at me for a while as if I were out of my mind, and then offers some more of the same: The Father's good pleasure is served; humanity is taken up into the exchanges of the Trinity. And I say again, Yes; but how does the story end *in fact?*

No answer. I try another tack: *Where* does the story end? Still no answer. All right, I say, I'll give you a hint: Where can you *read* the end of the story? And eventually someone says: In the book of Revelation — but who understands that?

I'm not asking you to understand it, I say. I just want to know what you read there. What is the last thing that happens?

And, slowly and painfully, it finally comes out: *The New Jerusalem comes down from heaven to be the Bride of the Lamb.*

They never see it till they fall over it! It's the oldest story on earth: boy meets girl; boy loses girl; boy gets girl! He marries her and takes her home to Daddy. The Word romances creation till he wins her: *You are beautiful, O my love, as Tirzah, comely as Jerusalem, terrible as an army with banners.* By his eternal flattery, he makes new heavens and a new earth; the once groaning and travailing world becomes Jerusalem, the bride without spot or wrinkle. And finally, as she stands young and lovely before him, he sets her about with jewels, and she begins the banter of an endless love: Jasper, sapphire, a chalcedony, an emerald; *Behold, you are fair, my love.* Sardonyx, sardius, chrysolyte, beryl; *You are fair, my love; you have doves' eyes.* A topaz, a chrysoprasus, a jacinth, an amethyst: *You are fair, my beloved, and pleasant: also our bed is green. Let us get up early to the vineyards; let us see if the vine flourish, whether the tender grape appear, and the pomegranates bud forth: there I will give you my love. The mandrakes give a smell, and at our gates are all manner of pleasant fruits, new and old, which I have laid up for you, O my beloved.*

Hunting the Divine Fox

An Introduction to the
Language of Theology

Ad Jerusalem:

Si oblitus fuero tui . . .

Preface

Answering theological questions is like trying to straighten up an unmade bed: the only way to do the job properly is to strip the problem at hand all the way down to its basic elements and start again from the beginning. Unfortunately, most inquirers — like most bedmakers — are in such a rush to get results that they simply make a casual pass at the lumpy dilemma in front of them and then cover it over with any tattered theological bedspread they can put a hand to.

Such an approach obviously makes for an uncomfortable intellectual bed. Theologians are asked, for example, where the soul goes between the death of a human being and the general resurrection of all at the last day. But no responsible theologian can simply give a short answer to that question. To say "purgatory" or "limbo" or "some intermediate state" or "nowhere" is as unhelpful as saying "Dubuque" or "the Bureau of Standards." Instead, we should deal one by one with all the tangled theological sheets and rumpled biblical mattress pads that underlie the inquiry. People must be led to examine not only what *soul* and *death* and *resurrection* and *last day* can possibly mean but also how, if at all, human language works when applied to God — or to anything else, for that matter.

In short, there is no way to answer a theological question without going back to the very foundations of theology itself. This book does just that. Its first half is simply the front end of a theology course — presented, however, not in the form of dry lectures but with all the whimsy the writer could muster. It *plays,* as it were, with the words and images of Scripture in order to bring the readers to cheerful but serious insights into both their limitations and their glories. The second half applies those insights to certain specific "religious" questions — the deity of Jesus, the nature of sacraments, and the role of the church, to name a few.

Fortunately, *Hunting the Divine Fox* has been well received. It has been used on the college and seminary level, and it has provided a springboard for any number of church discussion groups and adult education programs. On the one hand, it is a fast and enjoyable read; on the other, it profoundly challenges most people's theological assumptions and leads them to deep considerations indeed.

I am delighted that Eerdmans has seen fit to reissue the book in this new format, and I hope it will continue to help thoughtful people grasp with joy the things they accept in faith.

1. *Fable*

Once upon a time, in the mud at the bottom of a tidal pool, there lived an oyster. By oysters' standards, he had a good life: the sea water was clean and full of plankton, and the green warmth of the light at low tide made him grow and prosper.

Next to him lived a stone with whom he sometimes talked. It was very much the same size, shape, and color as he, and was good, if undemanding, company. As a matter of fact, their conversations gave the oyster a definite feeling of superiority. He loved to dwell at length on the differences that underlay their apparent similarity. Rocks, he would say, are merely mineral. Oysters may be mineral on the outside; but inside, they are bona fide members of the animal kingdom.

One day, however, the stone surprised him by coming up with a rejoinder. It pointed out that there were nevertheless some advantages to being further down the evolutionary scale. Rocks had fewer enemies than oysters. Starfish and oyster drills, it observed, were no threat to stones; to the oyster they were a matter of life or death. Furthermore, the stone told him, it was getting just a little tired of being put down by an oyster with airs. He might get a lesson in humility if he would listen to some of the things starfish say about oysters — things which the oyster never heard because he was too busy being mortally afraid, but which the stone heard regularly, and with amusement.

Starfish, it seems, have a very low opinion of oysters. They eat

[243]

them, but they always refer to them as "nothing more than a rock with a stomach." In fact, what passes for humor among starfish is rather like Polish jokes, except that the punch line invariably has to do with how stupid it is to be an animal and not be able to move about. The worst thing one starfish can call another is "sessile creature."

The oyster terminated the discussion huffily and went into a state of profound depression. To have everything he had been so proud of become the butt of underwater ethnic wisecracks made life not worth living. Existence, he concluded, was nothing but a cruel joke. All the faith he once had in the grand design of the evolutionary scheme forsook him. Better to believe in nothing than dignify this farce of a world with pretensions of order. He became an anti-evolutionist and stopped saying his prayers.

For a while, righteous indignation made the losing of his religion rather fun, as it always does; but as summer wore on into fall and the water began its slow progress to winter's cold, he became merely sour — angry at the universe, but even more angry with himself for having let it turn him into a grouch. Finally, in desperation, he decided he would pray once again; but this time with a difference. No more mumbling of set pieties. He saw himself as a Job among oysters: he would open his shell and curse his day.

And the oyster spoke and said, "Let the day perish wherein I was spawned, and the night in which it was said, 'A seed oyster has appeared.' Why is light given to him that is in misery, and life to the bitter in soul? Why do I live my days in doubt and darkness? O, that one would hear me, and tell me openly of the glories above. Behold, my desire is that the Almighty would answer me."

And, to his utter astonishment, a voice said, "All right, all right. But I have to make it short. It's Friday afternoon.

"It's all true. There are things you never even dreamed of. All kinds of stuff. And with moves you couldn't imagine if you tried. As a matter of fact, that's your problem. There you sit with a rock on one side and a starfish on the other. My apologies. It's a limited field of vision, I admit, but in the evolutionary-scale business, you've got to put a lot of things near the bottom. Spoils the effect if you don't.

"Anyway, the moves. I'll tell you a few. Basketball. College basketball, especially. The best performers are so flashy, they make you laugh for not being able to believe the guy actually made the shot. And squirrels going through trees. One of my best effects. You know the last time a squirrel missed his footing? I keep track of these things. It was May 3rd, 1438. Definitely a record.

"And it's not all slapdash, either. I've got creatures so graceful they almost break your heart. When it comes to exquisite moves, my favorite maybe is girls' knees. Lovely. Some people think that's a funny thing to get excited about, but in this line of work, there's no substitute for enthusiasm.

"Seriously. If you take the knee thing and really go all the way with it, you get my absolute favorite for loveliness, a prima ballerina. Talk about moves. It's like Michael Jordan, Marcel Marceau, and Squirrel Nutkin all rolled together but as a girl, which makes it that much better. Terrific.

"Listen, though. It's almost sundown, and I have to set a good example. As I said, your basic problem is your point of view. There really are all these great moves, but you unfortunately don't know from motion. If you're going into business as the world's first philo-sophical oyster, it's OK by me. But just so you shouldn't get it all wrong, I'll give you one piece of advice: Think very carefully. Re-member that all this stuff really is, but it can't possibly *be* the way you *think*. Or, to turn it around: The way you *think* about things will never be exactly the same as the way they *are*. But enough. I really have to run. *Mazel tov*."

And with that, the voice ceased and the oyster was left alone with his thoughts. He felt both humbler and more elated than ever before. He resolved to philosophize no matter what the difficulties, and, in order to make the best use of the voice's advice, he decided to put himself in a methodical frame of mind. What follows is a transcript of his train of thought.

1. There is motion. I, as an oyster, can distinguish two sorts. The first is *being moved* (e.g., both the stone and myself can be moved by oystermen). The second is *moving* on one's own. The

stone cannot do this at all. I can move the part of myself within my shell, but I cannot move my whole self from place to place. The starfish can move from place to place.

2. The voice was quite clear on the existence of more mobile creatures than the starfish. Let me see what I can say about the prima ballerina:

> Starfish move; ballerinas move.
> Starfish attack oysters.
> Can starfish attack ballerinas?

This is problematical. Perhaps a tentative solution would be that since the ballerina's motion is apparently far more eminent than the starfish's, a ballerina would invariably move in such a way as to avoid starfish. There are unresolved difficulties, however:

a. I do not know whether starfish and ballerinas occupy the same medium.

b. I do not know whether starfish have any interest in attacking ballerinas.

3. Let me begin again:

> Starfish move; ballerinas move.
> Starfish are deadly to oysters.
> Are ballerinas deadly to oysters?

One line of approach would seem to be that, since the voice says that ballerinas are his absolute favorite for loveliness, and since loveliness and deadliness do not seem to be compatible, the ballerina cannot be deadly to the oyster. (This depends, of course, on what is meant by loveliness and deadliness. It also might depend on whether a ballerina's possible deadliness to the oyster proceeds out of her nature, as the starfish's does, or out of some accidental or acquired taste, as it were. If the latter were true, then it might be that not every ballerina is deadly to oysters.) In any case, there is not enough evidence to resolve the question.

4. Even though the voice's enthusiasm for the world of higher motion seems to have suspended my own doubts, it is disturbing to think how easily a skeptical oyster could argue from all this that ballerinas do not exist, but rather are nothing more than a distracting hypothesis invented by oysters who cannot face the grimness of existence without flinching.

5. Tentatively, I shall list the following as the chief properties of the prima ballerina:
    a. Mobility (like the starfish's, but better)
    b. Invulnerability to starfish (likely)
    c. Loveliness (on faith)
    d. Deadliness (possible, but not certain).
There is a good deal unresolved here. Perhaps it would be useful to consider next what ballerinas are for. This is fascinating but tiring. At least, though, the seawater seems refreshing again.

CHINESE PROVERB

He who hammers at things over his head
easily hits nail right on thumb

2. Analogies

— and he who hammers higher does it easier still.

Unless our philosophical oyster gets a firm grip on the truth that discourse about realities other than himself is always couched in analogies, parables, images, and paradoxes, he could very well conclude his definitive treatise *On the Prima Ballerina* by proving that ballerinas have five feet and glide along the ocean bottom at four miles per hour. And unless we, who are unfathomably further from our major subject than the oyster, are a hundred times more careful, we will say even stranger things about God — and be just as unaware as the oyster that we have almost completely missed the mark.

That is why the very first word in theology has to be not about God but about the way we ourselves use words. Specifically, it has to be a firm warning that no words of ours can ever be trusted to mean the same thing when predicated of ourselves and God. Not even the florid ones with Greek and Latin roots. True enough, God is merciful and God is good, and you may make him out to be as omnipresent, immutable, and omniscient as you please. But never think for a minute that you have anything more than the faintest clue to what it's actually like for him to be all those things. You may assume on faith that it is legitimate to use such words, but never forget the oyster and the ballerina: she can grasp his brand of motion better than he can hers. When you're on the low end of an analogy, be very slow to decide you know what the upper end is all about.

Once that warning is digested, however, the going gets a bit easier. Some people, for example, try to attack theology by claiming that human discourse about God is invalid because it is anthropomorphic. On examination, however, the apparently lethal paving block thus flung turns out to be a cream puff. Of course our language is anthropomorphic. We are human beings — *anthropoi* — and human words are all we have: even the Bible, as Word of God, is composed totally of human words. But for all that, no theologian seriously suggests that God is just a big man. The nature of analogy, scrupulously kept in mind, is a constant reminder that we are ignorant of more than we know about God — that we know far better what he isn't than what he is.

"Ah, but," the objector says, "if analogy is the only way you have to talk about God, why talk at all? Stick to statements in which words can be used with one meaning only."

Well, on that basis, nobody will make very many statements about anything. One of the biggest pieces of mischief in our thinking is the assumption that talk about God is a special case, and that the rules which apply to it apply to nothing else. Admittedly, God himself is a special case; but our talk about him is just plain talk. The objection to the use of analogies when talking about God presumes that they are a strictly theological device of questionable validity. The fact is that we use analogies not only when we talk about what is over our heads but all the time — whenever we talk about anything, up, down, or sideways.

When I say that my dog knows the way home from the other side of town, I am making just as full a use of analogy as when I say the Lord knows all things eternally. True enough, there is not as much temptation to think of my dog as a little four-legged man as there is to think of God as a big invisible one, but the same rules apply.

Consider. My dog is doing something. He's getting from the other side of town to his doggie dish just in time for dinner. He was not dragged home with a rope or mailed home in a box; he came home on his own. He alone, of course, is the only one who is really aware of the process by which he got there; but if I want to feature to myself how he did it, I am going to have to cast about for an analogue out of my own experience. Along with most of the human race, I don't take too long to find a good one: I say, he *knows* the way.

I would be foolish, of course, to think, having said that, that I have any direct, univocal understanding of how he knows. His ways are not my ways any more than God's are. But for all that, few sane people have much trouble with the device. And even those who go to insane lengths to avoid it invariably fall right back into it.

Suppose, for example, I decide to explain my dog's trip home for dinner, but to avoid the use of such anthropomorphisms as *knowing,* I cast about for something else. Ah, I have it. Some force propelled him. How shall I speak of such a force? Perhaps I shall say that the omnipotent will of God kept him unswervingly in right paths. Or, if you would like something less pious, I could say that an unbreakable chain of causes, programmed into the universe from day one, did the same job on him. But look what I have done. I have thrown out a really apt — and, above all, bare-faced — analogue like knowing and substituted for it a couple of silly and sneaky ones. For, after all, any will of God that a dog can't get away from is just a pious way of smuggling in the suggestion of the leash; and inescapable determinism is nothing more than Latin for a philosophical box to mail him home in.

Indeed, one of our troubles, not only in theology but all the way down the line, stems from our failure to use the best, most human analogues we have. Take the case of the sunflower, for instance. We are so impressed by the scientific clank of subhuman comparisons that we feel we ought not to say that the sunflower turns because it knows where the sun is. It is almost second nature to us to prefer explanations that sound like the speech of a troll with a large vocabulary. We are much more comfortable when we are assured that the sunflower turns because it is heliotropic.

The trouble with that kind of talk is that it is nowhere near analogous enough. It tempts us to think we really know what the sunflower is up to. But we don't. The sunflower is a mystery, just as every single thing in the universe is. The world is a tissue of beings, each of which, like Eliot's cat, is the only one who knows its own deep and inscrutable singular Name. We do indeed know each other, but only by knowing the names we decide to call one another. And we can indeed know what other creatures are up to, but only by featuring to ourselves what it would be like if we were doing it. And it's all legitimate. And it works like a charm. But the delicious mystery of the self-identity of each creature still remains the mystery it always was.

One of the benefits of theology is that if you ever get anything right on the subject of God, you immediately get a bonus and start getting things right about the world. As soon as you realize that it is possible to talk about God in human terms and still utterly respect the mystery of his being, you quickly find that if you take the same care for creatures, the taste of the mystery of their being comes rushing back. It's like blowing your nose when you can't smell a thing and suddenly discovering that the glassful of nothing you were drinking is Cos-d'Estournel '45.

Let us have, therefore, not less anthropomorphism, but more. We must remember the oyster, of course, and avoid the mystery-stealing silliness of thinking that cats actually conceptualize as we do, or that stones literally make up their minds. But having done that, we are in a position to reclaim that older, better reading of creation which only the best analogies give. Think of what it would be like to have with us once more dogs who *know,* sunflowers that *like,* great stones that *refuse* to budge, and rivers that *make glad* the City of God. Imagine getting back a universe moved by *love* for the good, full of creatures who are *priests* for each other, with heavens that *declare,* waters that *rage,* stars that *sing,* and a sun who once again can *rejoice as a giant to run his course.*

It really was a better world — and our foolishness about words is the only reason we have to put up with the sleazy substitute we're making do with right now.

3. *Proofs*

Before going on with the work of reclamation, however, let me offer you a few apologies and explanations.

Even this early in the conversation, you may have begun to suspect in me a tendency to assume the truths of Christianity without proof. If so, you are right — except that it is more a principle than a tendency. The important points from which dogmatic theologians work are seldom susceptible of proof — and the points which they can prove are usually not very important. I realize, however, that this runs contrary to what most people expect from a theologian. To them, projects like Proving the Existence of God sound like the theologian's proper work, and they seem to expect anyone who neglects such tasks to feel ashamed of himself.

As I said, I am constitutionally unrepentant on the subject; but I shall, nevertheless, offer you an apology of sorts for this absence of apologia.

To begin with, it is seldom understood how modest the results of any proof of the existence of God must necessarily be. (Not that I agree with the apparent majority of philosophers and theologians who say it can't be proved at all, or that, if it can, it can be demonstrated only as a probability and not as certainty. I am convinced that it can be demonstrated — and demonstrated beyond a doubt, if you use nice tight arguments like Saint Thomas's "Five Ways.") The important point to make about the proofs is that even at their convincing best, they just wing God on the earlobe, as it were. They don't tell you much.

Notice how they work. They take a look at the world and conclude that its nature is such that it absolutely requires, let us say, a first cause which is itself uncaused. So far so good. But then they take a turn that almost nobody bothers to notice. They do not say:

God is an uncaused first cause;
An uncaused first cause exists;
Therefore God exists.

The major premise of that syllogism is an impossible statement. Nobody knows beans about what God is. The best we can say is this: One of the notes of the Judeo-Christian concept of God is the notion that he is an uncaused first cause. What we have proved precisely, therefore, is that one of the notes of that concept actually exists. Notice what exceedingly minor stuff this is. You haven't reached God himself — you never do; you haven't really even nicked his earlobe. The most you can claim is that you have established the existence of at least one thumbprint which a lot of people have included in their dossiers on him.

Why then the enthusiasm for proofs? Well, a lot of it was due to the fact that too many Christians never noticed how the proofs proceeded and thought they proved a good deal more than they do. Aristotle was the first one in this philosophical tradition to think his way through to an uncaused first cause. As far as we know, however, he did not fall down on his knees and worship it. Rather, he just went on with his main point — which was, since he was a highly talented philosopher, to continue his virtuoso philosophizing.

Saint Thomas, however, was another case. His main point was not philosophizing but falling down on his knees to worship the God of the Judeo-Christian revelation whom he knew as, among other things, the Three Persons of the Holy and Undivided Trinity, the God of Abraham, Isaac, and Jacob, and the Uncaused First Cause of the world.

Now when Thomas, who also happened to be very good at philosophizing, came across Aristotle's proof of an uncaused first cause, he stopped dead in his tracks and said something that never could have occurred to Aristotle. He said, "Hey! I know who that is! That's my main point! Fancy being able to prove by reason the existence of something I held only by faith up till now." Reason does the proving, you see, but it's faith that's responsible for the enthusiasm.

That is why I give you only a halfhearted apology for not doing much proving. You will be interested in God's existence only if, in advance of proof, you care about the subject. And that depends on more than mere existence. What does it matter to you if I can prove that lobsters exist, if you're not interested in seafood at all? The theologian's real job should be to work up your enthusiasm for the Lobster Himself. Only after that can he talk about the Unlobstered First Lobster without putting you to sleep.

Theologians, therefore, are to be judged more by the quality of the information they give than by the evidential force of the arguments they make. You should demand of them discussions of the really important things you have to know in order to make up your mind. Not, Does God exist? Rather, What is he like? Is he nasty or nice? Does he wear overpowering aftershave? Does he force Chinese food on his friends?

What you will get from me, accordingly, is precious little proof, but lots of excursions into the fearful and wonderful world of what the Christian revelation has to say about God. Note, however, this does not mean that I am about to answer your questions. Any questions you — or I — could ask in advance of our examination of the faith would more than likely be just as oysterish as the ones I just suggested, even if they sounded much more sensible. What I am about to give you instead is a guided tour of selected spots in the bizarre set of answers that I believe God has given us. Then, perhaps, we may inch our way back to a point at which we will be able to ask better questions. I do it that way because I am convinced that accepting the revelation on faith is the really *interesting* enterprise.

Theologians of an earlier day, with just a little blowing of their own horn, called theology the Queen of the Sciences, because it dealt with the highest class of subject matter. Philosophy, they said, was great — the overarching science of all the sciences, even of theology — but it had, by definition, to deal only with what mere human beings could wring out of creation by force of reason. Theology, on the other hand, started from nothing less than the revelation of God himself. It began its trip on the road to knowledge well beyond the point at which philosophy ran out of gas.

Nowadays that has a quaint, old-fashioned ring to it; but something like it needs reviving. Perhaps the way to say it is that philosophy points the searchlight of intelligibility at God and comes up, at best, with a few sightings. Theology, on the other hand, doesn't hunt for God that way at all. Instead, it receives in the mail a gross of very odd flashlights from the Lux Invisibilis Flashlight Co. It then takes these and proceeds to point their mysterious light not only at God but also at creation and, in the process, discovers movements, shapes, and colors it never saw before.

Theology, therefore, is fun. The inveterate temptation to make something earnest out of it must be steadfastly resisted. We were told quite plainly that unless we became as little children, we could not enter the kingdom of heaven; nowhere more than in theology do we need to take the message to heart. Accordingly, what we shall be up to here is playing, even horsing around with the flashlights just to see what we can see. If you'd like a more sedate and respectable description of it, say we are acting in accordance with Psalm 36, verse 9, which also happens to be the inscription over the chapel of Columbia University: *"In lumine tuo videbimus lumen."* Or say that, in the words of the ancient Greek evening hymn, we are allowing the *phos hilaron,* the "gladsome light," to shine in our minds. (Do a little better than "gladsome" if you will, though. It sounds so moderate and Victorian. Maybe *hilarious?*) But whatever you do, keep it light, or it won't, obviously, be light at all.

One last apology. Among the many other things I shall not be offering to prove, there is one that lies at the heart of everything I have to say: it is the validity of our knowing process. Many philosophers who weigh in at a lot more than I do have exercised themselves on the subject — and so strenuously that I long ago decided to take the whole thing as a spectator sport. With TV tuned, therefore, and Barcalounger tilted back, my one comment on epistemology is that I root for any team that says human knowledge is valid, and never watch the others.

I do this because everybody I know acts as if it were valid, anyway. The skeptic is never for real. There he stands, cocktail in hand, left arm draped languorously on one end of the mantelpiece, telling you that he can't be sure of anything, not even of his own existence. I'll give you my secret method of demolishing universal skepticism in four words. Whisper to him: "Your fly is open." If he thinks knowledge is so all-fired impossible, why does he always look?

So, no epistemology here. A little attention, perhaps, to some of the light that theology can shed on the way our minds work, and a lot to what should probably be called theological semantics, but which I prefer to think of as fooling around with the intellectual images by which we pick up God, Human Nature, Christ, and the Church. But definitely no epistemology. And no more apologies, either.

4. *Words*

I t was on a Friday afternoon, back at the beginning of when, that God said the one thing that probably has given him more trouble than anything else: "Let us make man — *Adam* — in our image, after our likeness: and let them have dominion over the fish of the sea, and over the fowl of the air, and over the cattle, and over all the earth, and over every creeping thing that creepeth upon the earth." And because God can't even think anything without having it jump out of nothing into existence, the result was that God created human beings — *the Adam* — "in his own image, in the image of God created he him; male and female created he them."

In the old days, when theologians were less uptight about their respectability in the eyes of biblical critics, the odd, majestic plural of that fateful "Let us make" was always taken as one of the Old Testament evidences for the doctrine of the Trinity. Nowadays you lose your union card if you do things like that, but I still think it's nice. You don't have to be dead earnest about it all and work up a theory that the Jewish writer who put the first chapter of Genesis together was some kind of crypto-Christian, or that the Holy Spirit was deliberately trying to Tell Us Something. After all, the Spirit got in his decisive innings on the Trinity later on, with Jesus and Paul; and as far as Christians are concerned, the LORD God who made the world just had to be the Holy Trinity, anyway. What's nice about that "us" is precisely its oddness. It's the kind of mysteriously gratuitous detail that's so much fun to come across in the work of a master craftsman. "Hey!" you say. "Look at that! Why would he say such a thing? He must smoke chicken marrow or something."

See? You need to *play* with Scripture, or else you get it all wrong. Deriving the doctrine of the Trinity from the "us" is nothing more than a little bit of baroque ornamentation: it's legitimate as long as you keep things in balance. The people who object to it do so because they think it's a case of putting a big doctrinal construction on top of a little grammatical point. But they're wrong. In theology you're in the oddity and style business. Once you get that straight, then the "us" is no longer a minor point; it's a mark of style. You may not know exactly why it's there, but you feel it's trying to tell you something, trying to elicit some kind of response from you. It just *asks* for ornamentation. So when the old boys put in a few trinitarian trills, they weren't destroying the balance of the piece; they were just making it sound — well, *nice*.

Let me give you another instance.

God says, "Let *us* make man . . ." Nowhere else in the whole first chapter does he use this form. All the other creatures are sprung out of nothing with a rather impersonal "Let there be . . ." From light to firmament, to land, to herb; from sun to stars, to whales, to fowls, to cattle, God is interested, but he doesn't seem involved. But when he gets to humankind, he really puts himself into it. He rolls up his sleeves, rubs his hands together, and says, "Now comes the part *we* always love best!"

And that, Virginia, is why we are in the image of God.

You see? It's perfectly serious and perfectly silly at the same time. Which is just great. It's like making love: you can laugh while you do it. As a matter of fact, if you don't, at least sometimes, you're probably a terrible lover. Watch out for biblical commentators, therefore, who sound as if they're holding a sex manual in the other hand. And especially watch out for the kind who look down their long theological noses at Saint Paul for proving that the Gospel is above the Law from the minor fact that "Abraham's *seed*" is in the singular and not the plural. Dummies! He was not trying to make an intellectual fast buck out of Scripture. He was making love to it.

But enough pique. Before I was derailed by my annoyance at biblical critics, I was working up to the subject of human nature in the image of the Trinity.

According to Christian doctrine, creation arises out of a mysterious interaction within God himself — out of some kind of exchange between the Persons of the Trinity: Father, Son, and Holy Spirit. The Son and the Spirit, therefore, are in the act from the beginning. They don't wait until the New Testament to go to work; all three Persons create, because they are, all three, simply the one and only eternal God there is. (It's confusing, I know, but don't think about it. It's a flashlight. We're not going to look at *it;* we're going to point it at the world. Focus the beam a little more narrowly, though.)

When we talk about the role of the Son in the act of creation, we normally refer to him as the Word. We do this because, when the Bible shows God creating, it doesn't show him doing it with tools, like a carpenter, but rather with words, like a magician. Christians, therefore, have gotten into the habit of talking about the Father's Eternal Word — the second Person of the Trinity — as the actual agent of creation. To put it all as briefly as possible: The Father *thinks up* a world, the Word *says* its name over the *brooding* of the Spirit, and presto, there you have a world.

Accordingly, when God says, "Let *us* make man in *our* image," it is specifically the image of the Trinity he has in mind. Furthermore, while human beings can be interpreted as being made in the image of all three Persons, it is especially fruitful to consider them as being made principally in the image of the Word — of the Son, the second Person of the Trinity. This seems legitimate for two reasons.

When God shows up in the humanity of Jesus, we always say it is the Word who becomes flesh, not the Father or the Spirit. On the principle that God doesn't change his mind, and in view of the fact that Jesus is what God finally says he had in mind for humankind, it seems fair to conclude that Jesus is what he had in mind all along. And since Jesus is the Word, that means that human beings had some special relationship to the Word from the beginning. Therefore, it does no violence to Scripture to interpret the "image of God" as referring especially to the second Person of the Trinity.

Second, the account of creation in Genesis 2 tends to support this: "And out of the ground the LORD God formed every beast of the field, and every fowl of the air; and brought them unto Adam to see what he would call them: and whatsoever Adam called every living creature, that was the name thereof." *Naming* things is the crowning glory of the human race. Of the three operations of the mind — simple apprehension, judgment, and reasoning — only one of them is distinctly and exclusively human; and it's the one most people guess last. It's not reasoning; monkeys can figure out how to put a fishing pole together in order to fetch bananas from outside their cage. And it's not judgment; my cat may not be able to predicate *mortality* of *canary,* but he is definitely of the opinion that the *dried cat food* in his dish is *terrible.* No, the uniqueness of the human mind lies in simple apprehension — in our ability to form concepts, to extract essences, by means of words. Indeed, one of the best ways of thinking about the nature of a concept is to conceive it analogically and call it an internal word or mental name. Accordingly, it is not farfetched to see our ability to name, to make words, as yet another intimation of our being made particularly in the image of the Word.

All right. The theological flashlight is sufficiently focused. Now point it at Adam — at us — and see what you can see.

Adam, obviously, has dominion over the world. In earlier ages, this had to be taken largely on faith, because the world was so big and human beings were so small that there was not much evidence to prove they had the upper hand. To be sure, they arm-wrestled some forests into farms and some hillsides into building stones, but the minute they turned their backs, nature started going her own willful way again.

In our time, however, the dominion of humankind over the world can be proved by unaided human reason. While the earth may still succeed in bucking us here and there for a while, it won't do it for long at the rate we're going. It's sad, of course, to have to prove it that way. It would be nicer if we, with all our present power, could point to a world that our dominion had loved into beauty and life. But it's quite enough, for the purposes of proof, to note that we have successfully converted most of the beauty and life it had into ugliness and death. And there is no doubt that we have the power to kill it off completely. And only a little doubt that we will.

Dominion, then. But how does our dominion over the world operate? What is its nature? Well, if we are in the image of the Word, perhaps it will be most fruitful if we see our power over creation as verbal power: for good or ill, we rule the earth by words.

Consider. Housebuilding was impossible until someone, some-where, spoke a word. The human race was provided with no instinctive architectural faculties. The bees built hives, the birds made nests, and the beavers worked like beavers, practicing housebuilding and stream control at the same time. But no one built houses until the day when one fellow who had sense enough to come in out of the rain sat down on a fallen tree he had dragged into his cave.

And it was so damp and dark and unpleasant that he got to thinking how wonderful it would be if he could arrange things so that he never saw the inside of a cave again. And as he thought, his eye fell on the tree on which he was sitting, and all of a sudden, an internal word sprang up noiselessly in his mind. He wasn't thinking the word *tree,* and he wasn't thinking the word *seat.* He was thinking a word he had never thought before. So he opened his mouth to hear what it was and, lo and behold, out came the word *lumber.*

It was such an odd word that he just sat there for a while. And all of a sudden, it happened again. Two new internal words in one day! Wait till his wife got home! But he couldn't wait, so he opened his mouth again and, this time, out came *house.*

Well, he was so enthused that he picked up the phone and dialed a friend. "Irving?"

"Speaking."

"Irving, have I got news for you! You and I are going to make a bundle. You know that axe of yours? And all those trees you've got in that *yard* I thought up for you last week? You're going to split them up, and we're going to sell them for *lumber.*"

"For *what?*"

"No, Irving. Not for *what.* For *lumber.*"

"What good is *lumber?* Who'd buy it? Nobody even knows what it is."

"Irving, Irving. Think big. When there's no market, you create one. We're going to sell the lumber to people who want *houses.*"

"What's *houses?*"

"It's the plural of *house,* Irving. I just thought up both words this afternoon."

"What have you been smoking over there?"

"Nothing. I've just been thinking."

"That's even worse. Every time you think, I end up working."

"Believe me, Irving, this time you'll thank me. I've even got the name of our business picked out. In honor of your place, we'll call it The Lumber Yard. So hang up now and start chopping. I'm going to think up *writing* so I can letter the sign."

Obviously, it was a winning idea. And all the credit goes to the words of the earthly image of the Word. It is by words that we build. A house is a creature of words: stud, shoe, plate; king post, tie beam, ridgepole; jamb and lintel, mullion and meeting rail, board, batten, soffit, and fascia. And houses themselves are called forth by words: Cape Cod, split-level, ranch; apartment, condominium, high-rise. It is words that turn houses into cities: street, avenue, plaza, park; dogcatcher, councilman, mayor, judge. And from the cities of humankind come those strange words — those renamings of creation and those namings of utterly new ways to name — that give the sciences the aweful power they have: acid, alkali, hydrogen ion concentration; diglycerides and butylated hydroxyanisole; trinitrotoluene, deuterium, and U-235; indeterminacy, non-Euclidean geometry, entropy, and curved space.

God's Word alone, of course, has the ultimate bark in it. When he says "Be!" there is nothing that has any choice but to jump. And when he hears his own eternal internal Word — when he knows all things in his dearly beloved Son — there is nothing that he doesn't know, no back part, no inner fold, no smallest speck at the heart of any smallest thing that the Word has left unspoken.

Our words do not have power like that. And yet, they have all the power we need, and more than we can handle. Not power enough to call things out of nothing, but enough to make Jerusalem of the world; not power enough to grasp things as they are, but power enough to wreck them as they stand.

In the beginning was the Word. . . . In the end, all it may take may be one word.

5. Images

Having gotten this far, I am in a position to deal with an objection I have been anticipating.

Many people are put off when they are exposed to theologians plying their trade. This refining of concepts, this making of distinctions, this juggling of texts — it all seems like a mere word game.

I concede every point — except one.

It all seems . . . It does indeed. And on some days, more so to theologians than anyone suspects. As a matter of fact, the point could be made more strongly, and I would still concede it. It doesn't just seem to be; it is.

A word game. No disagreement. Except to point out that the same thing is true of every subject that ends in *-ology,* and of a great many more that don't.

And that, of course, is why I finally draw the line at the word *mere.* Word games are the least mere games of all. They are power games; and the wise thing to do about them is not to write them off but to keep an eagle eye open whenever they are played. If you don't, you can lose a lot more than your small change and your Scrabble set. You can lose your way, your sanity, your money, or your life.

Accordingly, I overrule the objection as unfounded and go back to work investigating the peculiar power of theological language to shed light on the various projects that God and his creatures seem to have in mind.

Let me rather arbitrarily divide human speech into two categories: straight discourse and bent discourse; or, a bit more formally, into unrefractive and refractive uses of words. Straight discourse will cover all those uses in which words mean simply what they say. "Pass the salt," for example. Your mashed potatoes are too bland; you know salt will perk them up; you ask for it; and you get it. Everything is kept as literal as possible — and with excellent results. You can always count on words to sit still in this sort of discourse. No matter who uses it, the meanings remain the same.

Bent discourse, on the other hand, writes off this seeming advantage in favor of uses in which a single word may have several senses. *Analogy* has already been mentioned: it is perhaps the tamest, most disciplined sort of bent discourse. Here, however, I am interested in a far wilder and more fractious (or refractious!) way of talking: discourse by means of *images*.

"Pass the salt" got us salt and simplicity. "You are the salt of the earth" puts us in another ball game. We are now playing with *salt* not as a word denoting a thing, a mere intellectual handle for moving odds and ends about. We are tossing around *salt* as an image. The word is no longer simply a grip on the outside of what salt does; it has become a probe into the mystery of what salt really is — both in itself and in that dance of beings which we call creation.

Sharpen the distinction a bit. Calling it "a probe into the mystery" is slightly off the mark. Mystery is always inaccessible — by definition. What bent discourse actually does is take the word *salt* as an intellectual painting or icon. Then, on the basis of a firm belief in the power of words, it proceeds in one of two directions.

Sometimes it takes a very small corner of the painting and holds it up to view. For example: *Salt* perks up potatoes; life, unless it is perked up with a pinch of *bawdiness,* is flat and tasteless. Hence our hope (or our stuffy host's fear) that, with one more scotch, old Fred will let fly with some of his inimitably *salty* stories.

But at other, more important times, bent discourse takes the image not by parts but as a whole. It presents us not with a detail of the painting but with the entire word picture as an icon — as an almost holy sacrament, a powerful epiphany of all its meanings at once. The simplest, and perhaps the best, illustration is the image *Jerusalem*. Taken in its details, it can mean such things as the historical city, or the figurative hope of Israel, or the beloved of God, or the final destiny of creation. But used as an icon, it delivers all that freight of meaning in a single stroke. Take Blake's Jerusalem, for example:

> I will not cease from mental fight,
> Nor shall my sword sleep in my hand,
> Till we have built Jerusalem
> In England's green and pleasant land.

When you reach this level of refractive discourse, you have arrived at new heights of power. Straight discourse is potent enough: it delivers the goods, be they saltshakers or earth movers. But bent discourse is more powerful still, for it alone has light to shed on the Mystery that is our real home. True, it is inconvenient, volatile, and inflammable. Straight words are like so many billets of firewood: they are useful, they may be stored with relative safety, and they do not spill or leak. Refractive words are more like tanks of high-octane gasoline or nuclear reactors gone critical: they are much more useful but a hundred times harder to handle — and they create hazards all over the place.

Nevertheless, the human race, at its wisest, has never hesitated to keep them in quantity and to pass them dangerously from hand to hand. Their inconvenience is put up with because of their glory. And their glory is precisely that they don't just lie there all safe and fireproof with a single meaning. Every time they change hands, their meaning grows more complex. Every icon is holy; but some icons have done more miracles and been handled by more saints, and therefore are holier than others. So with images: the more poets who handle them, and the more pentecosts of power they make in the minds of those who hear them, the greater their iconic power to hunt the Mystery itself.

One of the chief concerns of theologians, therefore, must be an analysis of images. And not only of images themselves, but also of such general rules, if any, as they can formulate to ensure proper storage and handling of such potentially explosive material. This is particularly important nowadays because the education most of us have received has left us dangerously ignorant of how to think by means of images. Indeed, one of the reasons why the Bible is inaccessible to so many is that the Bible, at its deepest levels, is actually a tissue of images. The Word of God, when God most reveals himself, speaks with a bent tongue; if you have been brought up on nothing but straight talk and jargon, you will find him almost impossible to follow. Herewith, therefore, a few strictures on images, their use and their abuse.

Whenever you use an image, you will do well to think of yourself as standing in the middle of a plaza — one plaza among the many in the vast city of meaning that is human knowledge. Off this plaza run streets in many directions. These streets are the several distinct meanings to be found in the image itself. While you stand still in the plaza, you see all the streets at once; but if you decide to use the plaza as a way station to some other place in the city, you have to choose a street — a particular meaning — and follow it. Some of these streets will take you straight to your destination. But others will get you there only by detours — sometimes through the worst parts of town. Others still will turn out to be blind alleys with assassins lurking in dark corners. When you think by means of images, therefore — when you try to get somewhere in the city of meaning — choose your street carefully before you leave one plaza in search of another.

A simple illustration first. The relationship between the first and the second Persons of the Trinity is expressed in Christian theology in terms of the image Father/Son. Take that as the plaza in which we stand. Now look around and see what streets lead off it.

Father/Son. Fathers come first; sons come second. Fathers are bigger; sons are smaller. Fathers and sons are not equal. How does that sound?

It sounds like a street which, if followed only a little further, would lead you straight into saying that the Father *made* the Son, and that the Son, therefore, isn't really God. But that's not where you want to go. You want to get to the plaza called God from God, Light from Light, True God from True God, located right at the end of One Substance Avenue. Look around for another way.

Father/Son. Fathers love sons; sons love fathers. Love between persons can be equal without having to be the same. Ah! That sounds more like it. That's a street worth taking. Off we go: Paternal love/Filial love — and so on.

If, on the other hand, you want an illustration of how taking the wrong street can cost you a lot of time, lead you through the gashouse district, and almost get you mugged, turn to Saint Paul's Epistle to the Romans, chapters 9 through 11.

Paul has been proceeding nicely through the city of his argument that we are saved not by the Law of the Old Testament but by Grace through faith in Christ. At the end of chapter 8, he has reached the beautiful plaza of Nothing Shall Be Able to Separate Us from the Love of Christ.

Before going on to chapter 9, however, he formulates in his mind, but does not bother to express, a question that all of this raises: "If everything I have said so far is true, why is it that Israel — God's chosen people, the people with the true covenants, the true worship, and the true promises — has rejected Christ?"

His goal is to arrive at the plaza marked out by Romans 11:26: And So All Israel Shall Be Saved. You and I, of course, would have no trouble at all getting there. We never walk the streets of the city of images if we can help it. We would call for a helicopter from Straight Talk Airways, Inc., and fly there. Our answer to the question would be the usual easy out: "Who knows why people do the things they do? Some Jews accept Christ; some don't. If God really is going to save all of Israel, then we'll have to trust God to work out the logistics."

It's a cagey answer, and it's a dull one, but for all that, it's not bad. It was unavailable to Paul, however, because he was an inveterate walker, a man for whom thinking in the images of the Scriptures was as natural as breathing.

So he starts out of Israel Plaza, down Abraham Street, gets to

Jacob and Esau Place, and observes in passing that God chose Jacob just out of mercy and rejected Esau just because he wanted to. He stands there for awhile and asks the obvious question: "Is that fair?" He looks around, gets jittery, and dashes down Moses Street to Pharaoh Square: God Hardens Whom He Will. He asks one more question: "Why does God blame anybody, then? He's the only one responsible." And after that, he simply panics. He bolts down a side street and lands in a slightly seedy one-bench park at Isaiah 29:16, on the corner of Pot and Potter lanes: What Right Has the Pot to Talk Back to the Potter? From there, it's from bad to worse. His travels take him from Potter/pot to Vase/chamberpot: If God Wants to Make Israel the Recipient of All the Shit He Can Dish Out, So What?

As you can see, Paul has arrived in Hell's Kitchen, talking like a native. Let us leave him there. He did, of course, eventually get where he was going, but by an even more tortuous circuit of images. Unfortunately, because he was writing Scripture, the net result of his labors was that he left behind a permanent record of the disastrous detour. And — alas — many Christians, failing to see the powerful logic of images at work, refused to see it as a detour: they made each step of his wandering way just as important as the goal, and built monumental theological constructions all over the passage — their ultimate achievement being the glorious doctrine of Double Pre-destination, which said that God put people in hell just for the fun of it.

It just goes to show you that if you insist on taking everything literally, you end up with some things you shouldn't take seriously.

6. Willing

— which brings us to an instance in which all this advice can be put into practice.

Christians have carried on at length about the will of God, but they have often expounded the subject in ways that were, if not as blatantly embarrassing as Double Predestination, at least as inconvenient, uncomplimentary, unscriptural, and unbelievable. Has anything been said so far that can raise the level of the discussion?

Go back, for a start, to our insistence that all discourse about God is inevitably analogical. First of all, this forces us to say clearly that we don't really know what we're talking about. Whatever it is in God that we're trying to characterize by the word *will* remains a mystery. We must not pretend that we can either know anything directly or say anything univocally about it. But second, in spite of all that, the use of analogy allows us to insist that it is not only legitimate but essential that we talk about the will of God. If God acts at all, and if we are going to try to say anything about his action, we're going to have to feature it to ourselves in terms of some faculty of our own. Will is simply one of the highest analogues we have right up there between knowledge and love. If any of our verbal tools can do the job, will is bound to be among them.

But there is more than that to be said. The word *will* has been around for quite a while. It long ago graduated from the school of straight talk, if indeed it was ever in it. It may not yet be the sacramental icon that Jerusalem has become, but it is nevertheless an image of considerable power.

Webster's Unabridged gives *will,* noun and verb, almost two feet of fine print — and scatters its derivatives and compounds over four additional columns. By any standard, that makes a very large plaza of meaning, with a great many avenues (marked in capital letters) and streets (marked in upper- and lower-case letters) branching out on all sides.

Looking first at the southern, or warmer, side of the plaza, we SEE DESIRE, WISH, DISPOSITION, INCLINATION, APPETITE, PASSION, and CHOICE. Off to the east run: Something Wished For and REQUEST; off to the west: VOLITION, A Disposition Manifested in Wishing, and The Collective Desire of a Group. And finally, on the colder, north side lie SELF-CONTROL, SELF-DIRECTION, DETERMINATION, DECREE, COMMAND, and Power to Control.

Now with a range of meaning like that, it makes a considerable difference which side of the plaza you take off from. When I listen to some people talk about the will of God, for example, I detect a preference for meanings that lie on the northerly side. When they think of God as *willing,* they seem to have in the back of their minds a collection of images of a definitely austere sort. There is the king on his throne issuing decrees right and left. There is the iron-willed general determined to reduce the city to rubble. There is the willpower of the saint who touches no woman or wine and gets up at the same ungodly hour every day.

It's all pretty stern stuff. Even when they talk about God's will in milder terms, they still get in a coercive note. They may say "God's will is simply what God wants," but you can almost hear the unspoken "Or else!" in the back of their minds. It's as if they had been drilled in the old army rule that a request from a superior is to be considered an order. They never seem to escape from the area of power when they expound *will.* More than that, the kind of power they have in mind is usually conceived after the least human model. Their saint's willpower, for example, is thought of as being most perfect when it brings him to the performance level of a machine. Fortunately, since they are usually quite sensible people, the only damage this does is to persuade them to give that kind of religion a wide berth. Which proves, I suppose, that a mistake isn't always a total loss.

No doubt this picture of will as coercive, as the ability to Impose Patterns and Make Decisions Stick, strikes you as more or less the traditional Christian view. The church, perhaps, has seemed to you to have put into the words "the will of God" about the same tone as "Kinder, you vill all enjoy your oatmeal — zis very minute!"

Admittedly, this preference for the more northerly, not to say Prussian, meanings has been widespread; but for all that, there is plenty of evidence in the tradition that the streets on the southern side of the plaza have been well used. Scholastic philosophy, for instance, defines *will* as "a rational appetite whose object is the good" — thus making God's will a heavenly kind of appetite, a divine delectation. Followed just a little further, that gives you a will of God that, instead of being a chain of Divine Commands, is a series of Divine Lip Smackings. And that, of course, is nothing but what Genesis teaches on the subject: at the end of each of the six days of creation, God says *"Tov!"* — which is Hebrew for "Mmm, good!"

I suggest, therefore, that if we want to get rid of some of the unpleasantness that has crept into people's minds on the subject of the will of God, we should work the southern side of the plaza. I suggest we pay less attention to the military-academy snapshots people have habitually been carrying in their wallets — and more to those pictures that show a little warmth and toastiness — namely, Inclination, Desire, Wish, Appetite, Disposition, Passion, and Choice. Let us make ourselves a promise to talk for a while about the will of God as attractive rather than coercive, as a delighting more than a deciding.

That done, the rest is easy. There is no contest for the most promising set of images to do the job. Having left the Square of Will via the Street of Desire, we land smack in one of the most gorgeous parts of the city — the Grand Plaza of The Song of Songs: love as the right way to read will; will as the desire of the lover for the beloved.

The will of God now becomes not the orders of a superior

directing what a subordinate must do but the longing of a lover for what the beloved is. It is a desire not for a performance but for a person; a wish not that the beloved will be obedient but that she will be herself — the self that is already loved to distraction. The will of God, seen this way, is not *in order to* something but *because of* someone.

For after all, only a fool of a lover ever tries to change the beloved; it is only after we have lost the thread of our love that we start giving orders and complaining about lifestyles. For as long as we follow that thread faithfully, it is always a matter of, "I could never have invented you; how should I know how to change you?" Outrage at the beloved is possible, of course. But in a wise lover, it is never outrage at anything but the beloved's destruction of herself. Inconvenience, pain, sleeplessness — even rejection — are nothing. The beloved is all.

That suggests, among other things, that the will of God may well be not *his* recipe for my life but rather his delight in *my* recipe. It may well mean that he loves me in my independence, as any good lover would. Unfortunately, we have usually looked on the love of God for us as the love of a father for a small child. But that is not thoroughly scriptural. The grandest — and the final — imagery the Bible uses for his love is precisely that of lover and beloved, bridegroom and bride. It is the marriage of Christ and the church that is the last act of the long love affair between God and creation.

The love of father for child is the love of a complete being for one not yet complete. Even there, of course, the wise parent loves the child for herself, and never wills for a moment that the child remain a child. But the image is so colored by superiority/inferiority that it inevitably suggests that Doing What You're Told is what the lover really loves you for. Conformity, not independence, is the virtue it praises most. The lover's love for the beloved, on the other hand, suggests precisely the opposite. I think it is high time we took it seriously.

To illustrate: One of the difficulties in our thinking about the will of God has been caused by the crisis of change in the church. Everyone agrees, of course, that what we need most is To Do the

Will of God. The trouble is that very few people, unless they are faking it, know what the will of God for them is. There is a lot of pious talk about finding out about whether it is the will of God for you to marry Irving, or become a priest, or take the veil; but in all honesty, what you are really going to find out is what *your* will on the subject is and whether you have enough nerve to go through with it. A few special types with inside tracks may get their answers straight from God, but the rest of us get them from ourselves — and from Irving, the Bishop, and the Reverend Mother, respectively. God is notoriously silent; and when he speaks, it is usually in parables, just so no one will be able to claim too much clarity and insight. He runs the world not only with his hands in his pockets but with his mouth mostly shut.

In the old days, this shortage of communications from God was compensated for by a very talkative church. Once you had made up your mind to marry Irving, the church could tell you, in burdensome detail, precisely what you would be doing: You would be getting up at 6:45 every morning without fail, cooking Irving's 4½-minute egg for precisely 4½ minutes, kissing Irving good-by when he left for work, spending the day mopping up after Irving's children, having Irving's martini ready when he got home, feeding him his dinner, fetching him his slippers — and giving him a little action when he wanted it, no matter how deactivated you felt. And by doing all that, the church would assure you, you would be Doing the Will of God.

Ditto Irving, if he decided to become a priest — except that he would tend to get less deactivated than you.

The trouble with such advice was that it paid so much attention to what was to be done, it neglected the person who was to do it. It forgot that the Will of God for You included the word *You*. To be sure, you still celebrated your independence in theory, since it was you who freely chose to wipe all those dishes and bottoms; but in practice, you could hardly notice it.

In any case, however, times have changed, and we've all come a long way, Virginia. Nowadays, if you insist, Irving can set his own alarm, boil his own eggs, and stir his own martinis. He may even, on some days, have it strongly suggested to him that he go activate himself. And you? God knows what you should do. But God isn't talking. And while the church may still be talking, it pretty obviously doesn't know. So we'll all just have to wait and watch as you do it. You and me both, in our inconvenient freedom.

And Irving? Well, I have been a parish priest for the past forty-five years, and I wish him luck. It is the most undefined, ill-defined job on earth, and even the church is hardly pretending it knows what to say anymore. So he'll have to wing it, too.

We have, you see, been forced by change into a situation in which we are either going to have to stop talking about doing the will of God or else find a way of seeing it in a new light. Specifically, we are going to have to find a way of seeing our now almost inevitable independence as the heart of our calling — of discovering that our present condition of flying by the seat of our pants may well be Doing the Will of God.

And that is where The Song of Solomon comes to our rescue. The will, the desire of the lover is simply the beloved herself in her freedom: God just wants *us*. And the calling of the beloved is simply to love: the glory and the misery of the love affair is the master image for the understanding of our vocation. We are bidden not to some fairy-tale marriage in which all is settled but to a seeking and not finding, to the burning sense of loss in possession which only lovers know. "Tell me, O thou whom my soul loveth, where thou feedest . . . why should I be as one that turneth aside by the flocks of thy companions? . . . Stay me with flagons, comfort me with apples: for I am sick of love."

The will of God is not a list of stops for us to make to pick up mouthwash, razor blades, and a pound of chopped chuck on the way home. It is his longing that we will take the risk of being nothing but ourselves, desperately in love. It is not a neatly arranged series of appointments in a tidy office but a life of bad dreams, minor triumphs, and major disasters — of things that we did not have in mind at all, and of preoccupations that miss each other in the dark. "By night on my bed I sought him whom my soul loveth: I sought him, but I found him not. I will rise now, and go about the city in the streets, and in the broad ways I will seek him whom my soul loveth: I sought him, but I found him not."

Might it not be, then, that it is by bearing for love the uncertainty of what we are to do that we come closest to his deepest will for us? In our fuss to succeed, to get a good grade on the series of tests we think he has proposed, we miss the main point of the affair: that we already are the beloved. We long ago wound God's clock for good. "Thou hast ravished my heart, my sister, my spouse; thou hast ravished my heart with one of thine eyes, with one chain of thy neck. . . . Thou art beautiful, O my love, as Tirzah, comely as Jerusalem, terrible as an army with banners."

It is our thirst for success and our fear of the freedom that he wills for us that keep us the poor lovers we are. If the cross teaches us anything, it should be that the cup doesn't pass from us, and that agony, bloody sweat, and the pain of being forsaken on a dark afternoon are the true marks of having said, Thy Will Be Done. He is no less lost in this affair than we are. What really matters for us both, though, is not the lostness, not the doubt, not the fragile, mortgaged substance of our house — only the love as strong as death that has set us as a seal upon each other's hearts.

7. *Figuring*

That, of course, is not intended as a full-blown treatise on the will of God. It is meant only to illustrate how a biblical flashlight of a warmer color might possibly illuminate our thoughts about a mystery we have come to find cold and forbidding. No doubt it creates more problems than it solves. But then, I never promised you answers.

Furthermore, it must not be allowed to give the impression that the butt of the theological enterprise is just talk about God. As a matter of fact, any Christian theology that talked only, or even predominantly, about God would be, by just that much, untrue to the revelation. Theology is not, as the old manuals had it, "the science of God and things divine"; properly speaking, it is not about God but about the mystery of God's relationship to the world. Accordingly, I want now to spend a little time refreshing some imagery that will get us out of the excessively "heavenly" perspective we may have sometimes had on the subject.

If you were to take a poll and ask the question "What is the Bible about?" the chances are you would get a majority of answers to the effect that it was about God, or about God's directions on how to get where God is. In other words, people would tend to think that Scripture is either about spiritualities or about a morality that leads to spiritualities. No doubt this is due in part to the fact that many people are simply ignorant of what is actually in the forbidding black book with the bowling alley down the middle of every page.

[277]

But for others, it is due to something more complicated. Many who have read the Bible — including some who know vast stretches of it by heart — hold the same overspiritualized view. Mere familiarity does not necessarily produce understanding. It is perfectly possible to know something (or someone!) all your life and still never really comprehend what you're dealing with. Like the Irishman in the old joke who received a brand-new toilet from his American cousins: he used the bowl for a foot washer, the lid for a breadboard, and the seat for a frame around the pope's picture. Or, less humorously, like the man who, when his wife of twenty years up and left him, wrote a long, sad piece in which he never once referred to her as a woman, or as a person, or by name.

Getting something right, you see, depends on more than just picking it up: you must also pick it up by the right handle. Accordingly, since the Bible consists entirely of words, that means picking it up by the right verbal handle — by the right set of images. And when you come at Scripture in that light, you quickly realize that no little shorthand intellectual formula like "spirituality" or "morality" will do.

First of all, the Bible refuses to tell you, in plain, simple words, what it is about. If you look for such capsule comment, you are bound to be mightily disappointed: Scripture, approached that way, seems only a potpourri of history, myth, poetry, prophecy, and commentary. Second, when it finally does consent to tell you, it insists on using a profusion of images, types, and figures to do the job, which leaves almost as many unsatisfied customers as does its refusal to speak plainly. To be sure, it has a theme, and it is articulated by a logic of the most rigorous sort. But the logic is the logic of images and is unavailable to the literal-minded.

This is not to say that nothing in the Bible is literally true. Many things are, without any doubt. It is only to insist that, even when things are literally true, they still have to be interpreted by means of images before they yield their theme. Take the fact that Jesus ascended. Take it as literally true. The chief question still remains, So what?

At Hampstead, in the year 1562, a "monstrous pig" was born. So what?

Abraham, at the age of one hundred, had a son in Gerar, between Kadesh and Shur. So what?

Jesus floated up into a cloud from the top of a hill. So what?

It isn't until you start picking these things up by means of images that you can begin to differentiate and interpret them. It is only, for example, when the author of the Epistle to the Hebrews says that Jesus, in his ascension, is the Great High Priest entering into the Holy Place Not Made with Hands that the mere wonder of going up into the air like a balloon begins to yield a theme. The literal facts simply *are;* they don't mean a thing until you *figure* them.

There is an additional complication, however, when you come to deal with Scripture. The Bible makes up its own figures as it goes along. Events that at one point are mere events later become so loaded with meaning that they are used to interpret other events. When the Passover and the Exodus, for example, first occurred, they were just a miraculous escape act. But as the Jews carried that experience with them through the wilderness and beyond, they came to use it as a master device for interpreting to themselves their unique calling to be the chosen people, the body of the Mystery. And when Christians looked around for a symbol with which to figure out what Christ's death and resurrection were all about, they picked up the Passover and the Exodus, too: "Christ our Passover is sacrificed for us," they sang at Easter; "therefore let us keep the feast."

This use of biblical events and persons as images, figures, or types is called, appropriately enough, typology or typological interpretation; and it is essential to have some grounding in it, because the unity of Scripture can hardly be grasped without it. It is precisely by means of typology that this apparently random collection of books is seen as a single book with a single theme.

It is important, however, to make a sharp distinction between typology and mere allegory. Allegory is the symbolic expression, by means of fictional figures, of generalizations about human conduct. Bunyan's *Pilgrim's Progress* is a good example. The validity of allegory derives from the skill of the allegorizer; everything depends on how apt his figures are. Typology, on the other hand, does not involve making up arbitrary figures to illustrate already known generalizations; rather, it involves picking up already given figures from one part of the revelation in order to interpret events in another part — events in which the same unknowable Mystery is at work. Its validity derives not from the skill of the interpreter but from a connection in reality between two events. To be sure, the connection is a theological one, and it is on the underside of the events, as it were; but it is taken as real nonetheless.

To illustrate: The Exodus is a type of the Resurrection of Jesus. This is so not because I, or anyone else, find it to be a kind of ready-to-hand allegory of some generality called deliverance or rescue, but because of the theological presumption that the God who acted in the Resurrection was the same God who acted in the Exodus — and because of the further presumption that, as the unique God he is, he has left some telltale marks of his style in both events. Both events, if you will, are manifestations of the same Mystery — fingerprints from the same hidden hand. The Exodus bears the print of God's little finger, perhaps, and the Resurrection of his thumb; they may be used together because they already are together.

Or, to change the illustration slightly: Scripture is the *Word* of God; you should expect, therefore, some persistent tone of voice to keep turning up. Detecting it, of course, will be largely a matter of having a good ear; but every now and then you can get, in different passages, nicely matching voiceprints. These are the antitypes: two different sets of words, two different conversations with the unseen caller; but they give a very clear impression of just Who is on the other end of the phone line. That is how Saint Paul comes to hold that the rock from which the children of Israel drank in the wilderness was none other than Christ — and why the compilers of the King James Bible took the liberty of sprinkling Christ's name all over the page headings of the Old Testament.

All right. Enough focusing of flashlights. Back to the question of the theme of Scripture.

If the Bible is not simply about generalizations like spirituality or morality but about the Mystery of God's relationship to the world, what figure shall we use in order to grasp so elusive a theme? Well, on the assumption that almost all authors give themselves away in their last chapter, the choice is obvious. The image of images is Jerusalem, the City of God. Let us say, then, that the Bible is about the Mystery by which God turns the world into the City, about how his sword does not sleep in his hand until he has built Jerusalem in the whole earth's green and pleasant land.

From that, the rest is easy. Herewith a cram course in the unity of Scripture.

8. Covenants

The Bible presents us with the Mystery of God's work under two dispensations. It describes these dispensations by means of the image of a covenant or testament between God and his chosen people. The Old Covenant, strictly speaking, runs from the receiving of the Law by Moses on Mount Sinai to the birth of Christ; the New Covenant, for all the remaining years of our Lord. If you like references, the Old Covenant goes from Exodus 24 to Matthew 1; the New, from there on.

Before the making of the Old Covenant, however, three preparatory covenants can be distinguished: one with Adam, one with Noah, and one with Abraham. This makes five covenants in all, and five great pivotal figures around which the complex workings of Scripture are ordered into a single engine of the Mystery: Adam, Noah, Abraham, Moses, Jesus.

In each of these covenants, you can distinguish a demand, a promise, and a sign.

The *demand* is the same in all five, though the details of it vary widely from one to another. For the sake of simplicity, let us call it obedience: the demand of God is that his people should do his will.

The *promise,* too, is the same in all five. It is that the City will be built, that the world will become Jerusalem — or, in straighter language, that God's experiment of a free creation will be a success after all. This promise, however, appears in its fullness only when we come to the covenant in Jesus; in the earlier ones, it manifests itself by degrees.

The *signs* of the various covenants all differ, but they are by no means without a special unity of their own: when they are interpreted typologically, they put on an electric, mind-blowing display of theological arcs and short circuits.

I. The Covenant with Adam

The demand for obedience is voiced affirmatively. Adam and Eve, like all the rest of creation, are good. God tells them, "Be fruitful! Multiply! Enjoy, enjoy! Dress and keep this hint of the City, this garden I have given you, and make Jerusalem of all the world." The Tree of the Knowledge of Good and Evil is indeed set out; but only as the guarantee of the power of their freedom. The only negative demand is: "Leave *that* alone. Don't do any funny, twisty things in your mind with the good I have given you. Love creation for itself and for the City, not for the mean things it can be made to mean."

The promise is that Jerusalem will indeed be built. "I have given you everything. When you get it all named, it will be a City you never dreamed of. And I'll help you. When I walk in the garden in the cool of the day, we'll chat about how things are going, and then have a Cinzano and watch the sunset."

The sign is — well, you can take it a couple of ways. It's the whole garden, seen as the hint of the City. Or it's the Tree of Life in the midst of the garden. (Note — there are two trees: one forbidden; one, presumably, allowed.) In any case, both the garden and the tree are clearly signs of the covenant because, when the covenant is broken, both are withdrawn: cherubim and a flaming sword are set at the east of the Garden of Eden to keep Adam and Eve from the openness and directness of their first calling. The City will still be built, but no longer straightforwardly — not any more in the simplicity with which an obedient human race might once have raised it up. The Mystery of Jerusalem will work itself out now, not in straight lines, but by detours; not by intelligibilities, but by paradoxes and absurdities.

II. The Covenant with Noah

The point of the story of Noah comes not at the beginning but at the end. It is not that God destroys the world because of human disobedience but precisely that he forever renounces destruction as an answer to the problem of sin.

The demand, as before, is obedience. But this time the promise is that even disobedience won't stop the building of the City. This is the covenant of God's perpetual mercy, which begins at Genesis 8:21: "I will not again curse the ground any more for man's sake. . . . While the earth remaineth, seedtime and harvest, and cold and heat, and summer and winter, and day and night shall not cease."

The sign of all this is the rainbow. "This is the token of the covenant which I make between me and you and every living creature that is with you, for perpetual generations: I do set my bow in the cloud. . . . And I will remember my covenant . . . and the waters shall no more become a flood to destroy all flesh." God unstrings his deadly bow of wrath and hangs it up forever on the wall of heaven. Or, if you like, he leaves it strung and points it not at us but at himself. In any case, this sign is not withdrawn: his mercy is forever. Sin is behovely; but all shall be well. All manner of thing shall be well.

III. The Covenant with Abraham

Again, the demand is obedience; but this time, not to the sweet reasonableness of settling down in a garden and making a city of it. Now, beginning at Genesis 12:1, it is "Get thee out of thy country, and from thy kindred, and from thy father's house, unto a land that I will show thee." Obedience has become absurd; only faith in the Mystery remains. The City is to be built by a pilgrim on the run; Jerusalem will rise up among the nonexistent children of a man too old to have any.

The promise, too, is refined: not only will the City be built in an absurdity; it will be built in a scandal. It will not be raised up, even mysteriously, everywhere at once: the covenant is not with all humankind; it is only with Abraham's seed. But in that seed shall all the families of the earth be blessed. This is the covenant that specifies the means of the building of Jerusalem. In Adam, we saw the pure promise of the City; in Noah, the promise that it would be built in mercy; in Abraham, the promise that it will be built through a sacramental particularity, through a chosen people — through a church.

The sign? Circumcision. Forget the critics and their undoubtedly correct assertion that circumcision didn't really come into use until later. The author of Genesis puts it here as an interpretive device. Typology again. Only this time, read backward into the past instead of forward into the future. The point is that the family of Abraham are the body of the Mystery. They are not a club of like-minded religious enthusiasts or a learned society of Friends of Yahweh; they are the vessel of God's purpose, marked in their flesh as the place of the hiding of Jerusalem. "And ye shall circumcise the flesh of your foreskin; and it shall be a token of the covenant betwixt me and you."

IV. The Covenant with Moses

The demand for obedience now takes the form of the Law from Sinai. The Mystery, for a time, assumes the appearance of a plausibility: Do all these things, and you will inherit the promise.

And the promise? It, too, seems to lose its absurdity (Exod. 23:31): "If thou shalt indeed . . . do all that I speak, then I will be an enemy unto thine enemies, and an adversary unto thine adversaries. . . . I will send hornets before thee, which shall drive out the Hivite, the Canaanite, and the Hittite, from before thee. . . . And I will set thy bounds from the Red sea even unto the sea of the Philistines, and from the desert unto the river." It is the Promised Land: Jerusalem, not in mystery but in fact.

The sign is manifold. At first it is the Blood of the Covenant, sprinkled over the people at the reading of the Law. But that is quickly overshadowed by the Ark of the Covenant, the sacred box in which the Tables of the Law were carried, and over which, between the cherubim, dwelt Yahweh, God of Israel, whom the heaven of heavens could not contain but who, himself a pilgrim, deigned to pitch his tent among his people. And therefore, the Tent — the Tabernacle, the portable temple in which the Ark was kept in the Holy of Holies — becomes part of the sign, too. And so, eventually, does the Temple at Jerusalem, which replaced the Tabernacle when the wanderings were over.

And yet. The wanderings never really ended. A pilgrim God demanded a pilgrim people. The absurdity only seemed to depart. Jerusalem became an intelligibility only for a time, during the reigns of David and Solomon. David, Solomon. That was about the extent of the glory. From there on, it was all downhill — a deeper descent into the Mystery than ever before. The kingdom divided; Jerusalem destroyed; her people led captive to Babylon. Ten centuries of the gradual defeat of every plausible hope; a whole history of being run over by every steamroller in the ancient world: Damascus, Nineveh, Egypt, Babylon, Persia, Greece, Rome. The Old Covenant was still intact, but the only constant sign was the Blood of Israel itself, the Suffering Servant of Yahweh.

V. The New Covenant in the Blood of Jesus

The demand takes its final form: it is obedience not to the Law but to Grace by faith, to the ultimate absurdity of a God who gives Jerusalem for free.

The promise: New Jerusalem. A new heaven and a new earth. The holy City, prepared as a bride adorned for her husband. Twelve gates, twelve foundations. A street of pure gold, transparent as glass . . .

And the sign? The Blood of Jesus, the Blood of the New Covenant. More fully, the Sacred Humanity of Jesus himself . . .

I stop there, however. When imagery reaches that point, it becomes a critical mass. I want to save the fireworks of the ultimate explosion for the end.

9. *Priesthood*

We have been talking so far about the images with which we hunt the Mystery — about gardens and cities, covenants and blood. Time now to talk a little about the actual object of the hunt: about the habits and habitat of the Mystery itself.

All this discourse on the building of Jerusalem through covenants raises the question of the nature and extent of the operation. To begin with: Is it all an afterthought? Are the covenants merely adventitious — a supervening tidying up of a chaos that would never have become order without them? Are they extraneous transactions aimed at making a city of a world that is fundamentally alien to becoming one?

The answer appears to be no. The Mystery of the City enters at the beginning, not later on: the Garden is Jerusalem in the bud; Adam is the agent of the City from the start. At the very least, it seems better to view the history of the covenants as a long effort to get the original show back on the road — as an attempt to get Adam's agency back in business, so that the citifying of the world can go forward as intended.

But that raises a further question: Is Adam — is humankind — the only city builder? Does the world, apart from us, have no citifying tendencies? Or does the working of the Mystery go deeper? Does it lie, perhaps, at the very roots of all creation? And if so, how does it work in the orders below us? What images do we have that will shed light on cities which hide in the wordless dark?

Enough. That should keep us busy for a while.

Theology, as I said, starts from the top. When a theologian wants to find out something about humankind, he begins at Christ and works his way down by a series of analogical and sacramental handholds. Watch.

Jesus is Perfect Man. He is what God always had in mind for humanity and finally succeeded in getting. What is true of his human nature, therefore, will be a sacramental showing forth of what is true of all people. Accordingly, if Jesus is the Great High Priest — the offerer of creation to the Father, the reconciler of the world to God — all human beings may fruitfully be understood to be, in some sense, priests, offerers, reconcilers.

Thus the Priesthood of Christ, the Mystery that he sacramentalizes when he at last ascends into the Holy Place Not Made with Hands, becomes the key to the very first thing that Adam does when God breathes into his nostrils the breath of life: he offers, he reconciles, he lifts creation into ever higher unities. Adam, therefore, may be viewed as a priest: he offers the garden into the City; he names the beasts into an animal kingdom that they, unreconciled and speechless, could never know; he lifts the common coupling of the world into the mystical union of marriage.

Moreover, having come that far with this interpretive device, you can even run it backward: the priesthood that Jesus shows forth at the end is simply the priesthood that Adam had at the beginning, brought to its proper functioning. This, you will note, is the same device by which Saint Paul calls Christ the Last Adam. Some people dislike it, because they see it as a case of circular reasoning — of assuming what you started out to prove, and then using the results as proof of your assumption. But those are the people who fail to see that word games, especially image games, are also understanding games, reflection games. The flashlight shines in the mirror, and the mirror shines back at the flashlight. The exercise doesn't create any new light, but it really does shed light where there wasn't light before. In both directions.

Accordingly, I shall make another unprovable assumption and go straight to work. I raised the question whether the creatures below us — the lower orders, as we sometimes snobbishly call them — can be better understood if we see them, too, as involved in the working out of the Mystery of the City on their own level. I shall assume that the answer is yes. And I shall further assume that, just as the light of Christ can legitimately be pointed at us, so the reflection of that light can be bounced from us to animals, vegetables, and minerals — for fun and profit.

To a degree, indeed, I have already done so. When I ended up in Chapter Two with a sunflower that knew where the sun was, I got there by predicating a human faculty — knowing — of whatever unknowable thing it was that the sunflower was really doing. I justified it then by saying that, since all discourse about beings other than ourselves is heavily analogical anyway, we might as well use *de luxe* analogues. On that same principle, I want now to take an even more *de luxe* analogue and predicate it of the lower orders — an analogue taken this time not from philosophy, as knowledge was, but from the symbols of revelation. I propose to try the image of *priesthood* on the idea of *evolution* and see if it fits.

One slight further justification to get us going. From a theological point of view, there are reasons to expect this to be valid. When we say that humankind is made in the image of God, we immediately open the door to saying that creatures other than human beings may be made in the image of God as well. Three lines of reasoning lead to that conclusion.

First, earlier theologians held that the image of God in us was evidenced by our possession of knowledge and free will (as symbolized in Genesis by the naming of the animals and the command not to eat the forbidden fruit). If you take that stand, however, it is plain that knowledge and will exist below us — at the minimum, in most of the animal order and possibly also in the vegetable. A human being, accordingly, should not be viewed as a lonely sketch of God tucked into a book full of meaningless scribbles. Rather, he or she should be seen as the best self-portrait in a whole exhibition of self-portraits. Everything in the world looks like God, to one degree or another.

Second, even if you come at the image of God in humankind as more recent theologians have, you get the same result. They locate it by means of such phenomena as love and sexuality: to be made in the image of God means to be made in the image of the Trinity; accordingly, our inveterate mutuality is the visible evidence of the Mystery. Again, however, we are not all alone making love in the upstairs bedroom of the world; there's a lot of sex going on in the basement: "Birds do it, bees do it, even educated fleas do it." Ergo, et cetera.

Finally, if you take the image of God in us as referring preeminently to the image of the Word, the second Person of the Trinity, you arrive once more at the same point. The Word, in the solemn interchanges of the Trinity, is the one who offers creation to the Father — he is a priest forever, not just since the Incarnation but before all worlds. Humankind, therefore — Adam, from the word go — is a priest. But the priest business cannot be limited to us any more than the love business can. The world is full of little shops and cottage industries going full tilt at the work of offering up. Furry bodies lifting vegetable cells into animal tissue; tomato plants lifting mineral matter into vegetable stuff; even, this time, minerals strangely lifting themselves into shape: the formation of crystals is pretty odd, if you think about it for a while.

Priesthood, therefore, may not be a bad image at all with which to tackle the question of why this is an evolutionary world. At the very least, it ought to be given a try, because the images that modern thinkers have been using on the subject are, all of them, grossly unsatisfactory.

Consider the various explanations that have been handed us. They fall into two categories: chance theories and program theories. The chance theory is worthless as an explanation, because chance never explains why an individual event happens — it only describes the general pattern of events. My insurance company bases my premiums and its profits on the statistical certainty that not more than x sixty-nine-year-old males will die in a given year. I take some comfort from the fact that this enables the Prudential to come to my wife's rescue in the event of my sudden demise. But I learn nothing from it about the possible causes of my death — such as, for example, a little conspiracy between her and the Prudential man to put prussic acid in my birthday box of marzipan.

The chance theory does have one virtue, however. By the very fact that it does not explain the individual steps of evolution, it at least leaves room for the idea that, somehow, individual things really act on their own, even when they take an evolutionary flyer. It leaves a place in our philosophy for the concept of a radically free creation.

It is precisely the denial of the real and obvious freedom of everything to act for itself — and the transfer of the agency of evolution to a bunch of strong-arming theoretical spooks — that makes the *program* theories so unacceptable. It doesn't matter which one you take. They all come to the same fundamentally unbelievable conclusion — namely, that the whole history of the growth and development of the world was predetermined. The secularist version says that it was determined by an unbreakable chain of causes and effects: from the dawn of creation, everything had to happen the way it did because the material sequence of causes simply had to go the way it did. That, obviously, is not a scientific theory but a philosophical article of faith. It is not so much an explanation as a bald assertion. If it has any advantage, it is that it so plainly explains nothing that only a believer can hold it.

The religious version of the program theory, however, is even worse. It is indeed an explanation, and a great ham-handed divine one at that. It does, as the secularist theory does not, assign a sufficient cause for the programing: if God isn't enough, then nothing is. But when you say that God predetermined the entire natural history of the world and punched the program into some kind of built-in computer, your explanation hits the bull's-eye but on the wrong target. You explain the world perfectly. Only it's not this world you explain; it's one you made up in your head.

In your world, my dog pees on the second lamppost from the corner because he could not, in the nature of reality as programed by God from all eternity, do anything else but pee then and there, in full and on time. In this world — and admittedly, I mean my world — my dog pees where he damn well pleases. And the weeds in my garden grow where they damn well please. And the tree that fell and broke my fence fell where it damn well pleased. And I have damn well damned all three of them. Because the hallmark of a free world is every sane thing's deep inner conviction that it is metaphysically proper, practically useful, and socially acceptable to give a damn. God does. I do. And so does my dog, if you catch him in a foul mood. So compute me no computers, secular or divine. I'll bet you my world against yours any day of the week.

One more thing. The program explanations of evolution all have an unexpressed common assumption which ought to be damned while we're at it. It is that if, by any chance, you could manage to do the history of creation over, you would get the same result. Of course, no one ever will, so the assumption is safe from having to pass any experimental test. But haven't they learned anything from the tests they've done? They've been breeding fruit flies for decades now, and they've gotten some pretty bizarre fruit flies in the process — but nothing much besides fruit flies. That doesn't speak very well for their penchant for plastering philosophical necessity all over the upward thrust of the evolutionary process. Why doesn't it occur to them that maybe there never was any obligation to evolve? Desire is just as respectable a philosophical concept as necessity. Why don't they try that on for size? My theory is that when, as, and if the fruit flies decide to put on an evolutionary spectacle, they're not going to pull out of the barrel some script they used the first time around. They'll just wing it.

Because the world is, mercifully, not TV. There never has been a rerun and there never will be. Even things that repeat themselves don't repeat themselves: today's sunrise is not yesterday's — and today's sun itself is just a wee bit colder, one small step further along the road to the home for retired stars. The world is not a film that can be re-run; it is a single impromptu performance, a piece of street theater by a pickup company who never saw each other before or since, who did what they did, tossed off whatever lines came into their heads, barged into each other, punched each other, kicked and bit, or kissed and made up, as it seemed convenient at the time —

and closed to rave reviews with a rousing improvisation of *New Jerusalem* that made everyone go shivery all over.

You see? That makes a better world. Evolution as a fact is fair game. So is the investigation of the physical mechanisms by which it operates. But evolution explained as a philosophical necessity is malarkey. The explanation is either worthless or dreadful — or else it's a dodge to avoid talking about history. Which is even worse, because history is the real key to the subject after all.

We used to go at it that way. We used to talk about natural history. History was a nice high-class, human analogue, and it made for a sensible view of the world. But then we got into the habit of using the neutral word *evolution* and interpreting it — *figuring* it — by means of subhuman images. We filled our heads with pictures of machines and computers. And, inevitably, we blew it.

Let's go back, then, and talk history. In one sense, history can be taken as nothing more than chronicle: the bare sum of all the interactions of persons and things from the beginning of time. But in the most important sense, history is not an attempt to record everything; it is a quest to discover, by means of words and images, a shape in the course of time — to figure the Why and How of events. And when you come to that task, you do it badly if you attempt it by talking about external or internal forces. You do it well only if you use more elevated and uplifting language — only if you try to see the shape of events as due to the character of the various and several participants, human and nonhuman alike.

It was, for example, because of the relentlessly alpine character of the Alps — and the so remorselessly hannibalistic nature of Hannibal — that the world got the particular war movie that those two collaborated to produce. Without the unique actions that freely flowed from their distinctive characters, it would have been another picture. It was characteristic of Hannibal to *think big* but to be, regrettably, *unable to fly*. It was characteristic of alpine passes to have *fresh snow* on top of *old ice* in October. Put the two together and you get lots of scenes with sliding elephants. There was, however, no danger of getting another picture. What was, was; what might have been just wasn't. The history we got is the result of all the characters who were mixed up in it. If you are serious about asking Why and How, you will just have to study character.

Which is where priesthood comes in. In trying to figure an evolutionary world — to find an image that will shed light on the reason for evolution — we need something that will be characteristic of every creature in the process. For this is a very peculiar world. By all odds, it should, like everything else in the universe, be running downhill toward absolute zero. Indeed, like everything else, it is. Why then is its most obvious historical characteristic the glorious evolutionary march uphill? Why the boats-against-the-current theme over and over again? Why, in the face of entropy — in a universe in which the ultimate degradation of matter and energy leads to a state of inert uniformity of component elements, to the absence of form, pattern, hierarchy, or differentiation — why, in the face of all that, is the story of the world always more differentiation, greater hierarchies, splashier patterns, more gorgeous forms? Why does the nicely uniform primeval slime end up less uniform? Why ants in the hill? Why bees in the hive? Why stags fighting on the plain for the leadership of the herd? Why men who would run over their grandmothers to get somebody elected President? Why? Why? Why?

Well, I suggest that it is because, in some sense, everything in the world, every Jack and Jill in the cast of billions involved in this piece of improvisational theater we call history, is a priest. God has built into everything he made not a disk obedient to an external programer but a bent for offering on its own, a yen to lift for itself, an insane craving to make things more complicated just for the personal pleasure of doing so. Everything that hangs around this crazy performance watches like a hawk for a chance to make its move of offering up. On most days, it does its offering within the ordinary limits of its present nature. Ants offer up sand into anthills, bees lift nectar into honeycombs, and little slimy things do their thing with the slime. But on those rare days when the out of the ordinary happens, when, as a result of something fairly jazzy, things change — when there is an increase of radiation due to a storm on the sun, and a funny thing happens to somebody's DNA on the way to the theater — then that somebody doesn't just stand there. Like a running back looking for a break in the line, he shouts "Light!" and tears through. He moves out not because he was programed to do so by some coach but because he knows in his bones the object of the game — and, on his own, he makes his move.

Last step. Since all the running backs in creation are priests, the name of the game is offering, lifting, moving things up. That, I think, is what Teilhard de Chardin was saying, at least if you interpret his omega point as the target I believe he meant it to be. In any case, it makes more sense than determinism. It leaves you with Christ the Offerer *out there* as the goal of creation, and with Christ the Offerer *in here* making everything in his priestly image so that nothing fails to know the object of the game. Best of all, it leaves you with every single thing, top to bottom, free to play.

10. Computers

U sing the image of priesthood to illuminate the concept of evolution shows how good images can protect us from being robbed of our heritage of Mystery and, incidentally, keep us from solemnly mouthing a lot of sillies. But there are bad uses of images, too. The power of words is such that they can do nasty things. A horrible example is in order.

Consider the love affair that we are currently carrying on with the computer. It is a perfect instance of how we get in Dutch philosophically. Note, first of all, that I am not talking about computers as such. From the abacus on up to tomorrow's generation of supersophisticated electronic jobs, they are useful gadgets. I am talking here about what we think of the computer — about the way the image of the computer has developed in our minds, and how we have done ourselves a philosophical mischief with it.

The abacus seems not to have been much of a problem. People simply used it and let it go at that. They didn't turn it into an image and apply it to themselves. Nobody said admiringly that young Sneed had a mind like an abacus — probably because they knew the remark would be used as a straight line for "Too bad he's lost half his marbles." Back in those days Sneed Junior would most likely have been complimented for having a mind like a steel trap.

The hand-operated adding machine was no problem, either. Like the abacus, it worked at roughly human speed; no one was seriously tempted to look up to it or to figure out the mysteries of human nature by means of it. However, with the introduction of electrical and, later on, electronic machines, trouble began to brew. The computer acquired the virtue of speed. Sneed Secundus took it kindly when the Boss told him he had a brain like an adding machine.

But then, things went even further. The manufacturer added information storage and retrieval capacity to his already speedy piece of hardware. The Boss found himself tempted to transfer his compliments from Sneed to the machine. He praised it for its marvelous *memory* and for its ability to *figure things out*. He said it *thought* more clearly than Sneed, and in a final, idolatrous burst of enthusiasm, he punched in gossip about his political enemies and rubbed his hands in glee, because now it *knew* which senators liked boys better than girls.

But notice how things are getting badly out of control. On several fronts. For one thing, the reductionist fallacy is on the attack: we have substituted brain for mind — the *instrument* by which we know for the *faculty* of knowing. This has been done for so long now that "brains" is simply common speech for "intellect." "But," you say, "what's so dangerous about that? It's no different than substituting 'heart' for various functions of the will, as in 'have a heart,' meaning be 'merciful,' or 'miles and miles of heart,' meaning 'very sympathetic.'"

Don't kid yourself. Heart is an old giant among images; it's big enough to handle mystery with some resourcefulness. Brains is a midget — and a latecomer to boot. It is dangerous because you can't make an image of something that minor — with so little accumulated iconic content — without beefing it up a bit. Unfortunately for us, by the time "brains" was common usage, the most tempting image we had to figure it with was, lo and behold, the computer. Consequently, we started tossing off lines like "The brain is nothing but a computer made of meat" — which is reductionism rampant, nothing-buttery *in excelsis*.

But that wasn't all. Besides replacing mind with brain and brain with computer, we also lost track of which operations of the intellect came first. We substituted *thinking* for *knowing*. In spite of the fact that for ages we had them in the right order (1. simple apprehension; 2. judging; 3. reasoning), we carelessly talked ourselves into substituting the last for the first. "I think so" used to run a weak second to "I know so," but we spent so much time prattling on about reasoning as the principal ornament of the human mind that we lost the ear for the distinction.

The sad thing about such confusion of tongue is that it leads straight to confusion of face: it leads us into the reductionist's hall of mirrors, where we can no longer see ourselves as we really are. We take the fact that many animals obviously think, and the fact that the thinking of some of them comes amazingly close to reasoning, and we jump to the fanciful conclusion that human thinking is nothing but a special case of animal thinking — which means, of course, that it's nothing very special at all. Obviously, then, when somebody produces a machine that can reason circles around people, we are sitting ducks for the ultimate folly: we seriously begin to think about resigning our membership in The Animal and Vegetable Country Club and joining The Mineral Chowder and Marching Society.

Of course, our disgrace is entirely our own fault. Because the one thing the computer doesn't do is *know*. "Ah, but just a minute," you say with a wicked gleam in your eye. "This time I've got you. Why can't I say the computer knows? *Knowing* is simply an analogue. You applied it to sunflowers; why can't I slap it on my 486 laptop?"

You have a point. Knowing is indeed an analogue; and you may, if you like, predicate it of a machine. As a matter of fact, I want to reserve myself the right to predicate it, in some sense, of everything — all the way down to the bottom of the mineral kingdom. What you are forgetting, however, is that people who say the computer knows and then proceed, on a reductionist basis, to attack the uniqueness of human knowing are, by definition, using the word not analogically but univocally. Analogy is a way of shedding light on things that are really different, but alike in some respect. It predicates the concept *knowing* of a person and a computer, but it never kids itself for a moment that it means the same thing in both cases. Univocity also predicates a single concept of two different things, but it does so in exactly the same sense: *black* is the night; *black* is the color of my true love's hair. Clearly, since reductionists always end up saying that a human being is nothing but a computer, they are not using analogy at all. They are really no better than the old lady who believes that her cat actually conceptualizes the way she does. The only difference is that she pays the cat an undue compliment, while the reductionists give human nature a nasty slur.

But that's not all. Even a good analogue, used with due respect for the rules of analogy, has to be handled with discretion. I am obviously in favor of great boldness in this matter, especially after the last chapter, in which I set myself up for the job of explaining what in the world the priesthood of oysters and stones could possibly be. But a little prudence never hurts. Remember, when you apply an image to something, you release iconic power in both directions. To be sure, shining the light of knowing on the computer mightily enhances the computer. It takes the word a giant step closer to becoming an icon in its own right. But by that very fact, the computer now has power to reflect *its* light on knowing. And that's where trouble can start. Unless you keep careful track of which was the prime analogate, you may wind up rubbing Mother Nature the wrong way.

For, after all, there is a hierarchical grain to these things. Witness: I *know*. And my dog *knows*. And the lobster *knows*. And the sunflower *knows*, and the stone *knows* . . . But as you go further down the ladder, you run an ever-increasing risk of charley-horsing the long arm of analogy. The predicate takes a much safer hold at the top than at the bottom.

That is why I am reluctant to predicate *knowing* of a computer. It's a collection of mainly mineral junk. It's not even as far up the ladder as rutabaga: it's a machine, not an organism. (There's another pair of images that have been used in the same reductionist way: "Your body is a machine; fuel up with Chaff Flinkies for breakfast!") Organism, not machine, is the prime analogate; the machine is made in the image of the organism, not vice versa. For my money, I'm even prepared to say that a sunflower knows better than a computer. Not knows more; knows better. For when we use the phrase "it knows," we refer at least as much to the *it* — to the unique "selflike" quality which is the hallmark of an organism — as we do to the operation of knowing. The computer "contains" knowledge, perhaps, and can be programed to follow the steps of the thinking process; but what does the computer itself know? What does *it* think? Does it have any self-consciousness, any personal convictions? Does it have a heart? Even an eighth of an inch of one? *Chat fance,* as they say in French. And if you don't believe me, wait till the tender mercies of the IRS computer catch up with you. Instant conversion.

One of the tests that should regularly be applied to the results of any thinking process, however plausible, is: Would I like to sit down and have a vermouth with this thing I have just talked myself into? On that scale, ballerinas, oysters, free speech, and romantic love come off just fine. Computers, the Modern Presidency, National Honor, Protective Reaction, and Keeping America Number One make terrible drinking companions.

A man is not only known by the company he keeps; he is influenced by it. Evil communications corrupt good manners. And if all your communication is with nothing-butters, the corruption doesn't stop at bad manners. You yourself become frequently bad, usually sad, and, almost invariably, mad. Bad, because the root of all sin is the perversion of the priesthood by which we offer the world into the City. That *civilizing* priesthood is, as I said, principally verbal. The longer you persist in saying that things are not what they are — that Sneed is not a human being but a computer, that the computer is not a piece of hardware but a god — the more you are tempted to make wicked and uncivilized offerings. To do bad things long before you yourself have become a bad person.

People profess to wonder how men with such nice tailors, barbers, and family lives could become a plague of Waterbuggers. They don't seem to understand evil. They expect horns, hooves, and the gestures of blatant villainy; but that's not the way it works. With evil, in a classic paradigm of perversion, the beginning is in the word: it starts with the verbal abuse of reality. Adam sinned after Eve said that the tree was something to be desired to make one wise. We got Watergate and the secret bombing of Cambodia after we got NASAspeak and Nixonese — after the Pentagon abolished four-square talk. Not that we weren't warned: "The tongue is a fire, a world of iniquity . . ." No one can tame it. "It is an unruly evil, full of deadly poison."

But besides making you bad, it makes you sad. There you stand, next to a computer which you know is less than you, but which you have come to think knows more than you. Apart from accidents, the thing that makes people sick or well, glad or sad, is their own deepest belief about themselves. Shame came into the world only after Adam and Eve thought they were naked; sadness enters when they — the *domini mundi,* the lords of this world — cease to believe in their own kingship. Even an oyster gets sad when he loses his religion. How much sadder, then, must it make human beings when they talk themselves into thinking they are just little punks, no better than a machine?

Sad enough to make them mad. Angry mad, because they have been robbed of something precious and have so tied the hands of their minds that they can't get it back. Crazy mad, because angry people are dangerous and always do something when they can't do the right thing. And finally, stark staring bonkers mad, because they have reached behind their backs, picked themselves up by their belts, held themselves over their own heads, and are now occupied with the problem of how to change hands.

The Word always creates. And words always create. The idiot, by definition, is simply a person who has talked himself into a world of his own.

11. Souls

Ic should be noted, however, that the mischief done by the
creative power of words is not always the result of such wretched
usages as the one in the last chapter. Some of it comes from the
mishandling of perfectly good words and images.

One of the ground rules of all thinking, especially in philosophy
and theology, is that none of us gets very far unless we are willing
and able to make distinctions. There are times when my first-year
theology course turns into one long harangue on the theme "If you
don't distinguish, you can't theologize." After all, reality is a mystery
inaccessible to our minds. You can't form a concept of existence; you
can only affirm or deny existence of some known essence. Horses
exist, are real beings. Centaurs *do not exist;* they are only mental
beings. What our minds deal with directly are *essences* — the intelligibilities *by which* we grasp the act of being. We should regularly
expect, therefore, that a great deal of refining and distinguishing of
concepts will be necessary before we arrive at the best mental grasp
of things in hand.

Do you see how inevitable it is? The last two paragraphs
contain six distinctions, tossed in without half trying: Wretched
Usage/Good Usage; Good Usage Well Handled/Good Usage Mis-
handled; Mystery/Intelligibility; Existence/Essence; Real Being/
Mental Being; and for the boys and girls in the philosophical back
room, a hint of the distinction within *essence* between *id quod est*
and *id quo est quod est.*

But for all its inevitability, it takes a heap of handling to keep the distinguishing business from driving you out of house and home. If you can bear with just one more distinction, our distinctions themselves can bankrupt thought in two ways: by defect or by excess. *Sex* is a good example of a concept practically in the poorhouse by reason of a deficiency of distinction. Originally it referred to gender: we distinguished in human nature two sexes, male and female. But in modern times, that usage has been almost completely papered over. *Sex* has come to refer not to the distinction between two things but to some third thing which is the same for both sexes — or, worse yet, to anything done, alone or with others, involving the physical organs by virtue of which the distinction was first noticed. The very word, therefore, that was supposed to be a sharp probe to explore the full range of the mystery of humanity as male and female becomes a dull tool that, more often than not, obliterates the distinction altogether. Thus the barbarisms that go unnoticed every day: "I wish I had a sex life"; "Sex without fear"; and "Lose weight through sex." And thus, too, the old chestnuts which, to do them credit, at least have the sense to poke fun at it: "Name: EVELYN SNEED; Age: 23; Sex: OCCASIONALLY." And the one about the fellow who came into the office looking for Sexauer: "*Sexauer!* We don't even get a coffee break!"

Abuse of distinction by defect, however, is often small potatoes compared with abuse by excess. Take a simple illustration first.

When we set about to do justice to what is distinctively human about us, we frequently try to pick up that mystery by means of a distinction between knowledge and will. We discern in ourselves not only a consciousness of *what* we are doing but also an ability to decide *that* we will do it. Every human act, of course, is a seamless whole: even if I just sit around and know, I nevertheless will to do it; and if I will to do something, it always has to be something I know. Nevertheless, the distinction has been with us right from the beginning — and it has served us well, as long as it wasn't pushed to the point of talking about knowledge and will as if they were separate departments sending interoffice memos to each other. For there is no such *thing* as knowing, no such *thing* as willing. The only *thing* in actual being is a human person — and we do our thing as wholes, not by parts.

The temptation to excess, therefore, comes in the form of a penchant for thinking of the two parts of a mental distinction as if they were separable and actually existing things. It is a temptation to let the creative power of words get out of hand — to allow the terms to *reify* themselves and act as if they had a life of their own. To some extent, of course, this is inevitable. But it is safe only if you continually remember the original purpose for which the distinction was made — namely, the competent handling of a mysterious wholeness.

Which brings me to a larger and more theological illustration: the distinction we make between *body* and *soul* when we talk about humankind. Faithful to my general rule, I shall try first to find out what led the human race to talk about body/soul to begin with.

Adam, in his undoubted exhilaration at having successfully named all the animals, probably imagined for a while that his naming days were over. He was wrong. We have already seen his son the caveman, naming away on level after level. But even before the tour de force that gave Irving so much trouble, Adam came up against a problem.

He has, let us say, named the following things: Meadow; Large Tree Standing Alone in Midst of Meadow; Cow. But then he comes up against his first Thunderstorm. Ever conscious of his priestly duties, he promptly names Rain and Lightning. Cow, obedient to the more limited dictates of her nature, proceeds to take refuge under Tree. Lightning strikes Tree and bowls over Cow. When Rain stops, Adam goes over to Cow and puts his verbal priesthood to work again.

He looks at the beast lying on the ground. At first it seems to be the same Cow he named last week — and which, only two nights ago, he learned to call Sleeping Cow. But then he begins to notice differences: no motion at all; no breathing. "Thunder and grindstones!" he cries. "A Dead Cow!" He puzzles for a while over the cause of this change and finally concludes that, since no more breath is coming out of Cow, she must simply have run out of breath.

So he fetches his bicycle pump and tries to give her a refill. No good. Maybe she needs real breath instead of air. He tries mouth-to-mouth resuscitation. Again no good. Maybe she's just got a vapor lock: he jumps on her ribs with both feet. A little breath comes out, but still no good. And then, in a flash of insight, he finds the right verbal handle with which to pick up Death of Cow: something absolutely necessary to Cow — something without which Cow turns decisively and permanently into Dead Cow — has gone out of her. Since her breath has done just that, he decides to use the word *breath* for it; but in order to prove he knows it isn't really plain breath, he calls it Breath of Life. Finally, when he gets his Latin down pat, he fastens on the word *anima,* or soul, to do the job. As bonus points, he gets the words *animation, animate,* and *animal,* and off he goes again.

You can take it from there: how he came to distinguish his own more loved and respected *rational soul* from the merely *sensitive soul* of the cow; how he invented the *vegetable soul* to explain the phenomenon of living, as opposed to dead, cabbage; and how, eventually, he started down the road to talking about all these souls — but especially about his own — as actually existing parts of the things they animated, as *reified* entities.

What must be carefully noted in all this is the fact that the further you wander from the original purpose of the distinction, the trickier the going gets. It is one thing to say that the soul has gone out of a living body and that, as a consequence, the body is now no longer a true body but a corpse. It is quite another thing, however, to reify the departed ghost and then undertake to answer questions about its subsequent travels. You are on fairly safe ground in the first case: you are talking about an observed fact, death; and you are figuring it by the not inappropriate image of breath or soul. In the second case, however, you are talking not about something empirically observed but about the image you used to figure it; and you are attributing to the referent of that image a real existence which, in all honesty, you know very little about.

There is nothing necessarily wrong about that, of course. There may well be a real something, invisible and immaterial, that answers to the name Soul. But you don't know that. Perhaps you will say you do. Perhaps you think that God, in the Scriptures, assures us of it. Well, don't be so sure. Some biblical language certainly points in that direction. But on balance, more of-the Bible's talk about human nature seems to dispense with the usage. The "immortality of the soul" is not a scriptural notion. When the Bible wants to get at the idea of our eternal destiny outside the confines of time, it has a strong preference for images like the Resurrection of the Body and Everlasting Life.

Apparently, therefore, neither God nor we ourselves provide any final assurance on the subject of the separate existence of the soul. Certainly we should not despise the ancient and widespread belief of the race that the soul survives the body's death. But for the record, it ought to be noted that, in Christian circles, this surviv-ability was predicated only of the *human* soul. Animal and vegetable souls were held to perish when the matter they animated perished. The human soul was indeed said to persist; but the reasoning behind that conclusion was based chiefly on the theory that, unlike all other souls, each individual human soul was directly created by God and then infused into a body provided by cooperative parents. That, however, is one of the most minimally scriptural notions of all. It derives mostly from highly spiritual and otherworldly religions that set up an antagonistic dualism between matter and spirit: the soul, as spiritual, is good; the body, as matter, is evil. The goal of human life is to get rid of the nasty old physical cocoon in which the beautiful butterfly of the soul is imprisoned, so that, unfettered at last, it can assume its true nature and fly to God.

I am sure that many Christians — and all cheap-john-funeral-parlor-poetry-writers — firmly believe that to be the true Gospel. But it isn't. It is a thousand miles from the Judeo-Christian tradition. The beginning of the true teaching is that God made human beings — and precisely what we ordinarily mean by those words: eyes, ears, nose, arms, buttocks, shin-bones, ankles, toenails — God made *all* that, not just a "soul," in his image. And the end of the true teaching is that God redeemed human beings — flesh, bones, and all things appertaining to the perfection of human nature — by the Resurrection of the Body of Jesus. For a Christian, there are no Souls (whatever that means) in heaven (whatever that means); there are only Risen Bodies (once again, whatever that means).

And there, at last, is one of the most important phrases in all theology: *whatever that means.* It should invariably be tacked onto every statement that even begins to predicate attributes of the Mystery: in the Godhead (whatever that means), there are three divine persons (whatever that means), subsisting (whatever that means) in one divine substance (whatever that means). For these are only our words — dim, groping, oysterish images that we point unsurely at something we cannot see and could not grasp if we did. We may indeed, as a result of our labors, come to some small understanding of what it is we are trying to say about the Mystery. And we may, perhaps, come to some slightly larger understanding of what it is we are trying to avoid saying. But even at our best, we remain light-years away from any understanding of what the Mystery, in itself, is really like.

As a matter of fact, the only words we can be precise about in the trinitarian example I just gave are the words *one* and *three.* And even there, I am a little tempted to add something like " — if three is the right number, and if number is what God had in mind to tell us about." For after all, while we can be certain that three persons is the burden of Scripture and the teaching of the undivided church — so certain that we may rightly drum out of the corps anyone who says there are four — we have no knowledge of why God, in talking to us through Bible and church, picked the numbers he did. In all honesty, they don't make too much sense. It is quite possible that no one yet, in the entire history of Christianity, has stumbled over the real point of the information. But it doesn't matter. The purpose of orthodoxy is not to tell you the whole truth but to deliver intact to every succeeding generation the official Boy Scout set of images with which to pursue the truth. Theology, therefore, is a hunt for the Mystery — and the theologians are primarily hunters: even though they know that as long as they live they will never get even one clear shot at the Beast, they are happy enough keeping their guns oiled and tramping through the woods. Why shouldn't they be? At the end, the Beast has promised to fall right at their feet.

Accordingly, the upshot of our investigation into the original purpose of the soul/body distinction is this: "soul" was invented to pin down the distinguishing characteristic of a *living* body; therefore, don't be too quick to come to conclusions about its existence or nature when all you've got for evidence is a *dead* body. The only evidence that gives is evidence of absence. It's something. But it's not much.

Having said that, however, we may take up our lawful freedom to go on at any length we like about the soul. It is no small plaza in the city of our discourse, and we will only impoverish ourselves if we make a vow never to pass an afternoon in the park there. Just as long as the serious talk about it is labeled as speculative — and the looser usages recognized as mere figures of speech — we can stay as long as we like and, when we leave, know better than to lose the wholeness of the Mystery in a blind alley.

Incidentally, speaking of "soul" as a figure of speech, some priest friends and I once spent a late afternoon over a bottle of vermouth. During the casual clerical chitchat, we wandered into the subject of columbaria. The church, as everybody knows, is on its financial uppers. Accordingly, some of the more resourceful clergy have hit upon a neat way to produce a little extra revenue: you set up burial vaults for cremated remains in the basement of the church and sell the spaces to your parishioners. All it costs you is the price of marble, or whatever, to make the niches and their surroundings into a nice little chapel. Well, a few of the brethren got to talking about how much space you would need for each individual vault. The one priest there who had already built a columbarium said each niche took up about 12" × 14" or so. In the space available in his undercroft, he claimed, that gave him room for some three hundred souls. I just couldn't resist. I said, "Souls! If that's all you're burying, you're missing out on a chance to make a million. For souls, all you need is a quarter-inch drill."

12. *Superman*

If we are going to be dedicated theological hunters, however —
if we're planning to do anything more than just shoot the breeze
and knock back the Cinzanos — we had better get on with the
job of selecting, cleaning, and oiling the guns we need for the hunt.
And when you put it that way, the most important rifle of all —
the great elephant gun of an image — turns out to be the whole
cluster of words and images that make up what we call the doctrine
of the Incarnation: the teaching which says that Jesus of Nazareth
is *true* God and *perfect* man in an *inseparable* but *unconfused* union in
one Person — whatever all that means.

I shall, of course, attempt a few shots with it by and by. But
first, one very fast but important reminder: I am not concerned with
proving whether it's true or not. I happen to believe it is; you may
or may not, depending. All I want to do here is take a fresh look at
it and see, first, whether we've got it straight, and second, whether
we can use it to figure anything. As I said, the theologian's real work
is not to prove that the Faith is true, only that it's interesting.
Decisions about truth are, necessarily, the province of the faithful.
Off we go, then.

First, Jesus is God. More than that, he is true God. That means
that even though we say it is the *second* Person of the Trinity who
is incarnate in Jesus, we are using the word *true* to remind ourselves
that since there is only one God, the Person who "came down from
heaven and was incarnate by the Holy Ghost of the Virgin Mary"

just has to be that same one God. He is all the God there is; there is no God at all that is not in him.

Confused? If you are, it may be because of the football-game image with which we sometimes try to figure the doctrine. As a figure, it's a bit thick in the flitch. It produces only fatheaded understandings of the Incarnation. Witness:

God the Father plays the first half of the game all by himself: the Son and the Holy Spirit sit on the sidelines from the dawn of creation right through to the end of the Old Testament. But then, in the fullness of time, the Father puts himself on the heavenly bench and sends in the Son for the third quarter. At the beginning of the last period, however, he decides he's got enough of a lead to risk using the rookies, so he pulls the Son and puts in the Holy Catholic Church to finish the game, now and then sending in the Spirit to kick field goals.

Put that baldly, of course, it sounds silly. But it, or something only a little less gross, is in many people's minds. And not without some justification. After all, that's the way it seems to have happened: the dispensation of Grace occurs historically, by degrees. And biblical phrases like "in the beginning" and "in the fullness of time" are extremely patient of "game" interpretation. Indeed, there probably isn't a third-grade Sunday School teacher in the world who doesn't do it just that way. And since the church has a poor record of getting its members very far past the third grade, that's about the level of understanding of most of the membership.

But it won't wash. Scripture won't support it, and the Faith of the church won't touch it with a barge pole. The Word and the Spirit, as we said, are in on the act of creation, and Christ is in the Old Testament, and the Spirit of the Lord is in Isaiah, and Jesus *is* before Abraham was, and he had glory with the Father before the world existed. And as far as the church is concerned, whatever "three Persons in one God" means, it cannot mean three parts or three divisions or three separable anythings. There is only *one* divine individual.

So if it's a game at all, it's got to be another ball game. One in which the whole team is in there all the way, working mysterious plays in which each takes turns carrying the ball, while one or both of the others block, run interference, or just plain go invisible. And therefore, while it is indeed God the Son, the second Person of the Trinity, who becomes incarnate in Jesus, there isn't any of the Trinity outside him. The Father and the Spirit coinhere in everything he is and does. (It really isn't even correct to imagine his incarnation as a showing up, since he, as the one God he is, was always everywhere already.)

More on that later. Just note now how this *coinherence* of the Persons in each other and in one divine substance solves the problem that some people have with language like "he came *down* from heaven." They profess to be embarrassed by the implication that heaven is in the top story and that the Father had to send the Son downstairs to do his work. But no good theology has ever taken such language literally. It's an image — something with which to figure the Mystery of God in Jesus. The fathers were perfectly clear that he never left heaven to get here. Witness the old Latin hymn:

> Verbum supernum prodiens,
> Nec linquens patris dexteram . . .

(The Word proceeding from above, / Yet leaving not the Father's side . . .) The spatial implication didn't worry them. They knew it was out of bounds.

As a matter of fact, this is as good a place as any to get in a general warning about the implications people go around discovering under every theological bed: most of them turn out to be either false alarms or pussycats. If you know the Faith and a couple of ground rules, they don't bother you at all. So panic not. You're dealing with a set of images, with plazas of meaning from which you can exit by many streets. Whatever *down* means, it can't mean downstairs. Maybe it means that he came down from his first price. Or down off his high horse. Try it any way you like; just stay off the staircase.

For after all, *down* is no more, or less, difficult than the rest of the phrase. Why don't they fuss over *he,* for example? Obligingly enough, some people do. There is a pious backwater in the women's lib movement where you can find people who write services in which God is referred to as *she*. And of course, there is a corresponding angry swamp in the traditionalist movement where there is much weeping, gnashing of teeth, and writing of letters to the editor about the outrage. Knuckleheads! Why don't they just remember not to leave the plaza *He* by way of the street marked *Male*. Take *Person* as the way out, and you're as safe as if you were in an armored car. *She,* on that basis, is obviously OK too. But by the same token, it's also totally unnecessary. It's no better and no worse than *he.* So if people with no theological horse sense want to lob rocks at each other, let them. Children must play. The rest of us should put away childish things.

All right. Jesus is true God, whatever that means. At the least, we've ticked off a few things it should not be allowed to mean under any circumstances. On to *perfect* Man.

It may be that there is no single word in Christian theology which has been more grievously misinterpreted than the word "perfect" when applied to the humanity of Christ. The original Greek that lies behind it is the word *telos: an end accomplished,* the *completion* or *fulfillment* of anything. Accordingly, even though "complete" may sound a little mild, I'm going to use it. "Perfect" has gotten so overblown that it needs to be taken down as many pegs as possible.

Therefore, when we say that Jesus is perfectly human, we mean that he is completely human: his humanity is everyday, common-garden humanity *in completion.* But see how alien that is to the common view. "Perfect" is like "spiritual." It sends people's minds straight out on extended ethereal trips. The old dualism of evil matter/good spirit is so much a part of us that, in spite of the promise of the resurrection of the body, we can imagine human nature as perfected only if we can somehow see it as abolished in favor of something spiffier. We can figure Jesus as sinless only if we flesh him out in something other than ordinary flesh.

When we imagine him as a child, for example, we somehow feel obliged to say that he was a little freak who never hid when his mother called him, who always put his toys away in his toy box, and who, when he got to the age at which boys have wet dreams, piously refused to have any. But that's theological folly. It's winning a minor battle at the price of losing the whole war. The big things to be defended about Christ are his Godhead and his Manhood. It would be far better to bend the concept of his sinlessness a bit than to lose sight of his humanity in the process of trying to say how good it is.

Indeed, it might even be a good idea to come down a peg from *completely* human just to make the point clear. Let's call him *merely* human. Not, of course, in some disparaging, proper sense of the word such as "merely stupid" or "mere boiled potatoes" but in the complimentary, slangy sense: "She was merely telling you the truth, Arthur," or "a mere five-carat diamond." Christ's perfect humanity, accordingly, is mere humanity: it's human, wholly human and nothing but human. (Jesus is God too, of course. But the first rule there is that, while you may never separate his two natures into two separate persons, you must not make a scrambled egg of him, either. He is not a blend of deity and manhood: his natures are inseparable but distinct. There is no manhood in his deity. And there is not one shred of God in his humanity, any more than there is in yours or mine — loose talk to the contrary notwithstanding. The union of the two natures is precisely a union, not an amalgamation.)

All this is necessary because almost nobody resists the temptation to jazz up the humanity of Christ. The true paradigm of the ordinary American view of Jesus is Superman: "Faster than a speeding bullet, more powerful than a locomotive, able to leap tall buildings in a single bound. It's Superman! Strange visitor from another planet, who came to earth with powers and abilities far beyond those of mortal men, and who, disguised as Clark Kent, mild-mannered reporter for a great metropolitan newspaper, fights a never-ending battle for truth, justice, and the American Way." If that isn't popular Christology, I'll eat my hat. Jesus — gentle, meek, and mild, but with secret, souped-up, more-than-human insides — bumbles around for thirty-three years, nearly gets himself done in for good by the Kryptonite Kross, but at the last minute struggles into the phone booth of the Empty Tomb, changes into his Easter suit, and, with a single bound, leaps back up to the planet Heaven. It's got it all, including — just so you shouldn't miss the lesson, kiddies — *he never once touches Lois Lane.*

You think that's funny? Don't laugh. The human race is, was, and probably always will be deeply unwilling to accept a human messiah. We don't want to be saved in our humanity; we want to be fished out of it. We crucified Jesus not because he was God but because he blasphemed: he claimed to be God and then failed to come up to our standards for assessing the claim. It's not that we weren't looking for the Messiah; it's just that he wasn't what we were looking for. Our kind of Messiah would come down from a cross. He would carry a folding phone booth in his back pocket. He wouldn't do a stupid thing like rising from the dead. He would do a smart thing like never dying.

If you don't believe me, look at the whole tradition of messiah figures in popular fiction. Superman is a classic, but there are others just as good — and one that's even better — for illustrating our hunger for a nonhuman messiah. How about the sheriff in the typical "salvation" Western? Matt Dillon can be wounded but not killed, daunted but never defeated. He looks like a man, but he's really the avenging angel in drag. Just to prove it, the same old device is trotted out: you know Miss Kitty's business, and I know Miss Kitty's business, and it's a safe bet Miss Kitty knows her business. But Matt might as well be a Martian for all the good it does him. The only belt he gets out of her comes in a little beer glass with a lot of talk.

Ditto the Lone Ranger, heigh-hoing around the days of yester-year with Tonto, a white horse, no women, and a beltful of silver bullets, yet. Do you see? Everybody else is human: Doc, Festus, Quint, Kitty, the drovers, the sodbusters, the townsfolk, the bad guys. But the Messiah who saves them all is unbendingly, unflinch-ingly Divine.

Not convinced yet? That's because I haven't given you the clincher. These Western sheriffim are a little misleading. They still, like Superman, have the appearance of humanity. It is not until we come to the ultimate popular messiah figure that we realize how much we despise our nature: we are so desperate to get rid of it that our imaginations will accept not only superhuman messiahs but subhuman ones, too. Maybe you think I'm going to give you an essay on our longing to be saved by something classy like Technology, or Science, or The Computer. But I'm not. I'm still reading *TV Guide:*

❹ LASSIE — Drama
Lassie's problems: a snow goose and an ailing poodle. Part 2 of a four-part episode filmed at California's Vandenberg Air Force Base. Garth: Ron Hayes. Chaplain: Jack Ging.

A dog, for Christ's sake! Literally! Little Timmie goes schlepping all over the countryside getting himself lost, strayed, or stolen, but he's practically the only human character in the show. Mother and Father are a couple of clowns who couldn't keep track of the movements of Mount Rushmore. And poor Jack Ging, having to play the Chaplain! Turn off the set. I can't stand to watch a grown man make a fool of himself. But no matter. Lassie *vincit omnia.* She will be beaten by bad men, bitten by alligators, clawed by mountain lions, and left for dead in the desert. But three days later! Home she comes with the snow goose on her back, the ailing poodle in an improvised litter, and in her mouth, Mother's wedding ring, Father's wallet, and a note to pick up Timmie at the supermarket.

I hope I have convinced you that we can hardly be too fussy about keeping our view of the humanity of Christ completely, merely human. In any case, however, the last question to be dealt with is now in front of us: If Jesus is one-hundred-percent human, how do you figure the union of his two natures in one Person?

Well, the old orthodox answer comes in the form of two rules of thumb. Rule 1: If you're talking about the *natures,* you give Jesus two of everything and you try your best not to mix them up. Rule 2: If you're talking about the *Person,* you can relax a little and let it sound as if you had forgotten Rule 1. (Rule 1 came out of the church's experience with the Christological controversies of the fourth and fifth centuries — especially out of her response to some gentlemen named Apollinaris and Eutyches. Rule 2 arose in connection with a theologian by the name of Nestorius; it is called the *communication of idioms*. I don't know if that helps you, but I do have to flash my union card once in a while.)

Rule 1. Example: Jesus has two minds, one divine, one human.

QUESTION: Why do you have to say that?

ANSWER: Because if you don't, you welsh on what you've already said about his being true God and perfect man. Human thought and divine thought don't mix. Asking "Did Jesus think divine thoughts in his human mind?" shipwrecks you on the rock of incommensurability. It's apples and oranges — like asking, "What does E-flat smell like?" If you sneak divine thoughts into a human mind, you make it superhuman. That can be a lot of fun, of course, but it messes up the realities of salvation. Jesus came to save *us,* in the bare-faced human nature he gave us. But if the final product of his labors is a jazzed-up third something that is neither honest-to-God God nor honest-to-man man, then he didn't save *us.* He gave up on us and saved something else he liked better.

Get on top of it and look down. Suppose *you* were the highest thing in the universe, the cause of everything below you. And suppose that the frogs had eaten of the Lily Pad of the Knowledge of Good and Evil and messed themselves up royally. And suppose you decided to save them by becoming incarnate among them. How would you have to go about it? (Just for the sake of neatness, we should get the Latin formation straight: *Carn-* means "flesh"; *incarnation,* therefore, is enfleshment. Frog, in Latin, is *rana;* enfrogment should be *in + ran-* or *irranation.*)

In your irranation you must, above all else, take care not to foul up the frogginess of the frogs. After all, that's the very thing you're out to rescue from the detestable unfrogginesses they have committed. Accordingly, you will have to come down and dwell among them without intruding your nature into theirs in any way, shape, or form. You, as you, must not be revealed among them, because that would violate the way *they* live. Your thoughts of political science, economics, and chemistry must not be thought in their substance, because that's not their style. Your taste for fine wines, *escargots,* pepperoni pizza, and bawdy songs must not once be indulged through the whole of your irranation; you will have to content yourself only with the best insects you can find, the jolliest croakings you can manage. Only that way could they rebuke you, as we rebuked Christ, for being "a Croaker and a Bug-Eater."

For if you were to violate any of those conditions, the Christfrog in whom you would be irranated would be just a freak — a frog whose mind, for example, had two compartments. The lower chamber would be merely froggy, but the upper one, gloriously human. And between them would be a trapdoor so that, even though your Christfrog would not really draw his thoughts only from the froggy part of his mind, he would always be able, in a pinch, to reach up through the trapdoor and get any human knowledge he might like or need.

But once again, that just won't wash. Go back to Jesus: if you posit a trapdoor through which his divine mind can leak heavenly secrets into his human mind — if you give his human intellect an inside track that no other human intellect has — then you simply make it nonhuman. And you come up with a lot of sillies. Like the human mind of Jesus in A.D. 20 knowing who shot John Kennedy. Which is just plain unreal. His *divine* mind knew, of course. But you don't ruin his humanity just for the sake of some easy synthesis you'd like to effect. The rule in theology is: When you've got two truths that you can't hold in harmony, you don't solve the problem by letting one of them go. You hang on tight and hold them both in paradox. At least that way you don't end up sweeping jewelry under the rug in the name of compulsive neatness.

"But," you say, "it's so hard to imagine what it would be like for Jesus to be both God and man."

Wrong. Once you know any theology at all, you make a distinction: if you're trying to imagine what it's like for God the Son, as he is in himself, it's not hard; it's impossible. So give up. But if you're trying to imagine what it was like for Jesus, in his humanity, it's a lead-pipe cinch. Just imagine that he felt just like you, because that's exactly what the doctrine says: he was perfectly, completely, merely *human.* And if you insist on looking for an answer to the question of how the divine works on the human in Christ, seek it in some way that doesn't, on the one hand, make a mishmash of them, or, on the other, turn Jesus into some kind of committee of two locked in a thirty-three-year-long executive session. Perhaps the best way of figuring it is to say that in Jesus the divine operates on the human in the order of Grace and not in the order of nature. Which, of course, is to say of Jesus' human nature exactly what we say of our own — even when we talk about miracles.

Jesus didn't cast out demons by some superhuman power nobody else had. He did it by the Grace of the Holy Spirit, which everybody else has, and which lots of people have used, if you believe the miracles of Scripture. And he didn't get driven into the desert to fast and pray by some special high-octane intellectual gas that leaked through the trapdoor in his head. The Spirit drove him. Just as it drives us — except we mostly get off the bus too soon. And when he was little, his knowledge of Aramaic, and his knowledge of Scripture, and his knowledge of carpentry all came in the same way: humanly, not superhumanly. If he got any heavenly help, it was the same help of the Holy Spirit you and I get — which, in all honesty, is not too much when it comes to memorizing verbs or learning how to use a drawknife.

"But," you say, "didn't Jesus know he was God?"

FIRST ANSWER: Yes. Because what else could he mean by a statement like "He that hath seen me hath seen the Father?"

SECOND ANSWER: I don't know. He didn't say so in so many words.

THIRD ANSWER: No, at least not for part of his life. When he was a baby, he didn't even know he was a baby. How could he know he was God?

FOURTH ANSWER: No. As a Jew, that formulation of his mission was unavailable to him. He figured his identity in other ways: Son of Man, Son of God, Son of David, Christ, Lord, Brazen Serpent, Greater than Solomon, Bread from Heaven. It even took the church a couple of hundred years before it could say, "Jesus is God."

FIFTH ANSWER: You don't need an answer. It makes no difference whether he knew or not. He *was* God; and he *knew* how to save. Nothing more was necessary.

SIXTH ANSWER: It's a dumb question. Haven't you been listening to what I've been saying about the mere humanness of his human mind? Of necessity, he had to figure the answer to "Am I God?" with the human images he had at hand. Which he did. In the Gospels. The answers are all there; figure them out for yourself.

CORRECT ANSWER: Take your pick. I'm not in the question-answering business, anyway.

I apologize for taking so long with my one example of Rule 1. I shall atone by giving two exceedingly brief examples of Rule 2.

The *communication of idioms* is theological shoptalk for the idea that, since the divine and the human in Christ are, in spite of all the difficulties, still to be taken as united in *one Person,* then you may attribute the idioms or properties of either nature to the one Person they both in fact are. As I said, you get some more relaxed usage this way: God died on the cross. Well, obviously, God, as God, can't die. But if God is one Person with human nature in Jesus, then when Jesus dies in his human nature, the Person, the one Identity he is, may correctly be said to die too.

Again — to take the great original of this kind of talk: Mary is the Mother of God. Clearly, God as God neither needs nor has a mother. But it is a matter of record that when God decided to become human, he used a mother, just like everybody else. Therefore, since he is one Person with Jesus, and since Mary is the Mother of Jesus, the correct answer to the question "What was the name of the Person who was born of Mary?" can be either "Jesus" or "God," as you like. The answer "God" made people like Nestorius nervous. It still does. I happen to like it; you may not. Fortunately, it's one of those matters of taste we don't have to fight about — unless you try to tell me I am bound by some metaphysical necessity to dislike it.

If you do that, I shall call you a Nestorian and throw empty wine jugs at you.

13. Bookkeeping

Am I mistaken, or do I detect a note of annoyance? "Some nerve!" you mutter to yourself. "Where does he get off, threatening me? I feel like throwing a couple of bottles myself. Back in Chapter Nine he promised to begin talking about the Mystery. Here he is now at Thirteen, and all he's given me is more talk about language and four chapters full of pronouncements on what the Mystery is not. People who live in glass houses . . ."

All right. Pax. Fins. King's X. Be a Nestorian if you like. This is the only way I know how to do it.

Because as far as our minds are concerned, the Mystery remains stubbornly, maddeningly mysterious. Not that we don't have an existential grip on it: we touch it all the time — and not just in religious ways. It isn't only by anointing the feet of Jesus while he was on earth or by receiving the Sacrament of his Body and Blood that we grasp it. It is in us, with us, and under us every moment of our being — and in, with, and under everything else, too. And not that *it* doesn't have a grip on *us:* it is precisely the hand of the Mystery that holds us so alarmingly and gloriously *outside nothing* and *in being.* It's just that when we try to talk about it, we inevitably find that we can be clearer about what it isn't than what it is. The best we can do is refine and sharpen the paradoxes by which we state it, reassess and reinterpret the images by which we figure it — go over our figures, if you like, and check them for false results.

At the end of the last chapter, I slipped into a usage which, while practically unavoidable, is particularly in need of re-examination. In talking about Mary as the Mother of God, I used the phrase *"when God decided* to become human." That, and the fundamental question it raises about the nature of the Mystery, are what this chapter is about.

On one level, saying "when God decided" is perfectly all right. It is an anthropomorphism, just as every other usage is. To use it wisely, you simply have to bear in mind constantly that *deciding at a certain time* is not the best image of what God does. He doesn't sit around wondering and then *one day* make up his mind. He just wills. And whatever he wills, he wills from all eternity. His mind is never anything but fully made up.

On another level, however, the phrase is bound to make trouble, because the "time" imagery is so strong that it keeps knocking at every door in the house until somebody lets it in. Perhaps you think that's all right — that as long as it doesn't track its time-mired feet into the front room, where God is, it can be let into the kitchen, where creation is. For after all, the world is temporal, and God acts in history, and revelation comes by degrees. Why can't you just put an unexpressed parenthesis in the phrase to clean it up? Why can't you say: "When *(from our point of view)* God decided"? Doesn't that succeed in keeping the mud out of the parlor?

No, because even with its feet thus parked on a mat, it's just biding its time. The minute you turn your back it will roam all over the place. Watch.

Jesus of Nazareth was born in the back of a stable near Bethlehem in the year 4 B.C. (That's correct. Mercifully, though, it's not another paradox. It's the result of a mistake somebody made when the calendar was changed.) In any case, Christians believe that this same Jesus is the Word made flesh; he is God become man. Accordingly, it seems perfectly safe to hold that his birth is the beginning of a new departure in which God himself comes on stage in the Incarnation — that "when (from our point of view) God decided to become human," a new Mystery went into effect.

For most people, no doubt, that sounds cautious enough. It predicates time of God only in connection with something he did in time. He always willed to do it; but in this world, he did it on a certain day. But hold on. There is an implication there just itching to put its muddy feet all over your theology. If you don't watch it, you will quickly find yourself saying that, accordingly, this Mystery became operative only in 4 B.C., and only in Jesus.

Does that still sound all right? Watch some more. If this Mystery first went to work in 4 B.C., then it was unavailable to all the people who lived before that date. And if it is operative only in Jesus, then that means that Jews, Turks, and Infidels who died in 200 B.C., or Eskimos who died in A.D. 29, were never in touch with it. And that in turn means that the whole untimely lot of them are out of luck as far as getting hotel accommodations in the New Jerusalem is concerned. And that means they can all go to hell.

Notice how nicely we're progressing. We have now arrived at one of the more detestable enormities in the history of theology. And we have run smack into opposition with Jesus' own words: "I, if I be lifted up . . . will draw *all* unto me."

Since most of the theologians who embraced this monster were basically nice people, they had the grace to feel bad about not having room in the eternal Holiday Inn for so many people. So they proceeded to build, not with the hard cash of Scripture but almost entirely on speculation, a couple of cheap motels along the Jerusalem road. These were run by Conrad Limbo, Inc. There was the *Limbus Patrum,* or Limbo of the Fathers, for all the ancient Greek worthies like Socrates; and there was the *Limbus Puerorum,* or Limbo of the Children, for all the little tykes who cashed in their chips before they had a chance to commit any sins.

Things are going swimmingly. We have reached the point of saying that God will give you cut-rate bliss on the outer marches of his favor, just for being a good egg. Which, of course, is exactly what Jesus did not say: "*I* am the way, the truth, and the life: no one cometh unto the Father, but by me." Morality, not forgiveness — Law, not Grace — has become the promise of your gospel. You are about to skid yourself into the world's all-time worst pile-up on the Jersey Turnpike of theology: A dump truck (Galatians) and a tractor trailer (Romans) owned by Paul & Co. are going to jump the divider and clobber you. Reformation Brothers' Towing will take a hundred years to unscramble the mess, and not even Twentieth Century Body and Fender will be able to get the dents out. All because you thought it was safe to take your eye off "when God decided . . ."

Let's go back, then, and make the run again. Only, this trip, not quite so recklessly:

"When (from our point of view) God decided to become human," he chose to be "incarnate by the Holy Ghost of the Virgin Mary." This time we shall avoid the pothole of assuming that the birth of Jesus is the beginning of a new departure in the way God works in the world. Let us say instead that it was the culmination of a whole series of transactions between God and Humanity — transactions by which the one, unchanging Mystery works toward the building of Jerusalem, the City of God.

That sounds better already. It fits nicely with the history of the covenants, and it obviates the necessity of seeing Jesus as the sole transaction in which the Mystery is at work: on their own level, all the earlier transactions — Adam, Noah, Abraham, Moses — were true steps in the building of the City. The Incarnation is simply the supreme transaction. The Death and Resurrection of Jesus are the effective fulfillment of all that went before.

Accordingly, we may now view the proclamation of the Gospel in a different light. In Jesus, God has made the ultimate transaction, after which no other transaction will ever be needed. God has, as it were, perfected a saving product, and he now proceeds to distribute it. This is good, too. It makes sense of the scandal of particularity we saw in Abraham: God *particularizes* salvation, first in Israel and finally in Jesus, precisely in order to *universalize* it. He cuts out everybody just so he can eventually draw in all. He excludes, but only to catholicize.

We're holding the road pretty well. But how does the result of the ultimate transaction become catholic? How is the finally perfected product distributed to all? Well, in the first instance, this is accomplished by a fellowship of baptized people that is universal, for all people — by the one, holy, catholic, and apostolic church, sent to proclaim everywhere the Gospel of Jesus' full, perfect, and sufficient sacrifice, oblation, and satisfaction offered once for all on the cross.

How, though, shall we deal with the problem that, last time around, eventually caused the crash? How do we get the perfected product to those born too soon or too far away from the Holy Catholic Chain Store? Let's try it this way: let's say that, while the church is the normal outlet for the fruits of the transaction, it's obvious that the distributing operation of Jesus is not limited to the church. This has the virtue of having some scriptural and creedal foundation: after his death on the cross, and before his resurrection, Jesus *descends into hell,* into *the place of departed spirits.* He goes and preaches to *the spirits in prison.* He offers them an opportunity to accept the free gift he has just perfected in the ultimate transaction.

Good enough. That takes care of everybody who died before A.D. 29 — and without a single jerry-built limbo, at that. But what about the Eskimo in A.D. 29 who didn't even have an Eskimo's chance of getting preached to at all — who died in the frozen North while the church was still basking in the Mediterranean sunshine? What about all the poor souls who were too late for the early show and too early for the late one? Well, perhaps we can hold that the descent into hell was meant to be taken not as a single excursion but as a perpetual visit. Maybe it should be taken to mean that Jesus is always there, continually offering his salvation to all who die without having heard it: if you don't get a chance to pick up your free gift at one of his franchised outlets during your lifetime, he will personally distribute his product door-to-door after death.

It's holding nicely. No limbos. Nobody left out. But what of the final question? What does it mean when we say that the *souls of the departed* will have a chance to accept or reject the free gift? The souls of the departed, if they exist in reality at all, are not human beings. A human being is soul and body; if you separate the two, you get a ghost and a corpse. Furthermore, in the tradition in which this usage of *soul* was most common, the soul after death was viewed as a poor, passive thing, incapable of doing or deciding anything. And worse yet, there is 2 Corinthians 5:10: "We must all appear before the judgment seat of Christ; that every one may receive the things done in his body, according to that he hath done, whether it be good or bad."

Oh, oh. Things are beginning to sound as if we've got a front wheel out of balance. The argument is up to speed, but it's developing a shimmy. Perhaps if we push it a little harder, we can cure it. Suppose we try saying that the descent into hell means not a standing order by which Jesus offers the benefits of his saving transaction to the souls of the dead, but rather a willingness on his part to take some of the "deeds done in the body" — things done while people were still alive and, therefore, still people — as the equivalent of acceptance or rejection of the gift.

That only makes it worse. Apparently both front wheels are in bad shape. On the one hand, we are slipping from theology into bookkeeping: we are now obliged to work out a system for converting purely natural earthly deeds into acceptance of Christ. On the other hand, that turns out to be a tricky proposition. If we're not careful, we'll steer ourselves right back into the same situation that caused the awful pile-up on the last trip: we're on the verge of saying once again that morality, not mercy, is the key to the City — that Law is, after all, the touchstone of Grace.

Of course, we might try to work up some way of saying that the "good deeds done in the body" are to be taken not as good deeds that have power to earn salvation but as evidence of a willingness to accept mercy. How about a system for converting the coin of morality into the scrip of forgiveness? Of course, that will involve a lot more bookkeeping. As a matter of fact, it will probably involve keeping two sets of books . . .

Hey, listen. The shimmy is getting worse instead of better. I've got an idea. This heap we're driving has had it. Between the front end and the dents, it's going to nickel-and-dime us to death. Why don't we pull into the next dealership we come to and trade it in for a new model?

14. *Transacting*

As I analyze the troubles we ran into in the last chapter, it strikes me that they were caused — as most theological calamities are — by unexamined assumptions. On the first trip out, we made the mistake of assuming that the Incarnation was a *new departure*. Inexorably, that led us into a struggle to find a way of getting it to tag up with all the people whose times or places were such that they missed the boat. For if it really was something new, then old human nature had to be viewed as totally cut off from its benefits. From the birth of Jesus onward, we had to see "natural humankind" as a disaster area fit only for condemnation, and "redeemed humankind in Christ" as the only locus of the Mystery. Simple decency, of course, led us to posit limbo in order to soften the obvious injustices of such a view — and from there on, it was all downhill.

The second time around, we took the history of the covenants seriously and refused to see the Incarnation as a new departure. But we went right on assuming that it was fundamentally a kind of *transaction,* that the events by which it was manifested — birth, teaching, miracles, crucifixion, resurrection, ascension — were so many steps, the sum of which constituted the totality of a rescue and salvage operation. We did indeed manage to hold that this operation was in the works before Jesus: we caught on to the fact that the same Mystery is at work in all the covenants. But spreading the working of the Mystery over the length and breadth of history deals with only half the problem. The other half is the question of how the Mystery works. Is it completely contained, as it were, in the events of salvation history? Or would it be better to say that the saving events are contained in *it?* Are Jesus' death and resurrection, for example, the only communication of Atonement? Or is Atonement a vast Mystery of which Jesus' Death and Resurrection constitute just a single true, full, effective, preeminent communication?

Obviously, we opted for the former. We assumed that the Mystery was contained in the transactions by which we learned about it — that it could safely be spoken of as if it were operative only in the *pieces of business* presented to us in the revelation. And that, of course, led us straight back into the old problem of tagging up: how does a merely transactional Incarnation extend its effect to those who miss it? That, in turn, took us from theology to bookkeeping, and if we had kept on with it, we would soon have joined forces with the types at the end of Chapter Ten who were holding themselves up in the air at arm's length and trying to figure out how to change hands.

I suggest, therefore, that we take a much closer look at the connection between Mystery and transaction — that we re-examine the assumption that the operation of the Mystery can be equated with a series of shticks that God did at various times in the history of creation. My thesis is that transactional views of Christianity have caused more problems than we suspect, and that if we can manage to correct them, a lot of heretofore unresolvable conflicts may well just disappear. On with it, then — beginning, as always, with a distinction.

The Mystery does indeed manifest itself through transactions; for this is, after all, a totally transactional world. Nothing happens here that isn't *done* somewhere, sometime, somehow, by somebody. If the Mystery wants to tip its hand among the likes of us, it's going to have to work up its shtick just like everything else. And it has. The covenants — from Adam to Jesus, from the Tree of Life to the Tree of Calvary — are all pieces of business. So there is no way of escaping transactional language when we talk about the Mystery — or transactional behavior on our part when we respond to it.

On the other hand, the Mystery is not only in the world, busy with piecework. It is also in God, totally busy just *being*. The Mystery as it is in God, however — before, during, and after all worlds — isn't inching its way toward a goal it hasn't reached yet. In God, the end is fully present at the beginning; the beginning is fully realized in the end. God, in his mysterious relationship with the world, never changes his mind or his manners, never does anything he didn't have in mind before, never drops a stitch, pulls out a row, reverses engines, or slams on the brakes. And therefore, while in one sense everything he does in creation involves doing business with somebody, in another sense he never does business with anybody. He doesn't trade. He doesn't transact. He doesn't haggle. He doesn't even really *do*; he just *"bees."*

That sounds strange until you look at the Gospels. Then, suddenly, it sounds right: salvation as a gift given, not a bargain struck. A father who does not trade forgiveness for good behavior but who kisses the prodigal son before he gets his confession out of his mouth. A vineyard owner who pays what he pleases, not what the laborers earn. A shepherd who allows no sensible business considerations to keep him from leaving ninety-nine sheep in jeopardy to bring one to safety. A wheat grower who runs his farm not for profit but for the sake of letting everything grow as it pleases till the end. An Incarnate Word who won't talk to Pilate; a Carpenter of Nazareth who saves the world by nailing down his own hands; a Risen Lord who takes care of everything by going away. A God, in other words, who does all things well by doing practically nothing right, whose wisdom is foolishness, whose strength is weakness — who runs this whole operation by being no operator at all and who makes no deals because, in the high Mystery of his being, he's got it made already.

There is, perhaps, no topic in theology on which more barbaric, fatuous, dumbfounding things have been written than on predestination. I am not about to add to the confusion here, but I do want to insist that, in spite of its wretched history, the subject must be kept in the hopper for discussion. At the very least, it keeps before our minds this incomprehensible intractability of God. Much more than that, of course, needs to be said about it — and a good deal of it will have to be in paradoxical opposition to anything that pre-destination could possibly mean. But the impossible doctrine itself must never be skipped over. It is theology's star witness to the non-transactional nature of the Mystery at its deepest level — to the truth that even though creation may be mightily out of hand, God has got it all together from the beginning, without moving a solitary muscle or trading a single horse.

But enough. That's another hunt, and another beast. Time now to draw a bead on the Mystery through our newly purchased one-hundred-power non-transactional sight. Aim high and bring the gun down slowly on the subject.

Consider first how the act of creation is not a transaction, even though we ordinarily imagine it to be one. When we think of God as the cause of the world, we almost invariably figure the Mystery involved by forming a sentence whose main verb is in the plain, unvarnished past tense. We speak of his creating as if it were a piece of business he once did: Last summer, I *made* a boat, *closed* on a house, *played* a gig. In the beginning, God *created* the heavens and the earth.

But that isn't really the case. It is a usage that conceives of the act of creating as an act of *starting up* — which seems to say that all you need God for is to get things going, and that once he has created, the world needs no more causing. He could, of course, destroy it, but short of that, it continues to be on its own steam.

As Saint Thomas pointed out, however, that's not so. If God wanted to destroy the world, he wouldn't have to do anything; he would have to stop doing something. God is not only the initial cause of the world at its beginning; he is the present and immediate cause of the world at every moment of its being. Things exist not because he made them but because he *makes* them, everywhere and everywhen: of course he made them at the beginning; but that's only one moment in the billions of instants of time to which the Mystery of his creative act is eternally contemporary.

Examine next, therefore, what that means as far as his relation-ship to the world is concerned. It is not as if he once made the world and then turned it loose. That is a view which allows you to see history as something the world did largely apart from God. And it allows you to see his repair and rehabilitation of history as a super-added transaction — a new shtick by which he gets back into a show from which he was mostly absent after the opening number.

Once again, though, that can't be right. God creates everything at every moment. The freedom of the world to wander at will is a freedom it has not after it gets loose from God but while it is locked forever in the viselike grip of his creative power. That means that all its sins, all its enormities, all its bloodshed, all its savagery occur right in the palm of his hand because his hand is what *lets it be*. (The phrase, you will note, is pregnant. In its prim and proper sense, it refers to his actively creative power: *Let there be!* "Light! Firmament! Sun! Moon! Stars!" But the divine Wisdom also makes a fool of himself with creation. He leaves it free. Within the aggressive *Let it be!* he includes a slangy, laissez-faire *Leave it be*. "Whales? Birds? Cattle? People? *Leave 'em be*. Anything they want is OK by me." The Infinite Card Sharp, the master of every deal, is also just the Infinite Kibitzer, hanging around doing nothing. The Ultimate Agent is also the Ultimate Patient.)

But notice what kind of world that produces. The ordinariness we see around us and take for granted turns out to be an illusion; and the strangeness, the fingerprints of the Mystery, turn out to be the reality.

There are three possible views of the world, each of which is true. The first is that the world consists entirely of winners: every single thing that exists is a triumph of being, shouting from the housetops its praise of the Mystery by which it stands *extra nihil* and *extra causas*. The second view is that the world, at any given moment, consists of fifty percent winners and fifty percent losers: the river is wearing down the rock; the weasel is doing in the goose; these shoes are killing me. The last view is that the world is all losers: the shoes go to dust, the dust goes down the river, the river is evaporated by the sun, and the sun itself goes cold. The last course at the banquet of creation is frozen entropy — with no chocolate sauce.

On any given day, of course, you and I will be in such a mood as is appropriate to one or the other of these *Weltanschauungen*:

Exultant, as we and the surf frolic together. *Game,* as we take up arms against slings and arrows. Or stone-cold *sad,* when we sit by the waters of Babylon and the songs of Zion stick in our throats.

But on every given day, with every given thing — and on all the ungiven, unending days of eternity — *God is in all three moods at once.* Do you see what that means? He is always winning, always struggling, and always losing. He doesn't win and lose by turns, in transactions. He doesn't simply win on Sunday, simply struggle on Thursday, simply die on Friday, and simply rise again on Sunday. He does all three on all days. He loses on the first Sabbath because creation is free to defeat him at the Tree. And he reigns from the Tree on Good Friday because, in the Mystery of predestination, it is precisely by losing that he wins.

Therefore, the transactions by which he seems now to win, now to lose, are not, at their deepest root in him, transactions at all. They are rather revelations by degrees of what the Mystery is all at once. They are not bits of business that God transacts in order to get somewhere. They are sacramentalizations, outcroppings — effective and real manifestations under the *form* of transactions — of the one, constant, non-transactional Mystery by which he sets the world as a seal upon his heart, and forevermore has no place else to go.

The supreme outcropping of the Mystery, of course, is Jesus. But what happened in and through Jesus was not something new that God finally got around to plugging into the system. Rather, it is what God was really up to all along, finally and effectively sacramentalized. In Jesus, we see thrust up before our eyes what has always worked below the surface of the world. Looking at history without Jesus in it is like looking at the Great Plains and trying to imagine what the earth is made of: you never really catch on to the fact that, except for the surface, it's mostly stone. But when you come to the Rockies, you understand: there before you is a clear outcropping of what lies beneath the plains.

So with Jesus. Leave him out of the world's history, and people will simply spend their days being glad when they can and sad when they must. They will try to win until they finally lose, and then they will curse God and die. But put his Death and Resurrection into the picture, and suddenly all the winning and all the losing are revealed as God's chosen métier.

Follow that to the end and see how it eliminates once and for all the problem of tagging up with those who somehow miss the Incarnation. We call Christ's dying and rising the Paschal Mystery, the Passover Mystery. But seen in the light of a non-transactional view, this isn't just typology anymore. It's a flat assertion that the Passover and the Resurrection are, beneath the surface, *the same thing.* You don't have to work up some system for getting the Israelites in the wilderness in touch with Christ: they already were, long before Jesus turned up on the scene. And so were Adam, Noah, Abraham, Isaac, and Jacob. And so, to take it all the way, is everybody and everything that is.

Christ wins in every triumph and loses in every loss. Christ dies when a chicken dies and rises when an egg hatches. He lies slain in the wreckage of all Aprils. He weeps in the ruins of all springs. This strange, savage, gorgeous world is the way it is because, incomprehensibly, that is his style. The Gospel of the Incarnation is preached not so that we can tell people that the world now means something it didn't mean before but so that they may finally learn what it has been about all along. We proclaim Christ crucified — the formless, uncomely Root Out of a Dry Ground — in order to show all people, at the undesired roots of their own being, the Incarnate Word who is already there, making Jerusalem to flourish. We do not bring Jesus to people or people to Jesus. We preach the Word who already sends their roots rain, whether they hear or whether they forbear.

And so at last, the theological Rube Goldberg contraptions go into the trash can. At Auschwitz and Buchenwald, the Jews died in Christ and Christ in them. No limbos. No bookkeeping. If the church never got around to them — or if it did, but put them off with rotten manners — Christ still draws all to himself. He descends into every hell. The Incarnate Word preaches on all days, to all spirits, in all prisons. The Good Shepherd has other sheep, and he flatly refuses to lose a single one.

15. Reducing

We would be doing only half the job, however, if we were to stop our anti-transactional crusade at this point. To be sure, it helps greatly to see Jesus as the supreme outcropping — the grand Sacrament — of the Mystery of the Word's relationship to the world. It sorts things out. It reminds us that when we deal with mystery, we have to do justice to two things at once: the non-transactional Mystery itself; and the transactional plausibilities, the earthly signs, by which the Mystery makes itself known to us.

But Jesus is not the only sacrament. Once the process of sacramentalizing the work of the Word reaches the intensity it does in Jesus, it precipitates a whole shower of further sacraments: first the *church,* which is the sacrament of Jesus; then the *sacraments* properly so called by which the church celebrates the Mystery of Jesus. And if it was difficult to keep sign and Mystery in balance when we talked about Jesus, it will be even more difficult when we talk about the church: transactional views make mischief all along the line. The further down you go, the more trouble they make.

In Jesus, the union between the Mystery and its sign is unique. The Mystery, to put it still another way, is the immortal and invisible Wisdom of God, mightily and sweetly ordering all things into the City; it is the eternal Word, bringing creation as a bride to his Father's house. The sign is the humanity of Jesus, his very flesh and blood — the mere one hundred sixty pounds or so of meat and bone in which dwelt all the fullness of the Godhead bodily. But the union between those two natures is a union in one Person — in the Person of the Word.

It is not terribly important to know precisely what that means. The crucial thing to know is that it is meant to point to a uniqueness, to a situation in which, while we must be careful to do full justice to each nature (Rule 1 — remember?), we may also predicate the properties of either nature of the Person (Rule 2, the communication of idioms). Admittedly, there is the ever-present danger of either watering down his Deity so that he is no longer God or gussying up his humanity till he turns into Superman; but that danger is kept under some control by the fact that both are inseparably, unconfusedly one in him. When you pick up either of them with any deftness at all, you always say something appropriate about him. You may carry on for six weeks about nothing but his Godhead, or for a year and a half about his manhood alone; just as long as you don't say anything that violates the subject you happen to be on, you hit the bull's-eye on the subject of him every time.

This safety feature — this net so reassuringly rigged under the theological high wire — disappears when you come to speak of the derivative sacramentalizations of the Mystery. The Church, Baptism, the Eucharist, the Priesthood — all these should probably be spoken of with a little reserve. Jesus, on the one hand, may be seen as the great Sacrament of the Mystery — the Mystery itself supremely and personally present in the flesh. The church, on the other hand, while it may be seen as just as real a presence, should not be viewed as so eminent a one. The church is a sacrament once removed, as it were: Jesus is the effective Sign of the Incarnation; the church is the sacrament of that Sign.

In the long run, it's all the same, existentially. The church, for example, really is Jesus in his members: "He that receiveth you receiveth me." The Eucharist is nothing less than the fullness of Christ: "This *is* my body; this *is* my blood." But intellectually — that is, in the only way we can pick these things up theologically — it's not the same at all. There is no union in one Person to catch you if you slip. Whatever *Jesus* says, the Word says, because they are

[334]

one. That may give you some problems of interpretation, but they're not bad. However, it is simply not true that whatever the *church* says, Jesus says. And it is definitely not true that Jesus can safely be said to do whatever the church does. Mother Church has said and done some of the damndest things. She has at times been heavily into the cooking sherry. There have been centuries which found her pretty much confined to her room with the vapors.

When we come to speak of the church and the sacraments, therefore, the danger of overstatement or misstatement is with us in spades. First, we have to be more careful than ever to avoid reducing the Mystery of Jesus to some two-bit plausibility. Second, we have to resist far more strenuously the temptation to gussy up the sign and turn it into a substitute for the Mystery. And finally, we have to be supremely judicious about transactions: everything the church does is just a piece of business; but it is done as a communication of the Word, who, in his heart of hearts, is no businessman at all. Clearly, the possibilities for confusion, tomfoolery, fakery, and mischief are practically unlimited.

Take first the temptation to reduce the Mystery to a plausibility. It has been succumbed to so often and for so long that many Christians, and perhaps most non-Christians, actually believe the plausibilities to be the true Gospel. Consider, for example, the idea that the church is in the world to teach people the difference between right and wrong.

The president of the Rotary Club leans toward the clergyman on his right and makes small talk to kill time until the hour of the parson's speech: "Well, Reverend, it's good to have you here. We need to hear from you people every now and then. There's just no moral values anymore. I'll bet if some of these punk rockers went to church and heard what you fellows have to say, they wouldn't be messing around with sex and drugs, eh?"

The good father, of course, quickly tucks a heaping spoonful of rice pudding into his mouth and mumbles something like "Mmmh?!" His first thought, however, is probably more like "!@*#*&!@*#!!" And his second thoughts, while more printable, are even less tolerant:

"a. This guy hasn't darkened a church door all year. And it probably wouldn't help if he did. As far as he's concerned, the Gospel equals the Ten Commandments, and the church is society's moral cop on the beat. That's all he's prepared to hear.

"b. If I hear one more crack about punk rock, I'll scream.

"c. If I get one more knowing wink about teenage sex, I'm going to get every member of the Ministerial Association to promise to copulate in public at least once a week.

"d. Really though, it's probably just as well neither he nor the kids go to church: besides their being totally unprepared to hear that the Gospel is about Mystery and not morals, the church is almost as unprepared to say it. God help us all if we ever get religion.

"e. Now I have to get up and be polite to this monster of a misunderstanding. I think I'll tell proctologist jokes instead.

"f. I hate myself."

Morality, however, is only one of the plausibilities to which the Mystery is regularly reduced. It is just as likely that our short-suffering priest, had he been thrown to the tender mercies of the program chairman on his right, would have been regaled with an equation of the Gospel and philosophy: "We certainly need more religion, Father. If people only had faith, they wouldn't be so confused about the meaning of life. It's lack of faith that gives people ulcers."

And while the reverend gentleman was gagging on his rice pudding, he would, this time, have run the following mental course:

"Blech! People like him should be strapped in a chair and have the entire book of Job read to them very slowly in Hebrew, Greek, Latin, and English. The meaning of life, indeed! How many uncomprehending deathbeds has he hung around? How many total losses has he spent hours counseling? How many irretrievable misunderstandings has he had to admit he had no answers for? Phony baloney. And that bit about no ulcers. Hasn't he ever looked at a crucifix? Faith can punch as many holes in you as anything. As a matter of fact, given this mess of a world, anybody without holes in his gut should probably be written off as an insensitive clod, guilty of serenity in the first degree. As if the Gospel ever excused you from getting your tail kicked in: 'The disciple is several com-

fortable cuts above his master, alive and well in cloud-cuckoo-land.'
Gack!"

Finally, however, had our dominie landed next to someone more
honest and less earnest, he would undoubtedly have had it made
clear to him that his luncheon companion "never was, to be honest
with you, Father, very much when it came to religion."

But this would not displease the true shepherd of the flock as
much as might be expected. "At last," the pastor would muse to
himself, "one ray of hope. I get so sick of listening to malarkey. If
this guy only knew it, he's ready for the Gospel. Religion is a
necessary evil. It's the unavoidable transactional slop you have to
wade through in order to lay hold of the Mystery for yourself. But
in Christianity, 'religious' acts are not transactions in their own right.
They don't get you into heaven or keep you out of hell. They don't
earn you a nice wife, or good kids, or two weeks in Aruba, or the
combination to the superfecta at Aqueduct. They just deliver you
to the Mystery. Which is like being delivered to the lady or the
tiger: it could be great or it could be terrible; and in either case, it
might be both. But it is at least an adventure, and not some dumb
transaction by which the Great Bookkeeper in the Sky can be per-
suaded to fudge figures for you.

"If only they could see that Christianity starts by telling you
that you have no place left to go because you're already home free,
and no favor to earn because God sees you in his beloved Son and
thinks you're the greatest thing since sliced bread. All you have to
do is explore the crazy Mystery of your acceptance. Why do they
always want to do it the hard way?"

Let's leave the padre there. He's on the right track. The church's
temptation to welsh on the Mystery, to fake it, to reduce it to a
plausibility, to equate it with morality, philosophy, or religion, must
be fought to the death. For there is no escaping the consequences.
The church may think she is meeting the world on a basis it is
prepared to accept, but she's wrong. What the world is prepared for
on these subjects is mostly to hate them — and to hate anybody
who peddles them as well. The children of this world are wiser in
their generation than the children of light. They know that morals,

philosophy, and religion are not catholic tastes: they are the province of ideologues, scoundrels, interest groups, specialized talents, sincere people, and other fanatics.

But what the world in its wisdom does not know is that its only protection against these unwelcome sectarian plausibilities is the even more unwelcome foolishness of the Mystery. For that alone is catholic. That alone goes to the root of everybody's being. That alone, like spinach, is good for them, even if they don't like it. That alone is capable of nourishing the great unwashed generality of creation: the slob and the dilettante, the genius and the moron, the owl, the pussycat, and the beautiful pea-green boat.

If it is objected that Mystery is a dumb answer to the world's questions, the objection is sustained. On two grounds: Yes, it's a dumb answer, because all the world ever does is ask dumb questions like How can it get home? when it's already there, and How can it find favor? when it's already got it. And yes, it's a dumb answer, because it's literally *dumb:* sheep-before-her-shearers, silent-before-Pilate, still-as-the-grave, plain, unanswering, speechless, ask-me-no-questions-and-I'll-give-you-no-pious-pap, *dumb.*

But it is the answer!

16. Faking

I know. That's assertion, not proof. But listen, by this time, we're either friends or enemies. So, Three Cheers or Tough Luck, as the case may be. On to the temptations to fake the sign.

The gist of them all is that they resolve the tension between the non-transactional Mystery and the transactional sign by making the sign so spiffy that, for all practical purposes, it does duty for the Mystery. It's the old Superman temptation applied to the church and her institutions.

Simple illustration first: Jesus instituted the Sacrament of his Body and Blood by commanding his disciples to eat bread and drink wine in remembrance of him. Human nature being what it is, however, it wasn't long before somebody got the idea that the bread for the Sacrament ought to be something special. It wasn't enough, apparently, that by Jesus' own words any old bread would be nothing less than his true, risen, and glorious body really present in a high mystery. They had to have Superbread. And so, in accordance with Murphy's Law (if a mistake can be made, it will be), the angelic fish-food communion wafers were invented: snow white, unleavened, crumbless, odorless, and tasteless. And made by nuns. Out of rice flour. Without salt. In little waffle irons. With holy monograms on them.

And lest it be thought that this bent for spiritualizing the sign is just a bit of popery-jiggery, consider the Protestant Communion service. Store-bought bread is used, but the temptation to cut off the crusts is more than the elders can stand. So there sit the elements: piles of white cubes, totally bereft of the touch of fire that brought them into being; and trays with shot glasses full of grape juice so that the church can go Jesus not one, but two, better. She improves on his manners by being more sanitary, and on his morals by not using wine. Fearful and wonderful!

But not, in the long run, worth much more than a laugh. It's the purifying of other signs that makes more trouble. Take the Priesthood, for example.

The sign of the Ministry of the church is, quite clearly, the group of people designated as ministers. This designation takes place, for openers, at a service called ordination; but the important thing about it is that it continues. The Ministry is recognized in the church by function: the ministers are the people up there doing the bread-and-wine thing, or the baptizing-with-water thing, or the forgiveness thing, or the preaching thing. To do all those things, Jesus initially selected a ragtag lot of fishermen, tax collectors, peasants, and intellectuals. He told them that when they broke bread, he would be really present; that whenever they forgave anybody, he would stand by their decision; and that when they preached his word, they would move mountains.

Once again, though, it wasn't enough. By and by, the idea got around that just plain people wouldn't do for so holy a sign. They had to have Superpeople. So they started down the road to the present ruin of the Ministry. They did manage to avoid one pothole: except for a few fanatics called Donatists, the church never said that the unworthiness of ministers hindered the sacramental working of the Mystery. She kept, as her official position, the sensible view that a Mass said by a priest with his hand in the till, or a baptism performed by a minister who didn't believe in anything, was still valid.

But that was about it. For the rest, she went gleefully about the old business of going Jesus five, six, or a baker's dozen better. Priests had to be nifty people: at various times in her history she has, for various reasons, insisted that they be single people (because marriage is OK, you understand, but not that OK); male people (because women are swell, sure, but all that menstrual business is decidedly unpleasant); people without crime or impediment (because, of course, the church is composed entirely of forgiven sinners, but you have to draw the line somewhere to keep the riffraff out); and they also had to be smart people, good people, balanced people, charming people, diplomatic people, talented people, people who never got drunk, never swore, never told salty stories, never had mad loves, and who, in addition to all that, would be willing to work for next to no money at the job they did, even though they were not allowed to make a buck at anything else. There was even a time when lacking the *canonical digits* was an impediment to ordination: if some poor soul had lost a thumb or forefinger, he was considered unfit matter for the sacrament.

The result of all these nifty qualifications was twofold. First, it produced the poor, freaky, whacked-up thing that for centuries has passed for the ministerial sign of the Mystery of Christ. A list like that attracts a lot of nuts, rascals, and three-dollar bills. And when it does attract even moderately normal people, it drives half of them out of their heads when they try to fulfill all its contradictory requirements. And it drives half of the other half out of the ministry when they think they haven't fulfilled them. And half of the last quarter into smugness when they think they have. The remaining eighth — the group who know they have fulfilled them, and who also know the precise degree to which everybody else has not — become bishops, thus winning the game.

Second, however, the Superpeople list results in a situation in which not even bishops win. The sign becomes so important that the Mystery is lost in the shuffle. Since the church seems so insistent on all these *requisita* and *desiderata,* the world obligingly takes her at her word and judges her accordingly. She has advertised the omnicompetence, wisdom, and general niceness of her priests; when the world finds (as it always does) that the product is not as advertised, it complains loudly and boycotts the store. And it serves her right. She advertised the wrong product. She was in the Mystery business, but she took the easy way out and peddled plausibilities instead.

Once again, however, the damage done by this particular puffing up of the sign of the Mystery pales before the next example. A strung-out ministry and an anti-clerical world are nothing compared with the results of the aggrandizement of the church herself as an institution.

First of all, what is she, really? Well, she is the Body of Christ — an earthly society which, somehow, is Jesus himself in his members. She is not a club of Jesus enthusiasts or a sectarian fellowship of like-minded pals. She is a great, gangling hulk of a girl, a huge, catholic net dragged indiscriminately through the world. Her admissions' procedure guarantees that she will never be otherwise: she pours water over little babies about whose opinions and temperaments she knows absolutely nothing and blithely pronounces them full-fledged members.

From such a coarse screening process, no one in his right mind should ever expect more than chronic diversity, punctuated, with luck, by an occasional agreement or two. And yet. Murphy's Law. We did it again. We faked her natural multiplicity into a monolithic unity. We pretended that an institution composed entirely of sinners could somehow, as an institution, be pure. We talked ourselves into believing that a crowd of people who by necessity would hardly ever agree even about easy things would infallibly get all the hard things right. We made believe that the Holy Spirit would use a totally political entity without ever letting politics into the act. We turned an absurd, Gospel-proclaiming gaggle of geese into an efficient question-answering machine. And we fobbed off on ourselves — we who, like the rest of the race, can barely organize our way out of a wet paper bag — the solemn proposition that, because we were the church, we had access to some divine managerial competence that the world could never have.

What we forgot is that while the sign is always the sign of the Mystery, it also continues to be, in an important sense, nothing more than itself: it remains heir to all its natural ills as well as all its natural glories. The bread of communion can indeed be delicious, fragrant and warm from the oven; but it can also go moldy. So can priests. And so can the church: her political processes can be as good, or as corrupt, as any institution's. Her answers to questions may prove as wise as can be or as goofy as all get-out. As the sign that she is, she is not necessarily better or worse than the U.S. Senate, the American Bar Association, or the PTA. Except that, on the principle that what is good is difficult and what is difficult is rare, goodness in the institutional church — like goodness in violinists, cooks, and street sweepers — is bound to run a poor second to the sheer volume of mediocrity, ineptitude, and downright venality.

A couple of illustrations, therefore, of the fakery.

Take the idea of infallibility. Obviously, there is a legitimate sense in which we must say the church is infallible: she must have an infallible grip on the Gospel. If after two thousand years we are not perfectly certain we are supposed to be preaching that Jesus died and rose again, then we had best file for bankruptcy. But knowing for sure what the Gospel is, is a very modest business. All you need is the Bible and the creeds — which is precisely the slim but adequate area of agreement that most Christians have reached.

It is the step from that infallibility to a larger one that brings us to grief. It is one thing to claim that the infallible answer to "How long was Jesus in the tomb?" is "Three days." It is quite another to suppose that we have infallible answers to any and all questions which we or the world might choose to ask.

To do the church credit, she has so hedged about the doctrine of papal infallibility that it requires, as Chesterton pointed out, less of an act of faith than taking the word of your family doctor that his prescription won't hurt you. Infallibility has been restricted to the pope only, speaking ex cathedra only, and on faith and morals only. And as if that weren't cagey enough, all those conditions are open to interpretation to one degree or another.

But still, the hedge isn't tight enough. Point one: Why should the church be expected to have any infallible *machinery?* In a free world, God reveals himself without getting pushy. He does not override the nature of the earthly agents he uses; he works through them. He inspired the Epistle to the Galatians not by putting the author in a trance and speaking through his lips but by taking a very angry Paul and letting him rip. He gets the supernatural across by mysteriously allowing nature to do what comes naturally.

Now the church is a crowd of people. Its nature will be to operate like any other crowd of people: in its corporate judgments it will make mistakes. As a matter of fact, if we take history seriously, it will probably get more things wrong than right. Only the test of time will tell which was which. Why then, given that nature, should it be expected that somewhere in its fabric there will be a button that you can push to get infallible answers to your questions?

That's a poser. It was undoubtedly because of its manifest absurdity that a severe limitation was imposed on the types of questions for which infallible answers would be available: only Faith and Morals would get red-carpet treatment. But that's no less absurd. And it's a giveaway besides. First of all, questions of faith and morals have always been among the most hotly debated of all. Disagreements about them have been rampant and endemic, and agreements have displayed a tendency to be short-lived. To be sure, if you want to set up an administrative procedure by which a pope or a council can rule, supreme-court style, that x, y, or z is the church's official teaching and that gainsayers must henceforth shape up or ship out, all right. But if you go beyond that and claim that some basically political process of argument and pronouncement will automatically produce the Right Ruling, you're off base. Political bodies don't work that way; when they pretend they do, watch out. And it makes no difference what body or institution you select as your infallibility button. People have at times tried to claim that an ecumenical council, if you could manage to call one, would be infallible. But that's no better than the papacy. And, when you think about it, the papacy is no less political than that.

But second, the restriction of infallibility to questions of faith and morals is a giveaway because of the inclusion of morals. It betrays a fatal tendency to confuse apples and oranges, Mystery and plausibility. If two purveyors of infallibility would limit it to faith alone, maybe I would trust them. But when they tack on morals, I lose all confidence in their judgment. What's so all-fired important about morals? Why isn't it just as important for us to have infallible answers about economics? Or art? Or child rearing? Or cooking, for that matter? God knows, the number of evil cooks in the world is enough to make any reasonable human being long for guidance from on high.

I'll tell you why morals got up there in the Top Two. It's because they thought it was the church's real business. But it wasn't, and it isn't, and it must never be allowed to become so. The church is not in the morals business. The world is in the morals business, quite rightfully; and it has done a fine job of it, all things considered. The history of the world's moral codes is a monument to the labors of many philosophers, and it is a monument of striking unity and beauty. As C. S. Lewis said, everybody who thinks the moral codes of humankind are all different should be locked up in a library and be made to read three days' worth of them. They would be bored silly by the sheer sameness.

What the world cannot get right, however, is the forgiveness business — and that, of course, is the church's real job. She is in the world to deal with the Sin that the world can't turn off or escape from. She is not in the business of telling the world what's right and wrong so that it can do good and avoid evil. She is in the business of offering, to a world that knows all about that tiresome subject, forgiveness for its chronic unwillingness to take its own advice. But the minute she even hints that morals, and not forgiveness, is the name of her game, she instantly corrupts the Gospel and runs head-long into blatant nonsense.

The church becomes not Ms. Forgiven Sinner but Ms. Right. Christianity becomes the good guys in here versus the bad guys out there. Which, of course, is pure tripe. The church is nothing but the world under the sign of Baptism. It is the mixture as before, dampened. It contains as many scoundrels as any other sampling — and they practice their scoundrelism with as much vigor as the best of them. The rewards of divination, of course, are smaller nowadays than they used to be. But there was a time when the church could have bought and sold the Oval Office.

So hand me no infallible machinery. I can't believe it, and I won't trust it. It not only fobs off on me a transaction when it should be giving me a Mystery. It even gives me the wrong transaction. But lest all this be taken as anti-romanism, behold the Protestant parallels:

Parallel one: The Bible *only* is infallible.

Nonsense. The Bible is indeed God's Word Written, and it most infallibly contains all things necessary for salvation. But it is also a thing. It is not the Mystery; it is just another sign of it. And as the sign that it is, it obeys the law of its nature: it's a book. It came into being like a book: bit by bit. It lives like a book: in the mind of its readership. And it would die like a book, if it had no readers. How foolish, then, to think that the Bible alone can ever be anything. How idle to divorce it from its readership in the life-giving tradition of the church. I will grant you Bible-plus-church as the ground for some minimal but necessary infallible authority. But a lonely Bible machine pumping out answers? Never.

Parallel two: The Bible only, *in its literal sense,* is infallible.

With Geneva, as with Rome, make one error and you invite a second. Gussy up the sign, and the first thing you know, you start turning the Mystery into a plausibility. Rome went from an unreal, overblown view of the nature of the church to a forgetfulness of the church's real business. Geneva went from a book that never was on land or sea to a Word who communicates in simplicities instead of paradoxes and absurdities, and who, accordingly, within his infallible writings, gives you a world that began in 4004 B.C. and a rabbit who chews the cud.

Really! Is leaving the Mystery business to go into natural history any improvement over leaving it for morals?

17. *Delivering*

Lest it be thought, however, that the ravages of transactionalism are confined to the upper echelons of Christianity, I want to bring us down a bit to matters that affect more than popes and councils. All this backing away from Mystery and filling in with hoked-up signs has as bad an effect on the Indians as it does on the chiefs: in the end, we forget the breathtakingly paradoxical nature of the church. She is — always, everywhere, and at once — utterly the Mystery itself, and merely the sign that she happens to be. Unless both are done full justice, we reduce her to a plausibility and make her look ridiculous.

In the literal sense of the word. The church becomes a laughing matter — but laughed *at,* not with. The only fit response a sane person can make to a church that turns her Mystery into a simplicity and her sacraments into sacred transactions is ridicule. Explain the act of creation, for example, as an act of starting up, or the act of redemption as a transaction in which the death of Jesus literally buys off an angry God, and you give yourself so many problems that you can be blown out of the water with one well-aimed sneer. Or, alternatively, insist that the earthly details of the church's life — her services, her ministry, her day-to-day operations — have some *proper* efficacy, that they are, *as what they are,* blessings, things of beauty, and unqualified joyfers, and you turn the church into a laughingstock by the obvious preposterousness of the claim.

But besides turning the church into a bad joke, the twin

mistakes make the church's members hungry and sad. Hungry, because abandoning Mystery deprives them of their only real nourishment; and sad, because nobody likes to be laughed at, especially when the ridicule is aimed at overweening claims for merely earthly signs. More than that, the drift into transactionalism destroys their sense of balance and proportion. Having defined the church's work as the communication of heavenly transactions through the delivery of earthly transactions, they corrupt their definition of what constitutes success for the church. They become falsely elated over the pieces of business that prosper and needlessly depressed over the ones that fail.

All because they assume that the transactions have some proper efficacy and therefore will perform like gangbusters, if only they can get them right. For example: The sign of the church is people. So far, so good. However, on the assumption that the sign works in its own right, the temptation is overwhelming to define a successful church as one full of successful people, and then to proceed to work especially hard at catering to nice, moneyed, influential people. I don't care how saintly, how meticulously anti-transactional, how deeply grounded in the Mystery any Christian is: at the roots of his thinking, the success syndrome has trained him to prefer a full church to an empty one, a big church to a small one, a rich church to a poor one, and a church with clout to one without.

Not that any of those successes is something to be ashamed of. Let us leave no room here for a cult of unsuccess, for people who think there is something fine about being lonely, poor, and down at the heels. That's just one more missing of the point. The sign is itself and ought to be done justice. The church should have the best buildings it can afford, the finest music it can manage, the zingiest ministers it can find, and all the money it can rake in. Just because, if you're going to have such things, you ought to develop an intolerance for second-rate performances. But not because the best is any more effective a sign of the Mystery.

I have been, for years, conducting a one-man crusade against mean muscatel and New York State Port as altar wines. As long as the parish can afford it and the priest has his taste buds about him, we are going to celebrate the Holy Mysteries with a good medium-range port, imported from the only place on earth so far that produces what my upbringing taught me to call port. But I don't kid myself for a minute that it makes any difference in the efficacy of the Mystery. In a pinch, I am even prepared, at the price of a tautology and a sprained palate, to use the end of a bottle of cold duck. (Lucius Beebe, *ora pro nobis;* Crosby Gaige, *absolve me.*)

But having propitiated these lesser deities in our personal pantheons, we need to return again and again to Mystery as the governing consideration. We have so far referred to it as the building of the City by the Word. But the Bible uses another equally pregnant image: it speaks of the destiny of creation in terms of the kingdom of God; it teaches us to pray unceasingly "Thy kingdom come." The inveterate temptation of the church, however, is to turn the kingdom, too, into a plausibility — to assume that the church and the kingdom are the same thing, when in fact the best that can be said is that the church is the sacrament of the kingdom.

When yielded to, that temptation produces a veritable cornucopia of follies and iniquities. For example: Let us say for the sake of argument that the church may safely be equated with the kingdom and vice versa. On that basis, we may go on to say that, since the unbaptized are clearly out of the church, they are equally plainly out of the kingdom of God. Is that true or false?

It is false, false, very false. The kingdom has been at hand from Adam onward. Furthermore, since the King has been here all along, in complete, if paradoxical, charge of his realm, the kingdom has been here too. In the high Mystery of the kingdom, therefore, all people are somehow both in and out of it. Even the unbaptized are in, because it's always been operating; and even the baptized are out, because it hasn't yet cleaned up this grimy mess of a world. How much foolishness might we have avoided if we had kept that in mind? How much needless and arrogant bookkeeping? How many wicked prejudices? How many Jewish deaths?

Equating the visible church with the kingdom was a high church folly. Try a low church one instead: the true, invisible church (contradiction in terms there, but let it pass) is the kingdom of God;

it is made up of all those who have accepted Jesus as their personal Lord and Savior.

This substitutes a handful of internal, human transactions (prayer, thought, decision) for an external, sacramental one (Baptism). It is not, however, one whit less transactional. The Mystery of the Word does not come into anybody's life at a certain time, as the result of a specific invitation. The King does not wait to be asked into his rightful realm. He is there all along. The most you can say is that, on occasion, he sacramentalizes his presence so that the benefits of recognizing it can be enjoyed by his people. How much revivalistic charlatanism might we have been delivered from if we had remembered that? How much spiritual pride? How many boring, saved people? How many foolish campaigns in the church to ram the style of a few down the throats of the many in the name of evangelism?

But that is not the end of the matter. These follies tumble out only to be followed by iniquities. Equating the kingdom with the church, for example, was one of the sleepers in the much-praised nineteenth-century missionary movement. In the back of their minds, many quite admirable Christians conceived of their mission not only as a bringing of the church, the Gospel, and the sacraments to the heathen but also as a bringing to the heathen of their first contact with the kingdom.

It is instructive to reread the classic nineteenth-century mission hymns. I note in myself and others a deep reluctance to use them anymore. Every now and then, somebody tries to give us a bad conscience about that and says that they bother us because we've lost our missionary zeal. But I don't think that's the reason. I think it's because we have, in the light of history, caught on to the rather arrogant transactionalism that vitiated an otherwise noble movement.

> Can we whose souls are lighted
> With wisdom from on high,
> Can we to men benighted
> The lamp of life deny? (1819)

Fling out the banner! sin-sick souls
That sink and perish in the strife,
Shall touch in faith its radiant hem,
And spring immortal into life.   (1848)

What can we do to work God's work,
to prosper and increase
The brotherhood of all mankind,
the reign of the Prince of peace?
What can we do to hasten the time,
the time that shall surely be,
When the earth shall be filled with the glory of God
as the waters cover the sea?   (1894)

Not that you can't put a skin of non-transactional interpretation
on such poetry: some of the hymns actually state the Mystery quite
well. It's just that you can't sing that stuff for a hundred years and
not have it affect your thinking. It's hard to avoid giving yourself
the impression that the kingdom isn't going to get to the heathen
until you deliver it. Worse yet, it's doubly hard, once you start down
that line of thought, to avoid the ultimate language of delivery: war
and conquest. We'll do more than just hand it to them; we'll sock
it to 'em. Singing good, solid, four-four marching tunes as we go:

Each breeze that sweeps the ocean
Brings tidings from afar
Of nations in commotion,
Prepared for Sion's war.   (1832)

And from there, it's only a step to being sure you'll win — to
a conviction that by your agency (under God, of course, but by your
agency) your now rather strongly ecclesiastical definition of the goal
will be achieved:

Then the end! Thy Church completed,
All Thy chosen gathered in,

With their King in glory seated,
Satan bound, and banished sin;
Gone forever parting, weeping,
Hunger, sorrow, death, and pain;
Lo! her watch Thy Church is keeping;
Come, Lord Jesus, come to reign!   (1867)

Which means that the kingdom will finally come when the
church has finished her temporal conquest, and that it will be
marked, as every successful campaign is, by the total rout of all
enemies:

Let every idol perish,
To moles and bats be thrown,
And every prayer be ordered,
To God in Christ alone.   (1859)

It is victory in our time, at our hands. No heathen temple left
standing, no church left but The Church, not one Jew, Turk, or
Infidel left unconverted, and *no arguing about it, either:*

Let war be learned no longer,
Let strife and tumult cease,
All earth his blessed kingdom,
The Lord and Prince of peace.   (1859)

The Mystery of the Kingdom has been scratched and replaced
by Christian Chauvinism, out of Nineteenth-Century Evolutionary
Inevitability, Ecclesiastical Triumphalism up. But since that blood-
line never did have any staying power in the stretch, it quickly
petered out. The race was won by Manifest Destiny, out of Pax
Britannica, White Man's Burden up. Which, in turn, set us up for
the two German wars, and most of what we have had to accept in
the name of the only century currently available.

For none of that triumph-of-the-Gospel business was ever about
to come off, anyway. Even Scripture seems to say that the kingdom

will come not out of the victory of the church but out of the shipwreck of the world; that in the end, it is not the church that the Lamb marries but the whole of creation, the new heavens and the new earth: the holy City, New Jerusalem, coming down from God out of heaven, prepared as a bride adorned for her husband.

That, of course, is no excuse for welshing on the mission of the church. These earthly sacramentalizings of the Mystery must indeed be held up before every creature we can find. The transport and display of them is a perfectly feasible piece of business, and as with all such transactions, if it's worth doing, it's worth doing well. But it does excuse us from having to believe that the church (however defined, by Catholic or by Protestant) is either the sole instrument or the total extent of the kingdom of God. And that's not only a relief. It's a chance to start rethinking mission. But not here. I owe you an apology.

I am sorry if I have shot any of your sacred cows. I realize that it is considered bad form to take potshots at such things as the Missionary Enterprise, Evangelism, and the Great Commission to baptize all nations. But after all, I do have this new anti-transactional gunsight — and you were the one who painted those silly transactional targets on your cows. Anyway, theologians don't use live ammunition; those were tranquilizer darts. While the cows are still out cold, get the paint off them. Believe me, they'll look better without it, and they'll be much less likely to get shot.

For our transactionalism has cost us all dearly. Having faked the sign of the church and pretended it was something better than it ever could be, sticks and stones have broken our bones and we have been called all kinds of names. People get angry at us when they find that the church is full of priests who are lecherous, or stupid, or loutish, or mean, and that the pews are full of half-returned prodigals whose ideas about what constitutes good manners were formed mostly while they were slopping the hogs.

And we ourselves get depressed when we find that our cult of the successful church, our trust in the proper efficacy of our efforts, is just another batch of hogwash. We worry when people leave the church, we fret when they don't come in, only because we forget that the church's business has a *mysterious,* not a *direct,* connection with her life. People come and go for all sorts of plausible reasons. Some quit because they hate the priest; others join up in order to hate the priest. Some stay on in the hope of having their questions answered; others buzz off because they don't like the answers they get.

And we wear ourselves out trying to control the situation, trying to mollify this one, slug it out with that one, join forces with fellow partisans, or throw our favorite rascals out. And it's all fair game. And frequently lots of fun. And we might as well make a bang-up job of it while we're at it. But it mustn't be made to matter too much because, after all, it's only matter. It's our business, but it's not our life. We can do it so badly that we end up in the poorhouse. But we still rest secure in the possession of the Mystery that never fails.

So no faking of the signs, if you please, and no simplifying of the Mystery. No Chinese restaurant church where you eat plausibilities and feel hungry an hour later. Just the true church — the old leaky bucket, full of the water of life, from which we drink and never thirst again.

18. Dumping

I find that I have, more or less pardonably, slipped into usage which, while it is not necessarily wrong, can be dangerous if it is not recognized as slightly loose talk. In the interest of brevity, I have frequently said things like, "In Christianity, religious acts are not transactions in their own right." Properly speaking, however, I should have been more cautious. For if we are going to allow my contention that theology is a serious word game, a groping for the Mystery with verbal tools, statements like the one just cited should always be modified to read ". . . religious acts *should not be viewed, or not be spoken of,* as transactions in their own right." The point is that neither I nor you know anything directly about what the Mystery is or about what religious acts actually do. We are simply trying to find the most convenient — or, perhaps even more modestly, the least inconvenient, the least damaging — way of talking to ourselves and others about it.

Accordingly, with you thus forewarned that I expect to be given credit for that subtlety at all times, and myself thus forearmed against accusations of dogmatism, I return to my more relaxed usage and take up the subject of the sacraments properly so called. I propose to elaborate the following proposition: The sacraments of the church are not transactions, except insofar as the merely material outward sign is concerned.

Let's clear the board of one matter first. Every sacrament inevitably involves a whole string of transactions — of bits of business that set out to do something and, by proper efficacy, accomplish it. The godmother is a properly effective agent for handing the baby to the priest (though, in all honesty, most women who are not trained nurses can't do it deftly). The altar server is properly effective for conveying the wine cruet to the altar (though, infuriatingly, she leaves the stopper in more often than not). The priest's ear is properly effective for hearing the words of the penitent's confession (unless he's switched off his hearing aid). And so on. In all the materialities of the sacraments, we are on the plain, everyday, transactional level, dealing in the ordinary, earthly way with things like personnel, inventory, schedules, and logistics. There is nothing divine about them. While they may be fancier and more solemn tasks, they involve, qualitatively, no more problems than the work of getting the spaghetti wound around the fork: a proper investment in labor and materials gets the job done every time. You may — indeed, you should and you must — be as transactional as possible. On this level, any other course is fakery.

But on the level of the total effect of the sacrament as Sacrament — when you come to talk about the *benefit* of the sacrament, when you turn your attention from the mere outward sign to the mysterious *inward grace* — there, I contend, you must not be transactional at all. In spite of all the history of transactional talk about the sacraments, and in spite of the almost overwhelming temptation everyone experiences to go right along with it, thinking of them as sacred transactions is bad news. And getting them out of that category is a breath of fresh air. Let me illustrate first with the Sacrament of Penance.

If any sacrament has ever looked, felt, and acted like a transaction, it is the bit of business involved in making one's confession to a priest. There you kneel, with a conscience full of sins — with three trash cans labeled Thought, Word, and Deed, full of the garbage you allowed to accumulate since your last visit to the holy disposal pit. For a fee (the bother of going, the embarrassment of confessing, and the doing of your penance), the custodian of the dump knocks out your trash cans, puts in new, snow-white liners, and sends you out with the advice to live a neater life.

The exercise is transactional in the extreme — and on two fronts. On the one hand, a long-standing tradition held that the confessional was the only dump where you could get rid of really messy garbage, so you had to go there in order not to be caught dead with a rat-infested house. But you were also taught that it had another purpose: even if you were basically neat, so neat that your trash cans never contained much more than lightly soiled Kleenex and neatly rinsed-out tomato cans, you were urged to go in order that, by constantly practicing the act of emptying them, you would eventually become so fastidious that you just wouldn't make garbage anymore. Your trash cans would turn into planters, and you would grow geraniums in them.

Now in fairness, I must admit that the church's doctrine on the Sacrament of Penance has never been put quite as baldly as that. But in all fairness, you are bound to admit that at many times and places, that is precisely the impression that got about on the subject: it was a strange cross between an insurance policy and a self-improvement course. Above all else, it was a piece of business.

But seeing it that way made all sorts of trouble. Protestants accused Catholics of emptying their trash cans just so they could get back to the fun of loading them up again. Catholics accused Protestants of hiding their garbage in their closets. Protestants replied that they got rid of their garbage every night, not just once a month or once a year — and to the Great Dumpmaster Himself, not to some underling. But secretly, both sides had to wonder whether they had done the transaction right. The Protestant, whether he had really repented; the Catholic, whether he had let it all hang out; and both, whether the act they performed was sufficient. That is, they assumed that it took some properly efficacious spiritual transaction to get forgiveness. And they wondered, each according to his own lights, whether they had done it up brown. And even if they decided in their own favor, they still both felt the burden of cleanliness: the religious life consisted of feeling good until you felt bad. Which was always pretty soon. None of us takes long to cast the first cat-food can into the nice, clean liner.

It is a fascinating illustration of religious controversy — of how people can be so totally opposed to what they perceive as each other's errors and, at the same time, so utterly united in a third error neither of them sees at all. And it is an instructive lesson in how to resolve religious controversies: never take them at face value; if people could have made peace on that basis, they would have done so long ago. Instead, look for some unexamined, uncontroverted error in the back of both opposing minds and attack it. Nine times out of ten, if you demolish that, you cut the foundation from under the original argument and it collapses of its own weight. My contention here, and throughout the subject of sacramental theology, is that it is unrecognized transactionalism that lies at the base of our troubles. Watch what happens to the Sacrament of Penance when you get rid of it.

The first step is to render the transactional view of forgiveness suspect.

Item One. The parable of the Prodigal Son. As with so many parables, the popular name, because of our penchant for transactions, is exactly wrong. It gets the teaching of the parable a precise one hundred eighty degrees out of whack. This parable is not about the prodigal but about the father, just as the parable of the Laborers in the Vineyard is not about the laborers but about the owner of the vineyard. The prodigal is not forgiven as a result of anything he did. Of course, he thinks that's the way it works — and so he composes a terrific confession, full of self-deprecating malarkey about not being worthy to be his father's son anymore, and he hits the sawdust trail home.

"But when he was yet a great way off, his father saw him, and had compassion, and ran, and fell on his neck, and kissed him." He doesn't earn forgiveness by a transaction called Coming Home and Saying You're Sorry. He just walks in and finds he had it all along. The father doesn't forgive him because he made his confession, privately or publicly. He forgives him just because he's his father.

And when the elder brother — another dyed-in-the-wool trans-actionalist — shows up with his bookful of self-righteous Green Stamps and complains that his father never gave him any premiums, the father, with a touch of impatience, explains he doesn't accept trading stamps: "Look. He's my son; you're my son. Neither of you has to earn any of this stuff; you both already own everything I've got. So what the hell are you standing out here complaining for? Wipe that look off your face and go on in and fix yourself a drink!"

Item Two. The Nicene Creed: "I acknowledge one baptism for the forgiveness of sins." What does that mean? Does it mean simply that Baptism forgives all the sins you've committed up to the moment the water hits you? In that case, it's a bit hard on the kiddies. All the subsequent sins that a baptized infant commits during his entire life will have to be dragged, one by one, before some ticket window or other and processed. If that's the case, it would be smarter to borrow a page from that hardheaded businessman, the emperor Constantine, and postpone Baptism until just before death: one blanket policy covers all.

Or could it mean, perhaps, that in Baptism we are clothed with a lifelong, head-to-toe suit of forgiveness? Maybe Baptism is not a transaction by which forgiveness is given in return for repentance, but rather a sacramental proclamation of the fact that we're always forgiven, always welcome home, and that we will never have to do anything to earn forgiveness. We just have to shut up and accept it. That sounds more like the parable of the Forgiving Father. Perhaps that's what we're supposed to mean when we acknowledge one Baptism for the forgiveness of sins.

Item Three. In spite of her rather flagrant transactionalism, the church has always hedged a bit on a purely transactional view of Penance. When pressed, she usually admitted that if you couldn't get to the confessional, a sincere repentance would get you absolution anyway. That always looked like an inconsistent concession to the Protestant point of view, but it's at least possible that it sprang from an insight into the connection between Baptism and forgiveness. Maybe somebody took the view that all Christians walked in a perpetual cloud of absolution, and that all they ever needed to do in order to enjoy it was just breathe in.

And there's the word that leads to the second and last step: enjoyment. Once you get rid of the transactional emphasis, Penance takes on a new meaning. It's not a special piece of business by which you purchase something you couldn't get elsewhere, but a special kind of party at which you celebrate what you have always had but were lately, perhaps, guilty of neglecting. There are the two of you in the funny little box — priest and penitent, a couple of perpetually forgiven sinners — telling each other, from different points of view, incredible old stories about what a friend you have in Jesus.

Look how many problems that solves. It makes Penance a real sacrament again — a signal instance of something that is true everywhere but effectively manifested here. You no longer have to be afraid of taking too high a view of priestly absolution. Take as high a view as you like, because when you do, you will be saying that what is true in the confessional is just as true, and just as effective, clear across the board. Group confessions, solitary confessions, all confessions everywhere have exactly the same solemn high access to the Mystery of forgiveness as auricular confessions.

"Ah, but," the fool says in his heart, "why go to a priest then, if you can get it anywhere?"

Dummy! Why go to a party when you can drink by yourself? Why kiss your wife when you both know you love her? Why tell great jokes to old friends who've heard them before? Why take your daughter to lunch on her birthday when you're going to have supper together, anyway? Do you see? What the fool is really asking is, "Why be human, when you can be a jerk instead?"

The sacraments are there to sacramentalize. Because we are sacramental creatures and the world is a sacramental world. The Mystery is everywhere, present in every bit of business, sacred or secular. But you can't see it, taste it, touch it, smell it, or hear it. And therefore you can't know it. So just to make sure you don't forget it, God takes some agreed bits of business and tells you to make a very careful point of saying that the fullness of the Mystery is effectively present in them. Which of course it is, because it is effectively present in all things, times, and places. And he does that on the sound principle that, for the likes of us, nothing gets done unless we do something about it. The Mystery may be able to hold us without using its hands, but we can't hold it without using ours. And since our relationship with it is apparently supposed to be a two-way street, we need sacraments to keep up our end of the bargain.

I chose Penance for the first illustration because, of all the sacraments, it's the one that has always seemed to make the most overweening claim. But note how that impression got about — and how it is now clean gone. It got there not, as people used to think, because too high a claim was made for confession to a priest: "Some nerve!" they would say. "Where do they get off, having the Mystery of forgiveness funneled through a human being!" Rather it got there because of the incorrect, transactional rider Christians too often attached to their perfectly correct, high doctrine of penance: they said, "The Mystery of forgiveness is effectively present in the Sacrament of Penance, unlike anywhere else." Simply change that last phrase to "just as it is everywhere," and four hundred ever-hating, red-eyed years of sacramental controversy go whistling down the wind.

Why, it almost spoils the fun of being a theologian!

19. *Zapping*

Nevertheless, on we must — even if it costs us our paranoia.

The Eucharist is even better served than Penance by refusing to see it as a sacred transaction. It never did make much sense on that basis, anyway. Take, for example, the old assertion that Jesus *becomes* present in the bread and wine. Presto! One more Catholic-Protestant donnybrook, off to a roaring start. Protestants, made squeamish by what they perceive to be Catholic hocus-pocus, insist that Jesus never becomes present in the elements, only in the people who receive them. Catholics retaliate by digging in their heels and going themselves one better: not only do they say that Jesus becomes present; they take Saint Thomas's useful substance/accident distinction, turn it into a polemical device it was never meant to be, and go on to claim they even know how he does the trick.

But how foolish! The sleeper in that discussion is the big, fat, transactional word *becomes.* What they both should have said was what Jesus said: This *is* my body; this *is* my blood. Really, Truly, Absolutely. No ifs, ands, or buts. Be as high church as you like about it. Affirm his real presence. But don't start throwing around a word like *becomes.* Because that implies that his presence occurs after a previous absence. Keep it up long enough, and you'll get a theology in which Jesus *shows up* at Mass. And if you're silly, you'll get a "spot consecration" theory in which he shows up right between the "r" and the "p" in *corpus: Hoc est enim cor — ZAP! — pus meum.* And if you can manage to sucker some equally silly adversary into an argument, he will oblige you by proving that Jesus shows up not between the "r" and the "p" but in the heart of the true believer. Which gives the world two more flawless, perfectly matched, king-size wedges of baloney.

For in fact, there is no sense in which Jesus can be said to show up at Communion. Not in a natural sense, for the Mystery of the Word of which Jesus is the supreme sacrament was in the bread — and on the altar, and in the pews, and out in the parking lot, and down in the cesspool — twenty minutes before the Mass started and ten seconds after the world began. And not in a religious sense, because Jesus, in his Godhead and in his Manhood — crucified, risen, ascended, and coming again — is fully present in all the baptized. He doesn't show up in a room from which he was absent. He sacramentalizes himself in a room in which he is already present. The bread and wine of Communion are not a peephole through which the church checks out some mysterious stranger who wants to come in for a visit. They are a mirror that the church holds up before her face to see the Mystery that is already inside her and at home.

And likewise there is no sense, secular or sacred, in which Jesus can be said to show up in the heart of anybody, believer or unbeliever, true or false. And once you've gotten that straight, isn't it lovely to find the right reason for going to Communion again? You don't go because the tankful of Jesus you got last Sunday has now been used up and you need a refill. You go to do precisely what the church has always been smart enough — or lucky enough, or guided enough — to call it all along: you go to *celebrate* the Holy Mysteries. It's the image of the *party* again. You go to taste and see how gracious the inveterately hospitable Lord is. To share still another bottle of the great old wine he's always kept your cellar full of. And to relish once again the old tall tale about how he came to his own party in disguise and served the devil a rubber duck. You go, in short, to have a ball — to keep company while you roll over your tongue the delectable things that have been yours all along but that get better every time you taste them.

The several sacraments of the church, therefore, are the same party thrown in various circumstances. Call them the Mystery under the guise of a progressive dinner, with cocktails at the Baptisms', soup at the Penances', main course at the Eucharists', and dessert, perhaps with an orgy thrown in, at the Holy Matrimonys'. Or call them Christianity's oldest and longest uninterrupted floating crap game: always the same crowd, the church — militant, expectant, and triumphant; and always the same High Roller, the Paschal Mystery, betting everything on one throw and winning. Figure the sacraments any way you like. Just don't make them into a bunch of slot machines.

Notice next, however, how avoiding transactional imagery improves your understanding of those less easily defined sacraments that are, in effect, states of life: Holy Order and Matrimony.

If you conceive of a sacrament as a sacred piece of business in which something is cooked up, you quickly become preoccupied with the process by which it is confected. And you just as quickly get drawn off the true center of its sacramentality. The "spot consecration" theory of the eucharistic presence is an example of the distraction, but I want to call your attention to the "moment of Ordination" and the "moment of Marriage" theories, which do even more mischief in their respective bailiwicks.

As soon as you begin thinking of ordination to the priesthood, for example, as a transaction by which priesthood is somehow conferred on the ordinand, you are in for trouble. You begin to convince yourself that a Christian becomes a priest at a certain moment in his life — that priests are "confected" like so many batches of fudge. That done, you proceed to judge whether the priesthood is being exercised in a given church on the basis of the "validity" of the confecting process. And that, in turn, leads you to say that ministers who are not ordained by bishops are not priests. And when all is said and done, that means you are accusing the local Presbyterian minister of peddling bogus sacraments. Which is no way to win friends and influence ecumenical movements.

So take it from the top again and get the transactionalism out. Priesthood is not something you "add" to a Christian. By the baptismal presence of the Mystery of Christ in all of us, we already have the fullness of Christ's priesthood. The church is a whole kingdom of priests. Notice the benefits so far. We have revived one of the best insights of the Reformation, the Priesthood of All Believers, an insight on which Protestants muffed the ball because they ended up using it merely as a polemical shillelagh — "The Church of Rome can't turn anybody into a priest; every Christian is a priest already. Just to teach them a lesson, we won't have a sacramental priesthood at all" — forgetting that what's everybody's business is nobody's business, and that an unsacramentalized Mystery simply disappears. So the very people who rediscovered the universal priestliness of the church became the ones who lost all track of the notion of priesthood. This way, however, we get it back. Furthermore, we get, as an incidental bonus, the answer to the question "Are women fit subjects to receive the priesthood?" It is: "Your question is a little late. They've already got it."

But there are more benefits. Once you free yourself from the imagery of turning people into priests, you are liberated from the necessity of taking the ordination ceremony as the sign of the Sacrament of Order. You stop "confecting" priests, and you go back to older, better figures. Your priests are "ordained," "ordered" — that is, they are lined up into a sacramental *arrangement* within the church. The ceremony at which a person is admitted to that arrangement is indeed important — once again, simply because you can't do anything without doing something. But the focus of your attention now lies not on the confecting power of the ceremony but on the sacramental visibility of the arrangement.

Accordingly, the *sign* of Holy Order is taken to be not the moment of the laying of the bishop's hands on the head of a single ordinand but the ongoing acts of the entire crowd of those who are in the order of priests. The sign of Order is precisely the Order itself. The principal normal manifestation of it is not services of ordination, or letters of consecration that many Christians never see, but priests doing the ordinary priesting that all Christians always see. And that's a better view. It forces us to pay attention to what's actually happening rather than fuss about some quasi-legal entity left over from the past. It might even force us to think about using priests *as an order* — as a fellowship, in continuing mutual support — rather than sending them out one by one, as we do now, in the fond hope that the tankful of holy gas we gave them in ordination will take them all the way.

Another benefit is the one that accrues to our thinking about the ecumenical movement when we take a non-transactional view of the priesthood. "Moment of Ordination" theories have mired us for years in the problem of figuring out how to arrange a suitable service for the eventual unification of now-separated ministries. The problem, to put it bluntly, was how to get some presumably valid bishops' hands on the heads of presumably invalid Presbyterian clergypersons — a matter of finding a device for slipping the priesthood over on people who either didn't know they didn't have it or didn't want it at all. Suggestions ranged from having the benighted Presbyterians kneel humbly and gratefully before the True Successors of the Apostles to having everybody silently lay hands on everybody else and let the Holy Spirit sort it out.

But that's all unnecessary now. If the Presbyterians are already fully possessed of the priesthood of Christ by virtue of their baptismal possession of the Mystery of Christ, and if the sign of Order is the Order of Priests acting as such, then when they act as if they're priests, they'll have valid orders. In other words, all you have to do is concede the ecclesial reality of the Presbyterian Church (they've got no less of Christ than anybody else) — and the rest follows. Best of all, it puts the discussion of the ecumenical movement back where it belongs: it must be a grappling with the nature of the church's life, a wrestling with the question of what kind of sign the church herself is supposed to be. I happen to think that, among other things, it has to be a distinctly priestly sign. But that can't be provided by a service; it can be manifested only by a lot of priesting. As I see it, the job of Anglicans, in the pursuit of church union, is not to give Protestants the priesthood but to encourage them to exercise it. For my money, when they do that, the job is done — without any mergers, and with no new bureaucracy.

Refreshing, isn't it? Especially if the prospect of a Super-church gives you the willies.

Lastly, however, Holy Matrimony. Watch how getting rid of "confection" theories gets Mother Church out of the hot kitchen she's been enslaved in for ages.

Perhaps nowhere has the concentration on the "moment of doing the sacrament" done more damage than in marriage. We began by swallowing uncritically the apparently harmless statement that every marriage is contracted on a certain day, at a certain hour. But that was a piece of bait with a very large hook in it. See where it dragged us. The legal imagery of contract led us to see marriage as an extrinsic third something binding two parties together — when in fact a marriage is simply what two parties do to each other for as long as they do it. That, in turn, tugged at us until we endowed the marriage with a life of its own, and with rights over the parties that the parties could never abrogate — when in fact people with enough nerve have always abrogated any marriage they felt like abrogating. And that hauled us right up onto the beach of never-never land, where we pretended that two divorced people who lived a thousand miles apart, who never spoke to each other, and who were each married to somebody else were still, in the most important sense of the word, really married to each other. And that finally left us gasping the ultimate idiocy: namely, that a man who sleeps with no one but his second wife for the rest of his life is actually a rip-roaring adulterer guilty of mortal sin by definition, and therefore ineligible for absolution.

And this time our transactionalism got us into more than mischief. It got us into wickedness. Because this time we were dealing with people's lives. Not with bread and wine, which you can't hurt, or with the priesthood, where you mess up only a few people, but with warm bodies by the millions, whom you foul up royally if you teach them to pick up the biggest single arrangement in their lives by the wrong handle. The figure of a binding contract is deadly. The most important thing about a marriage is not its confection by a few words and a roll in the hay on some Saturday in June but the mutual life it brings into being for all the days thereafter. The sign of Matrimony, therefore, should be figured by some image such as Show Still on the Road, or Continuing Partnership, or Ongoing Business Venture: as long as the shop is open, you've got a marriage; when they close it down, you haven't. The business doesn't continue in some shadow existence. It doesn't go anywhere. It just ain't.

And the former partners don't have to ask anybody's permission to get remarried, because in fact they are free to get just plain married — having no present, continuing marriage to stand in their way. When the ongoing sign of a sacrament is gone, the sacrament itself is gone. If a consecrated host burns up, you don't have to wonder where Jesus went: the sign is gone, and the Mystery fends for itself until it finds another one. If the mutual life of a couple disappears, you don't have to do any more bookkeeping on the subject of their matrimonial sacramentalization of the Mystery. If they want to go out and provide the Mystery with a new sign, the church's job should be not to keep sending them bills on the old one but to help them set up a better shop the second time around.

But look what we did instead. We taught couples to see the weddings, not their marriages, as the sign of Matrimony. We told them that at that solemn moment, something vast beyond imagining was confected, probably in heaven. And then we blithely kissed them off. Out they went, thinking they were secure because marriage was going to take care of them — only to wake up, ten or twenty years down the road, confused and terrified by the discovery that there was no marriage at all because they didn't take care of each other. But they had been well taught: all appearances to the contrary, they went on pretending they had a marriage just because they'd had a wedding. And so the marriage that did no job at all of being a marriage became a prison that every year did a better job of being a prison.

And there they sat. Angry at themselves for having landed in the clink. Angry at us for helping to put them there. And above all, utterly distracted from the one thing they should have been thinking about all along: how to live their own lives, on their own four feet, with their own four hands. The final product of the church's disastrous captivity to the language of contract on the subject of Matrimony was an army of emotional cripples, trained from childhood to think that something that would never exist unless they themselves created it would step out of nowhere and run their lives for them.

If nothing else ever does, that should teach us how essential it is for the church to mind her tongue.

20. *Fireworks*

And there I come to rest. The theme of this whole book has been precisely the necessity of minding the Christian tongue when we talk about the Mystery. I urge it upon you.

I do not mean to suggest, however, that you become finicky to the point of being unwilling to use the old language I have criticized. I myself am perfectly happy to use any and all of it — to speak of the Atonement as a transaction, of Baptism as an instrument, of Marriage as a contract, of the elements as converted by consecration, or of deacons as made priests by the laying on of hands — and I am even willing, on some days, to say it is all done with a loud Zap! right on the dot of an *i*. For there is a large grain of truth in such phrases: they protect us from concocting for ourselves a religion in which nothing ever really happens. Which would be manifestly false; for while the Mystery itself is not a transaction, there is an important sense in which it is nevertheless the supreme happening at the root of everything.

I mean only to suggest that every word — and, particularly, every image — used in theology be examined with the greatest care and handled with as much judiciousness as we can manage. The language of theology is a pack of foxhounds, and theologians are masters of the hunt. Their job is to feed, water, and exercise their dogs so that they will be in peak condition for the hunting of the Divine Fox — and to keep them, if possible, from biting defenseless Christians. They ought to be constantly intent on improving the breed — ready to pay heavily for a promising new bitch, or willing to spend all the time necessary to nurse an ailing but proved one back to health. Above all, they must love dogs — they must be persons who delight in their kennelful of words. For language is the very substance of their profession: if anything can be called the key to the Scriptures, it is a loving study of the images by which all those miles of words are woven into the Word of God.

Someone once accused me of ending every book I have written in the same way and on the same note. I plead guilty. It is the best ending, and it is the ending of the best book. I shall, therefore, use it again: the endlessly refreshing image of Jerusalem, the City of God.

When I spoke, in Chapter Eight, of the various covenants, their signs and their promises, I promised you a fireworks display at the end. Sit back, put up your feet on the porch rail, and watch.

I have four rockets. I am going to fire them off all at once from the four corners of the lawn, make them come together at the zenith, and then explode them in a single giant shower of sparks. Rocket number one is the sign of the Old Testament: the Ark of the Covenant. Rocket number two is the promise of the Old Covenant: the Promised Land. Rocket number three is the sign of the New Covenant: the Humanity of Jesus. Rocket number four is the promise of the New Covenant: the New Jerusalem, the City of God. All set? Fire!

The *Ark of the Covenant* begins its flight as an image by rising and expanding into a larger image. It becomes the Tabernacle, the Tent of Witness in the wilderness. But it rises higher still, and when the Israelites actually settle in Jerusalem, it becomes the Temple. What began as a threatening, aweful box of laws becomes a lovely, graceful thing, the object of a centuries-long romance: "O how amiable are thy dwellings, thou Lord of hosts! My soul hath a desire and longing to enter into the courts of the Lord; my heart and my flesh rejoice in the living God."

The *Promised Land* takes off as nothing more than a promise in Abraham, but it becomes, in the wilderness, a beauty foreseen: the Land Flowing with Milk and Honey. Moses glimpses it from afar and dies; but the People cross the Jordan and enter it in fact. When they are established in Jerusalem, however, what began as a flirtation turns, year by year, into a love affair. The literal city itself becomes the Daughter of Zion, the beloved of Yahweh, the longing of Israel. Her hills, her gates, even the pools of rain in her streets ravish the heart: "The Lord loveth the gates of Zion more than all the dwellings of Jacob. Glorious things are spoken of thee, O city of God. . . . The singers also and trumpeters shall make answer: All my fresh springs are in thee." And when the captivity comes, the love only grows greater in the loss: "By the waters of Babylon we sat down and wept, when we remembered thee, O Sion. If I forget thee, O Jerusalem, let my right hand forget her cunning. If I do not remember thee, let my tongue cleave to the roof of my mouth; yea, if I prefer not Jerusalem above my chief joy."

The *Humanity of Jesus* starts as an unimpressive figure in the back of a barn and rises unobserved for thirty years. But gradually it becomes transfigured, multifaceted: He calls his body the Temple and promises to raise it up in three days. He calls it the Bread of Life and feeds it broken to his disciples on the night before his death. He calls it the Brazen Serpent and lifts it up on the cross. And then he raises it from the dead and ascends as the Great High Priest. But strangely, his body does not leave: he makes the church his Body Mystical and, in her, moves across the face of the earth.

The *New Jerusalem,* the heavenly City, makes the most splendid takeoff of all: It comes gloriously out of heaven, turreted, pinnacled, and gorgeous:

> Thy walls are made of precious stones,
> Thy bulwarks diamonds square;
> Thy gates are of right orient pearl,
> Exceeding rich and rare.

But then it rises shimmeringly into the image of the beloved: the City becomes the Bride adorned for her husband and comes in fine linen to the marriage supper of the Lamb.

And with that, all four rockets converge and explode. The Signs and the Promises detonate each other, and the freight of imagery, accumulated over a thousand years, bursts out in one blinding flash: for the Temple has become Jerusalem, and Jerusalem has become the Bride, and the Bride has become the Mystical Body, and the Lamb and his Wife are one. And everything is Christ, and everything is the Bride, and everything is the City where there is no temple, sun, or moon, but only the Lamb who is its light. And the River flows back from the dawn of creation, and the Tree of Life returns from Eden, and the Gates of Jerusalem are not shut at all by day, and there is no night there. The tears, the sorrow, the crying, and the pain are gone. It is all gardens, gallant walks, and silver sounds:

> There they live in such delight,
> Such pleasure and such play,
> As that to them a thousand years
> Doth seem as yesterday.

By the drawing of the Mystery, the world has passed from her lostness and found him whom her soul loves. The Beloved comes leaping upon the mountains, skipping upon the hills. The time of the singing perpetually begins.

"Vulnerasti cor meum, soror mea, sponsa; vulnerasti cor meum in uno crine colli tui. Si oblitus fuero tui, Jerusalem, oblivioni detur dextera mea. Adhaereat lingua mea faucibus meis si non proposuero Jerusalem in principio laetitiae meae."

Oh, Wow!